The Age of Post-Rationality

Val Colic-Peisker • Adrian Flitney

The Age of Post-Rationality

Limits of economic reasoning in the 21st century

palgrave
macmillan

Val Colic-Peisker
RMIT University
Melbourne, VIC, Australia

Adrian Flitney
Heathmont, VIC, Australia

ISBN 978-981-10-6258-2   ISBN 978-981-10-6259-9 (eBook)
https://doi.org/10.1007/978-981-10-6259-9

Library of Congress Control Number: 2017950579

Cover illustration: Pep Karsten/Getty Images

Printed on acid-free paper

This Palgrave Macmillan imprint is published by Springer Nature
The registered company is Springer Nature Singapore Pte Ltd.
The registered company address is: 152 Beach Road, #21-01/04 Gateway East, Singapore 189721, Singapore

To our respective surviving parents, Mr Radomir Colic and Mrs Hellgart Mahler-Flitney, a father and a mother who taught us the love of books and the value of thinking beyond the mundane.

Acknowledgements

This book was inspired by many people—not only by those who have asked and discussed similar questions to our own, including our friends, work colleagues, public commentators and authors but also those who have buttressed economic rationality as a twenty-first-century dogma by their public utterances, primarily mainstream politicians. The latter triggered many conversations from which this book emerged.

Closer to home, we are particularly grateful to our friends, Dr Peter Waxman and Mr John Inverarity, whose sustained interest in advancing drafts of the book chapters provided us with valuable feedback, from broad intellectual contention to the minute editing. We also thank another couple of friends, Dr Michael Simpson and Ms Jan Prislin-Planinc, who read an earlier draft and provided encouraging noises.

Acknowledgements

[illegible]

Contents

List of Figures and Tables

1

Introduction: Not Just the Economy, Stupid!

In 1992, Bill Clinton campaigned for the American presidency under the slogan 'It's the economy, stupid.' As you know, he won, but you may not be aware than he won against the odds. The slogan was a work of a marketing genius.[1] It outlived the elections and invaded public consciousness. It has been quoted and paraphrased ever since. Politicians take it for granted. The cheeky little phrase took over the world, expressing pithily what had already happened under Thatcher and Reagan over the previous decade. At this point though, in the Anglosphere at least, the 'left' and the 'right' sides of politics converged; both major parties now marched under the 'it's the economy stupid' banner. Left-leaning intelligentsia likes to call it 'neo-liberalism.' At the dawn of the Trump era, we are told that 'neo-liberal globalisation' has failed and its victims have raised their collective political fist by electing the loose-cannon president because he promised radical change. However, be sure: whatever Trump does and whichever way he tries to 'make American great again,' he is not going to throw the slogan out of the window. Which is a little ironic, given it is a Clinton slogan.

V. Colic-Peisker, A. Flitney, *The Age of Post-Rationality*,
https://doi.org/10.1007/978-981-10-6259-9_1

Rationality Versus Economic (Post)rationality

In this book, we ask whether the unchallenged rule of economic reasoning is a way to a bright future. How did the 'healthy economy'—synonymous with the one that grows forever—become the pivot of the daily news, indeed the foundation of our social reality? Is it rational that we should always want more, individually and collectively, regardless of how rich we already are? Do all social issues have to be presented in dollars and cents? Do we really need to know how much it costs 'the economy' to beat up one's wife? Does the action against domestic violence really need economic justification (Access Economics 2004)? Do we need to know how much it costs to raise a child? An undertaking that will, according to a calculation published prominently in *The Australian*, set you back a A$1,000,000 (Callaghan 2010, 6). Similarly, we learn the price of our life when we take out life insurance. Clever satirists have mocked the extreme application of economic logic by concluding that 'life is in fact not worth living,' as its 'cost clearly outweighs the benefits' (Onion 2005).

In this book, we will argue that economic rationality—the 'cost and benefit' analysis—has gone beyond its remit, pervaded all areas of life and created a one-dimensional reality. We entered the era of post-rationality. Politicians argue over policies exclusively in dollar terms, sport is about big bucks, art is about 'art investment,' universities are about attracting student-customers and selling them degrees, and working people are 'human capital' or 'human resources.' Ironically, Marxists are often criticised for 'economic determinism,' but neo-liberals seem to be the extreme devotees of this creed. Such an approach is irrational because (nearly) everyone knows that there *is* more to life and society than dollars and cents—even if politicians and their advisors, almost exclusively economists, argued their economics properly and clearly. Yet, they often retreat to 'econobabble,' a perversion and obfuscation of economic argument presented to justify their decisions while discouraging scrutiny (Denniss 2016). Even neo-liberal champion Fredrick Hayek, when he accepted his Nobel Prize in economics, was critical of the influence of economists: '[T]he influence of the economist that mainly matters is an influence over laymen: politicians, journalists, civil servants and the public generally.

There is no reason why a man who has made a distinctive contribution to economic science should be omnicompetent on all problems of society [...]' (1974).

If we leave the terrain of economics and look at the broader idea of rationality, it is a difficult concept to define. We have a sense that rationality is a uniquely human characteristic, perhaps central to our humanity. We use the word in everyday discourse, but its precise meaning may vary from person to person and situation to situation. We think we recognise when we, or those around us, act 'irrationally.' Most of us would agree that gambling money away or binge drinking is irrational. Yet, bars and bottle shops, gambling dens and shiny casinos are economically rational enterprises that live off people's irrational behaviour.

An everyday, common-sense meaning implies that rational behaviour is to one's advantage, and irrational to one's detriment. However, further questions instantly haunt this simple understanding. Our behaviour affects others, so an advantage for whom, us or the others? Certain behaviours can be advantageous, and therefore rational to an individual, a business, a family, a 'community,' a nation, but detrimental to outsiders. What about humanity as a whole, including future generations, as in warming up the planet for the sake of short-term rational economic goals? How do we reconcile local and global rationality, the rationality of short- and long-term goals? We can also ask what constitutes our ultimate 'advantage,' or 'rational goal.' Is it a pursuit of pleasure or happiness? Accumulating wealth? Leading a meaningful life? Or something else? And of course what is 'happiness' or 'fulfilment' is another million dollar question. Rationality is a complex concept; in this book, we step down from the most abstract, philosophical level and analyse it through several case studies highly relevant for the society here and now.

In his seminal 1945 book *The Open Society and Its Enemies*, Karl Popper (1973) argued that the readiness to listen to a critical argument and to learn from experience was the primary tenet of rationality. He defined rationality as 'fundamentally an attitude of admitting that "*I may be wrong and you may be right, and by an effort, we may get nearer to the truth*"' (p. 225, emphasis in the original). During the eighteenth and nineteenth centuries, when the West shed the last vestiges of theocracy and the secular elite dismissed God as the final arbiter of human affairs, human judgement was recognised as relative. In this context, Popper emphasised the social character of rationality; a particular type of rationality to which a society or an era adheres should be continuously tested through democratic debate.

There is an even broader meaning of rationality: an action is rational if the actor conceives a *rationale* (purpose, reason) and a (however basic) plan or method to achieve this purpose. We are able to define our goals, including long-term ones, and devise the means of achieving them. This is 'instrumental rationality.' Given the social nature of human existence, the purpose needs to appear reasonable to others—especially our 'significant others.' What is considered rational is dependent on social context, time and place. Consequently, an everyday meaning of rationality can be stretched almost endlessly. A 'rational' purpose of one's action, as well as the 'most efficient' method to execute it may have myriad variations, as well as a posteriori interpretations.

Arguably, the broadest as well as most fundamental meaning of rationality points to our individual and social survival. Actions, habits and behaviours that are likely to prolong our individual life are considered rational; the same applies to the survival of human groups and the human species itself. Following Descartes, we can start with the one essential condition of any deliberation, the existence of the thinking person: *Cogito ergo sum*. Therefore, the primary rational goal we should be able to agree upon is our collective survival. This point of consensus can serve as a basis in defining rationality as a social issue.

This book started from the need to have a close look at the rationality of the society we live in. Our desire to explore the topic was triggered by daily news and current affairs, and particularly by the global warming debate. The wrangling over whether climate change is anthropogenic or not should be a rational debate grounded in science and based on evidence, but it has degenerated into a quasi-religious tug of war between 'believers' and 'sceptics.' Even more importantly, because *it's the economy, stupid*, we seem happy to sizzle and freeze, drown and burn, due to an increasingly extreme climate in order not to hurt the economic 'bottom line.' Is this rational? Has the world gone crazy? Many middle-aged people have asked this question before us. But we do believe it is not just our mid-life crisis that led us to write this book.

We (Westerners[2]) highly value democracy and freedom from religious dogma and authoritarian repression, which allows us to have a free and open debate and be rational in the sense proposed by Popper. In this book, we argue that the 'free debate' has been locked within the iron cage of economic rationality. Wanting *more* has become a collective hypnosis. Yet, as a society, we would not want to be called anything but rational. Unlike irrational theocracies, some established (e.g., North Korea) and some threatening to take form (the 'Islamic State in Iraq and Syria'), we claim to inhabit a rational civilisation that relies on science and democratic debate as the basis for a good society. Yet, we choose to conveniently ignore science when heeding its environmental message may 'hurt the economy'? Is this rational?

In the following chapters, we step back and look at particular social domains where post-rationality, in the form of dogmatic economic rationality, has taken over. Even without the threat to the survival of the world as we know it, what is the point of being wealthy, as an individual or as a nation, if it is just a source of anxiety and an obsessive concern to become even richer? In response to these questions, we identify a pervasive orthodoxy, neatly expressed in Bill Clinton's campaign slogan. We express it in an even shorter formula: *more=better*. We discuss this unquestioned truism of capitalism in Chap. 2.

Economic rationality is a neat set of principles—it is clear and credible. However, it has hardened into a doctrine which disregards some common-sense facts. For example, that our economies can neither grow indefinitely, nor do they need to. Most of us (comfortable Westerners) do not *really* need to be richer (saying this is a terrible heresy!), but we do need fresh air and clean water. We also need physical activity and other people's affection to remain healthy. All this is essentially free—although also for sale, if you can be persuaded—as are many other important things. Of course, there is no denying that we need many products and services that are not freely available, and which we have to produce, sell and buy. As a society, we do this very efficiently. Our productive technologies are amazing and owing to these we reached the stage of the 'affluent society,' defined by J. K. Galbraith[3] (1974) in his bestseller by the same name, as the society where 'more people die of too much food than of too little.' This is even truer today, in the midst of the obesity epidemic.

The West and the Rest

We, the 'Westerners,' about 20 per cent of the world's population, are well-off and comfortable, and 'emerging' and 'developing' economies are rushing to join us. Through a process of globalisation, capitalism, usually in its early Darwinian form of the 'survival of the fittest,' has tightened its grip in these countries over the past couple of decades. Ruthless exploitation of workers, child and slave labour, slum living and other ills largely eradicated in the West by the early twentieth century are still prevalent there. Hundreds of millions of people live in the slums of Mexico City and *favellas* of Sao Paolo, scavenge on the rubbish fields of Jakarta or eke out their existence as *cartoñeros*[4] in Buenos Aires. Millions of young factory workers in populous Asian countries stare at tiny pieces of electronics for long hours, on paltry pay, so we can regularly update our iPods, iPhones, iPads and other gizmos.[5] Others, mainly women, sew our clothes in unhealthy and sometimes deadly sweatshops so our wardrobes can overflow with embarrassingly cheap clothing. In 2013, the Rana Plaza building collapse in Dhaka, Bangladesh, killed 1129 people and injured or disabled nearly 2000 (Butler 2013). The building was eight stories high and contained garment factories supplying Western markets.

Neglectful of where our consumer goods come from and under what circumstances, we enjoy a gentler, 'advanced' stage of capitalism. However, critics do not fail to remind us that much of the initial wealth accumulation of the West happened via brutal exploitation of the Rest: think of three centuries of the transatlantic slave trade, one of the most deplorable chapters in Western history. Yet, the story is complex and we aim to avoid the extreme views: neither the 'White Man's Burden' view nor the ideological penance of listing the horrors of ruthless imperialism is helpful in understanding the history of Western domination.

Over the past 60 or so years, since the West formally withdrew from its colonies, the global constellation of power has been increasingly dynamic, opening a possibility of a new, better, more equitable global order—hopefully to everyone's advantage. Advocates of capitalist expansion tend to emphasise that globalisation has pulled many people out of poverty. Indeed, the developing countries' economies are growing fast, but at a vast human, social and environmental price. Yet, they rightfully want to acquire what we already have and are adopting the irresistible, fateful maxim: 'It's the economy, stupid!'

Having eradicated most of the poverty-induced suffering and indignities, the West now has problems caused by abundance: one quarter of English-speaking children are obese, 20 per cent of adults are clinically depressed at some point in their lives, illicit drugs are endemic, and if you live in a large city, your car, however high-tech, will bring you nowhere fast. In one sense, this book is about the artefacts of civilisation that have escaped our control. But we are not talking about trivial 'First-world problems'—we have serious ones too. For example, the 2008 financial crisis exposed the vulnerability of an exceedingly complex system and, according to many economists, it is likely to happen again before too long. It also exposed the mindless rush to accumulate wealth and the rising inequality within developed countries, especially in the US and UK (Piketty 2014; Streeck et al. 2016, 176–179). The woes of the most prosperous parts of the world, Western Europe, US, Canada and Australia, are not trivial. What we're saying in this book is that they are not likely to be resolved within the dominant economic paradigm.

The English-speaking world (we will refer to it as the 'Anglosphere') has been the leader of global capitalism since the eighteenth-century Industrial Revolution and is today its 'neo-liberal avant-garde.' Great Britain and its empire steered the world through the nineteenth century; the US became the 'leader of the free world' in the twentieth century. Many say the twenty-first century will be the 'Asian century.' Globalisation, although still dictated from the West, is also where the Great Western Fear kicks in: losing global dominance, in particular, to a rising China. Well, the giant country may well soon call the global shots. There are close to a billion hard-working people in China producing nearly everything for the rest of the world, but still with a much smaller environmental footprint than the dwellers of Western countries. We do produce a lot but spend even more, while the Chinese produce a lot but spend little (on average). Therefore, the profligate West borrows from them in order to be able to buy Chinese products. Historian Niall Ferguson (2008, 283–340) named this mind-boggling economic symbiosis 'Chimerica.'

Still, the part of the world much maligned by grumpy lefties—'the West'—is also the part of the world where most of them live and are in no hurry to leave. Many people from the less fortunate parts of the world are keen to move to the West, thousands literally dying to get in: travelling across the seas in leaky boats, tracking through deserts, dodging physical and legal barriers. Millions of people migrate to the West each year. In spite of, and partly due to, some dark historical episodes, especially in its relationship with the Rest, the West has achieved much that is worthy of salvation. Capitalism is the most successful system in securing satisfaction of people's material needs as well as securing the highest so far achieved level of human freedom, security, opportunity and perhaps even happiness.[6] Yet, we should not avert our gaze from the distressing margins of society, where we find long-term unemployment, drug addiction, crime, child neglect, domestic violence, homelessness and indigenous populations in a state of social disintegration. But we have all the prerequisites to think our problems through and save ourselves: amazing technology, an educated population, democratic institutions. What is stopping us?

One of the often quoted problems with the neo-liberalism of the past several decades is the increase in inequality. This has indeed happened in most countries: developed, developing and, in particular, post-communist. The gap between the rich and the poor in the West decreased after the Second World War and reached its lowest point in the late 1960s, as Piketty (2014) elaborated and supported by copious data. Since then, the gap has increased considerably (Piketty 2014; Toynbee 2016; SMC 2016). But having said all that, we should not forget that the most egalitarian societies in the world can be found among developed countries (especially in the north of continental Europe and Scandinavia). In the West, 'absolute,' real poverty (as opposed to 'relative poverty') has been largely eradicated. Global capitalism churns out impressive numbers of new billionaires each year, and many of them are in developing and post-communist countries. The levels of inequality in those societies are staggering, and increasing. For example, according to the 2013 Global Wealth Report, in Russia, a country known for many unenviable records, just 110 people own 35 per cent of the country's wealth (CSRI 2013).

The 'developed' economies have grown up and cannot grow as fast as they used to after the Second World War. Historically, our growth rate is decreasing, which should make sense and not drive us to despair (Wallerstein et al. 2013). After all, we have enough *stuff* and should be able to devote a larger part of our lives to what Bertrand Russell[7] (1935) called 'intelligent pursuits': enjoying a more sociable and spontaneous, less anxious and overall a more pleasant existence, instead of working long hours in order to keep one's place in the rat race. Some wise people ('downsizers,' 'sea-changers') have seen the light, but the challenge is to do it collectively.

Western countries need leaders with a 'vision' who can shift the language of the public debate and introduce new perspectives. Our leaders are not inspirational reformers; they ride the economic orthodoxy hoping this will help them keep their jobs at the next elections. Many issues in the domain of politics, policy, economics and finance are made into complex mysteries, so that we give up and take for granted what we're told by various, often dodgy and self-interested, experts and politicians. Unconventional views and alternative voices do exist, but they are still at the margins, while econospeak reigns supreme. Our governments need to lead a relaxation reform rather than making us anxious to run the rat race ever more breathlessly. In a poor society, *more* indeed *equals better*, but not in the rich West. We may have reached the stage of post-rationality where, according to Galbraith (1974, 210), 'the behaviour of both the utterly rational and the totally insane seems equally odd.' Are we able to reinstate rationality, a collective common sense? Introducing new angles to the debate would help. We hope to contribute to this goal.

Crisis?

Over the past half a century, global capitalism, (still) directed from the West, has entered what many reputable authors see as its 'late stage,' perhaps also a crisis stage (Streeck et al. 2016; Wallenstein 2016). *Crisis* has long been one of the favourite media buzzwords: crises of various kinds are the meat of media reports. We would not question that the 2011 Fukushima nuclear disaster was a crisis; similarly the months surrounding the end of Gaddafi's tyranny in Libya or the bloodshed that has taken place in Syria in recent years. Violent rioting in six British cities in August 2011 was also a crisis point. The authors of this book live in Australia, a country where all political and economic indicators point to remarkable stability and prosperity, but we are also constantly kept on our toes by the crisis talk. The fear mongering usually boils down to the catastrophe of our 'growth rate slowing down' once the world's tough times and calamities inevitably catch up with us or China stops buying our iron ore and coal in colossal quantities.

The reason why we take heed of this message in spite of the actual state of affairs is that nowadays most Westerners, and certainly news junkies among us, have at least a vague sense that 'Western civilisation' has contracted some threatening, possibly even terminal, disease. In many people's minds, the sense of dynamic technological and social change is coupled with a feeling that things are in some respects getting worse. Our politicians happily exploit the sense of crisis and underlying public anxiety to advance their agendas. Paradoxically, this sense of social malaise and the crisis talk co-exist with Western triumphalism and a sense of superiority.

In some sense, the crisis talk has always been around. Contemporary warnings about global warming, ageing population and impending financial chaos were preceded by the post-Second World War decades when we stared down the barrel of nuclear Armageddon, not to mention the Great Depression of the 1930s, or the Spanish flu epidemic of 1918–1919 that killed more people than the First World War. According to Ferguson (2006), the twentieth century was the most violent in history in absolute terms—although relative to world population, the view is somewhat better (Pinker 2011). Can the twenty-first century be better, less shocking and bloody, given the increasing global interdependence, economic and environmental? So far, it does not look too promising. Apart from wars, conflict and a growth in terrorism, the problems of nuclear proliferation, overpopulation, resource depletion, environmental degradation and climate change demand serious global attention. Diplomatic posturing is insufficient. On the other hand, the anti-utopian scenarios laid out in many books and films have not materialised, at least not in the time scales predicted—although we have just learned that our televisions may be spying on us as predicted in George Orwell's *1984*. We may be able to deal with that particular challenge!

Out of Ideological Trenches

While trying to think outside the dominant discourse, we agree with the method of social change dominant in the Anglosphere: reform rather than radicalism. This may sound boring, but in the Anglosphere, people prefer radicals to inhabit historical anecdotes and novels rather than their neighbourhoods. We hope that many contented citizens, the category we belong to for better or for worse, share with us a readiness to think outside the received wisdom if challenged in an interesting way. This is our book's ambition.

By reform we mean going beyond the usual minor policy manipulations with the eye on the next election. The prescriptions of conventional economics do not seem to be addressing the current problems but rather they lead to them. We may need something along the lines suggested by economist and Nobel laureate Joseph Stiglitz[8] (2010, 238) who commented on the current American economic problems: 'Economics has moved—more than economists would like to think—from being a scientific discipline into becoming free market capitalism's biggest cheerleader. If the United States is going to succeed in reforming its economy, it may have to begin by reforming economics.'

We are neither apologists nor detractors of capitalism. The former, often referred to as 'neo-liberals,' consider global capitalism the pinnacle of human progress. They believe it is a system that can endlessly reinvent and fix itself through the magic of the market—the idea of a self-correcting market is their 'rational faith.' The extension of this ideology is an insistence on a global free market, that is, free international trade, where allegedly everyone benefits, multinational corporations as well as Third-world villagers. According to this school of thought, government regulation of economic activity is nothing but restrictive and ultimately detrimental 'socialism' because it not only slows down the economy but also endangers democracy; a powerful state means powerless citizens. The free marketeers also like to remind us how capitalism was vindicated nearly three decades ago when European communism caved in.

The doomsayers of capitalism, often labelled 'lefties,' 'greenies' or 'socialists' are generally an intellectually inclined and grumpy lot tirelessly issuing warnings about mounting problems (see, e.g., Streeck et al. 2016;

Amin 2011; Klein 2014). The scientific modelling of anthropogenic global warming currently supplies the most compelling evidence to the doomsayers. Most people, however, cannot see the crisis on a planetary scale, as long as they live their largely unaffected, comfortable lives. The crisis of capitalism may not yet be acute but it is nonetheless 'systemic.' This means that the system needs a carefully devised therapy rather than just regular painkillers.

Those in the middle see merit in gradual reforms and usually suggest stricter financial regulation, some redistribution of wealth through taxation and the welfare state and well-funded public services such as education, health and public transport. They say the turbo-capitalism of the Anglosphere could learn a few things from other cultures instead of pompously considering itself the pinnacle of civilisation. History has not ended—far from it. It's been churning out social change faster than ever. The debate continues and we are keen to contribute. We are in this camp, arguing that we do *not* live in the best of all possible worlds: political changes to restore rationality are necessary and possible. There is much research done on specific problems and possible fixes, but the big picture is usually carefully avoided. In chapters to follow, we are treading this rather difficult territory and develop some ideas that have escaped the straightjacket of conventional wisdom.

The Book, Its Authors and Their Friends

Our interest in the big picture comes not only from our educational and professional backgrounds but also from our life trajectories. More than two decades ago, Author 1, upon careful planning, joined many thousands of people who opted for capitalism over 'post-communism' by migrating to Australia from Croatia; so far, this seems to have been a good move. Author 2, having opted out of a career as an academic physicist, earns his living by the most capitalistic of pursuits, share trading. Among our close friends is a son of a British colonial officer in Africa who thinks the British Empire was a shiny historic period and not just for Britain; another is a fan of Maggie Thatcher and Tony Abbott (a staunchly conservative, recently deposed Australian PM); another couple of our close friends are conservative voters; several more work for evil multinational corporations; and a couple of others recently embarked on spending their retirement savings that are so big they'll need to live way beyond their life expectancy in order to whittle it away (what a problem to have!). We also have friends among impecunious ageing hippies; died-in-the-wool feminists; and artists who have succeeded in avoiding conventional work well into their 50s, which probably means forever. One friend detested capitalism so much he fled his native Australia for a nearby poor country and now lives among the locals, having married one. Our politically diverse friends all offer points worth considering and make for interesting debates.

In short, we do not think it is useful to look at the world from an ideological trench—like a 'frog looking up from the well,' as our Pakistani friend put it. Both schools of thought, apologist for the free market and its critics, seem to have become more extreme over the past decades and there is less and less dialogue between them, reinforced by internet 'echo chambers' (more on this in Chap. 7). Preaching to the converted provides small daily doses of catharsis to members of the respective camps but makes no real difference whatsoever. Importantly, in the everyday flow of a messy life, ideological positions are rarely clear-cut. Most people have some progressive and some conservative views. People barely ever think things through to the depth where their ideological mosaic would start to unravel. In every one of us, our ideological and other contradictions are more or less neatly patched together. Our British-Empire-enthusiast friend is also a barrister working pro-bono for Australian asylum seekers. The Thatcher fan is a most likeable and the least bigoted man imaginable, a respected educator working tirelessly for an educational charity into his seventies. Most ideological positions, apart from the extreme and violent ones, deserve to be heard because they reflect some profound truths about the society and the human condition.

Notes

1. In 1993, James Carville was declared the 'Campaign Manager of the Year' by the American Association of Political Consultants.

2. We devote more time to the idea of the 'West' in Chap. 2. This somewhat vague term seems hard to avoid. In this book, the West denotes the rich 'First World' of European extraction: the affluent societies of Western Europe and their rich offspring in the 'New World': US, Canada, Australia and New Zealand. A broader idea of the 'West' denotes the 'Christian world.'
3. John Kenneth Galbraith (1908–2006) was a Canadian-born American economist and a prominent public intellectual, the author of many best-sellers. In 1949, he was appointed a professor of economics at Harvard University. He served as advisor in Roosevelt's, Truman's, Kennedy's and Johnson's Democratic administrations and was the US ambassador to India under J.F. Kennedy. *The Affluent Society* was first published in 1958 and had several subsequent editions.
4. *Cartoñeros* support themselves by sorting through the city's 4500 tonnes of daily rubbish searching for recyclable items to sell. See Robinson (2014).
5. A recent documentary showed workers on 12-hour shifts falling asleep on the job in Apple's factories in China (ABC 2015).
6. Happiness is hard to measure but when this is attempted through international life satisfaction surveys, it does not seem to be related to wealth, or even security: Mexicans came on top as the happiest nation in 2013 according to the OECD *Better Life Index* (http://www.oecdbetterlifeindex.org/).
7. Bertrand Russell (1872–1970), a philosopher, mathematician and peace activist, was one of the leading British intellectuals of the twentieth century. Although born into a prominent aristocratic family, and a grandson of a Prime Minister, he was an outspoken social critic and even served time in jail as a pacifist during the First World War.
8. Stiglitz (b. 1943) won the Nobel Prize in economics in 2001 and is a former economic advisor to President Clinton and former chief economist at the World Bank.

Bibliography

ABC. 2015. Apple's Broken Promises. *Four Corners*, 2 March 2015. Australian Broadcasting Commission (ABC) TV.

Access Economics. 2004. The Cost of Domestic Violence to the Australian Economy. Access Economics report commissioned by the Australian Government Office of Women. Accessed 11 June 2017. https://www.dss.gov.

au/our-responsibilities/women/publications-articles/reducing-violence/the-cost-of-domestic-violence-to-the-australian-economy

Amin, Samir. 2011. *Ending the Crisis of Capitalism or Ending Capitalism?* Cape Town; Dakar; Nairobi; Oxford: Pambazuka Press. First published in 2009 as *La crise: Sortir de la crise du capitalisme ou sortir du capitalisme en crise* by Le Temps des Cerises.

Butler, Sarah. 2013. Bangladeshi Factory Deaths Spark Action among High-Street Clothing Chains. *The Guardian*, 23 June 2013. Accessed 11 June 2017. https://www.theguardian.com/world/2013/jun/23/rana-plaza-factory-disaster-bangladesh-primark

Callaghan, G. 2010. Million-Dollar Babies. *The Weekend Australian Magazine*, 6–7 November 2010.

CSRI. 2013. Global Wealth Report 2013. Credit Suisse Research Institute (CSRI) report, November 2013.

Denniss, Richard. 2016. *Econobabble: How to Decode Political Spin and Economic Nonsense*. Melbourne: Schwartz Publishing/Redback Quarterly.

Ferguson, Niall. 2006. *The War of the World: Twentieth Century Conflict and the Decline of the West*. New York: Penguin.

Ferguson, Naill. 2008. *The Ascent of Money: A Financial History of the World*. New York: Penguin.

Galbraith, John Kenneth. 1974 [1958]. *The Affluent Society*. Boston; New York: Houghton Mifflin.

Hayek, Fredrick von. 1974. Speech to the Nobel Banquet, 10 December 1974. Accessed 13 June 2017. http://www.nobelprize.org/nobel_prizes/economic-sciences/laureates/1974/hayek-speech.html

Klein, Naomi. 2014. *This Changes Everything: Capitalism vs. The Climate*. New York: Simon & Schuster.

Onion. 2005. Cost of Living Now Outweighs Benefits. *The Onion*, 13 April 2005. Accessed 11 June 2017. www.theonion.com/articles/cost-of-living-now-outweighs-benefits,1316/

Piketty, Thomas. 2014. *Capital in the Twenty-first Century*. Cambridge, MA: Harvard University Press. First published in 2013 as *Le capital au XXI siècle* by Éditions du Seuil.

Pinker, Steven. 2011. *Better Angels of Our Nature: Why Violence has Declined*. New York: Viking.

Popper, Karl. 1973 [1945]. *The Open Society and its Enemies*. London: Routledge.

Robinson, Kristies. 2014. Buenos Aires Embraces “Cartoneros” in Push for Zero Waste. *Citiscape*, 16 October 2014.

Russell, Bertrand. 1935. *In Praise of Idleness and Other Essays*. London: Allen & Unwin Ltd.

SMC. 2016. State of the Nation 2016: Social Mobility in Great Britain. Report by the UK Government Social Mobility Commission (SMC), November 2016.

Stiglitz, Joseph. 2010. *Freefall: America, Free Markets and the Sinking of the World Economy*. New York; London: W. W. Norton & Company.

Streeck, Wolfgang, Craig Coulhoun, Polly Toynbee, and Amitai Etzioni. 2016. Does Capitalism have a Future? *Socio-Economic Review* 14: 163–183.

Toynbee, Polly. 2016. Equality Looks Further Away than Ever in a Brexit, Donald Trump world. *The Guardian*, 17 November 2016.

Wallerstein, I., R. Collins, M. Mann, G. Derluguian, and C. Calhoun. 2013. *Does Capitalism have a Future?* Oxford: Oxford University Press.

2

A Rational Civilisation?

What was the foundation of Europe's, and later the 'West's,' unprecedented success in achieving economic prosperity and political freedom? Which material or cultural elements led to its global pre-eminence? This exceedingly complex question has been tackled from different angles with more or less persuasive results. The shortest possible answer, albeit incomplete, is rationality—asserting the authority of dialogical reason. The most fundamental shift was the one that shed the shackles of dogmatic (religious or otherwise authority-based) thinking and opened the door to rational (free and argument-based) thinking—that is, allowing free debate. This change ushered in the modern era, the age of global domination of the West.

The key principles that govern modern Western society developed and took hold over several centuries. Some of its fundamental features were formulated during the Renaissance that started in northern Italian cities in the thirteenth century. The Renaissance (literally: rebirth) has been conceptualised as the process of liberating human curiosity and the spirit of inquiry from religious and feudal limitations (Burckhardt 1990). The growth of cities, the nodes of economic and cultural exchange, was a sign of a new era dawning out of the 'dark' Middle Ages.[1] European medieval society was dominated by all-powerful feudal landlords who owned the

V. Colic-Peisker, A. Flitney, *The Age of Post-Rationality*,
https://doi.org/10.1007/978-981-10-6259-9_2

peasantry along with the land. This was a slow-changing rural world of subsistence farming and nearly universal illiteracy, culturally dominated by religion, which ensured massive political power for the church. From the ninth to the thirteenth century, those interested in science and intellectual inquiry headed to Baghdad, whose 'House of Wisdom' was the global centre of leaning at the time (Brentjes and Morrison 2010). Yet, historians do not agree on the level of 'darkness' of the European Middle Ages (Huisinga 1996). The year 1492, when Columbus reached the 'New World,' is usually considered the symbolic end of the medieval period and the beginning of the modern era marked by the global expansion of European powers.

Modern society started to emerge when manufacturers, merchants, artisans and bankers in the growing Renaissance cities formed the nucleus of modern capitalism, 'breaking through the crust of the traditional agrarian society' (Moore 1966, 174). The rising urban class carefully manoeuvred through the endemic political struggles and wars between the church and secular powers, Popes and Emperors, kings and nobility. Some European cities secured an autonomous status and flourished amidst the turmoil of rising and falling fiefdoms and empires. The city of Florence is a famous and perhaps the most illustrative case: early Florentine bourgeoisie can be credited not only with financing some of the most brilliant works of Western art and architecture to this day, created to immortalise rich patrons, but also with spearheading capitalism to the rest of Europe. Relative to its size, Florence may be the most important city in Western history.[2]

From Antiquity until the sixteenth century, the Mediterranean was the most advanced part of the 'Occident,' due to its maritime trade connection with the 'Orient' (the Arabic world, India and China), from where many key ideas and inventions were brought to Europe. For example, the Hindu–Arabic numerals replaced the cumbersome Roman numbers, greatly simplifying calculations and making modern mathematics possible. After the Reformation in the early sixteenth century, the baton of Western progress shifted from the Mediterranean to the north-western Protestant corner of Europe (Moore 1966). The Reformation denied the universal authority of the Pope and created churches considerably more tolerant to social and cultural innovations than the Vatican—a situation that remains to this day.

Fig. 2.1 With sword and cross: a statue of Cristóbal Colón (Columbus) in Buenos Aires,[3] Argentina

At that time, naval powers went about conquering extra-European lands: Spanish and Portuguese *conquistadors* invaded Central and South America, the British and the French settled in North America, the Dutch took the 'East Indies' (now Indonesia). European powers profited greatly from the exploitation of new lands and their indigenous populations. From the sixteenth century onwards, European metropoles were flooded by new ideas, foodstuffs and spices, as well as gold, silver and other riches coming from Asia and the Americas.

The 'discoveries' of overseas lands in the fifteenth and sixteenth centuries were matched by important scientific discoveries: Copernicus proposed that the Earth orbits the Sun, overthrowing two millennia of accepted wisdom about the Earth being the centre of universe; Galileo started the science of mechanics and supported Copernicus' ideas in a book written in Italian (rather than in scholarly Latin) which was therefore accessible to a wider audience; Kepler derived the laws of planetary orbits and Newton proposed laws of motion and gravity. These thinkers started a scientific revolution. The early development of capitalism, first the 'mercantile' variety that emerged in France in the sixteenth and seventeenth centuries, and then the 'industrial' one heralded by England in the eighteenth and nineteenth centuries, was simultaneous with the conquest of new lands and a spectacular development of natural sciences as the basis of modern technology. These were in fact aspects of the same process.

The European Enlightenment of the eighteenth century freed the most advanced Christian lands from the intellectual domination of religion and the political domination of the church. Its main programmatic intention was to free rational thinking and to establish the scientific method as the primary source of authoritative knowledge. This transformative cultural movement spread from pre-revolutionary eighteenth-century France to other European countries already seriously infected with the virus of modernity: Britain, the Netherlands, Belgium and Germany. From the most advanced countries, the Enlightenment ideas quickly spread further to the peripheral European lands and also European overseas settler colonies, especially North America. By the 1780s, 'the ideology of an individualist, secularist, rationalist belief in progress' was firmly established throughout the Western world (Moore 1966, 15).

The central idea of the Enlightenment was one of secular and progressive bourgeois democracy, a 'meritocracy' we know today, where all men (but not yet women) were 'born equal' and could enjoy the 'unfettered exercise of individual talent in a world of reason' (Hobsbawm 1962, 38). The 'common man' was to be liberated from the domination of traditional hierarchies of landed nobility and clergy. The historic distinction and merit of modern bourgeois society was its introduction of free competition for truth, wealth and power. Such a free competition proved the best system in advancing knowledge, technology, productivity, material welfare, democracy and the arts. The capitalist 'free market' guaranteed by the rule of law in the gradually developing and increasingly democratic nation-states of Europe represented the institutional framework of the West's epochal success.

The revolutionary political ideas of '*egalité, fraternité, liberté*' (equality, brotherhood and freedom), fermented in the eighteenth-century Enlightenment, finally asserted their power as the motto of the violent French Revolution of 1789. This was the crucial point of dismantling European feudal society, the *ancien regime*, and spreading the ideas and practices of bourgeois democracy across Europe. The French Revolution demolished thus far impenetrable barriers between the ruling First and Second Estates (nobility and clergy, constituting 2 to 3 per cent of the population) who did not pay any taxes and the Third Estate (bourgeoisie, urban proletariat and peasants—the working people who lived off their entrepreneurship and/or labour) who supported them. At the same time, the equally important Industrial Revolution in England was based on technological advances that led to an upsurge in economic productivity and material prosperity (Hobsbawm 1962). In his *Capital in the Twenty-first Century*, Piketty (2014) analyses the economic growth, capital ownership, returns on capital, labour income and inequality of the past 200 years. After long slow centuries, economic growth shot up during the Industrial Revolution. Technological superiority led to global Western hegemony through the establishment of settler colonies and colonial empires. This domination still holds in the most recent wave of globalisation triggered by the internet revolution.

Judging Vs. Measuring

The application of the scientific method was a crucially important development: it meant switching from *judging* to *measuring*. Judging is a process of truth-seeking through reliance on external authority. This means that only socially recognised authority figures—those invested with power through their public office (e.g., church dignitaries and secular judges) and those whose power to judge rests on hereditary rights (e.g., kings and feudal lords)—can exercise judgement and proclaim 'the truth' that others are obliged to follow. These authority figures sometimes have a written law to inform and shape their judgement, for example, the Holy Scripture for clergy or a written statute in secular legal determinations. However, by definition, judging is arbitrary to a considerable extent.

Until the Enlightenment, the ultimate judgement or *truth* was the one stemming from the authority of God, as interpreted by God's representatives on Earth. Anyone who opposed the judgement of clergy committed a heresy. The Inquisition was the Roman Catholic Church's 'thought police' in charge of arresting any unorthodox thinking. It was first established in twelfth-century France and later in Spain and Portugal (and their American colonies) in order to enforce the dogma throughout Europe. After the Reformation, the Inquisition was limited to the Catholic south-west of Europe, but heresy and witchcraft continued to be prosecuted in Protestant countries, including Iceland, England, Scotland, Denmark and German and Dutch lands. The seventeenth century was the peak of the European witch hunt which only ceased at the end of the eighteenth century.

Spaniards showed the most zeal in persecuting heretics. The same royal couple that united provinces of what we nowadays know as Spain, and funded Columbus' expedition to the Americas—King Ferdinand II of Aragon and Queen Isabella I of Castile—also established the Spanish Inquisition in 1478. Muslim and Jewish influences were relatively strong in the Iberian Peninsula, and powers-that-be felt compelled to keep their subjects under a watchful eye. The Spanish Inquisition was the most ruthless pursuit of ideological purity in Western history. If lucky to be judged as only committing a minor ideological transgression, heretics were excommunicated from the church; if the wrongdoing was deemed to be major, they would have burned at the stake, preceded by interrogation and confession in the torture chamber. The West has come a long way from those judgemental times, despite there being some recent examples of the use of torture and suggestions that it could be reintroduced.[4]

Unlike authority-based judgement, measuring is a basis for a process of autonomous truth-seeking. In natural sciences, the process of measuring starts with collecting data. Quantifying observable natural phenomena is the first step of the rational scientific method; data analysis, based on calculations, is the second. Logical argument based on the data analysis leads to scientific insights. Importantly, the scientific method is egalitarian and open to everyone to follow in the pursuit of knowledge and understanding of nature and human society. The insights scientists arrive at must withstand the free criticism of their scientific peers—or anyone else for that matter, as the debate on climate change clearly shows. In science, there is no heresy against the authority: finding flaws in the current argument is not a transgression but the way science progresses. Established scientific truths are continuously challenged, open to criticism and revision, and hence refined or discarded. Science is a cumulative effort of free-thinking human beings equipped by a step-by-step prescribed method. Its results, although never final or perfect, are formidable. Through measuring, quantification and calculation, Western science introduced the authority of numbers. In this context, words have become mere opinions, more or less persuasive speculation, but numbers have come to symbolise and represent undeniable, positive facts. In contrast to pre-modern societies, the culture of capitalism is embedded in radical quantification: the simple, elegant and persuasive ontology of numbers. Yet, Western science remains an effort of imperfectly rational, biased humans and embedded in its specific social context. It has been criticised from many vantage points, including non-Western (for appropriating contributions of non-Western cultures, implying Western superiority), feminist (for excluding women) and Marxist (for being subservient to technological interests of capital).

Even though the Enlightenment discarded the judgements by authority figures as subjective and fallible, remnants of the *ancién regime* are present on the margins of modernity. The dogma of the Pope's infallibility for example, formally declared at the Vatican Council as late as 1870, is still in principle followed within the Catholic Church. Another example of contemporary Western dogmatism is the European communism of the twentieth century with its many 'personality cults.' Communism is a bastard child of Western rationalism; its doctrine originated in the most advanced part of the enlightened, scientific West, but its implementation in the relatively backward Eastern Europe reverted to the authoritarian model. In a neck-breaking leap of faith, communist rulers proclaimed themselves infallible on the basis of the definitive Truth of 'scientific socialism.' However, given that science only advances through reasoning and debate, authoritarianism and rationalism can never be reconciled.

Economic Rationality

A simplest possible definition is: economic rationality is a logic guiding self-interested individuals who seek profit through optimising the cost–benefit ratio in order to reduce the costs and increase the returns of an economic activity. The goal of such rational action is wealth accumulation for individuals and economic growth for societies; in the Anglosphere, the latter is taken as a proxy for social progress. Economic rationality, focused on pecuniary gain, is the central pillar of capitalism's ideological structure, a pervasive and taken-for-granted way of thinking. 'It's the economy, stupid' sounds like a perfectly plausible claim, reinforced daily by politicians and business peoples. Yet, there are many who like to qualify this claim. Joseph Stiglitz, the 2001 Economics Nobel Prize winner, argued that 'economists have pushed their model of rationality beyond its appropriate domains' (Stiglitz 2010, 251). Indian-American anthropologists Arjun Appadurai (2003, 52) lamented that

> [...] anthropologists have essentially handed over the entire business of the future to economics. Culture [is] seen as a kind of rear-view mirror, habit, tradition, norm, etc. but always looking back. The question of the future—of people's wishes, choices, projects, visions etc. has been more or less handed over to the domain of economics.

Overly confident economic analysis nowadays ventures into explaining the calculation of mate selection (more on this in Chap. 3) followed by the economic inquiry into marriage. For example, the gender division of labour within marriage is considered economically advantageous, while parenthood is not, because it decreases parents' (usually mother's) earning ability. The gap in earnings of mothers versus non-mothers is larger than between men and women overall; childless women have earnings comparable to men. However, economic calculation may not be uppermost in people's minds when they think of having children as, apparently, many other things are involved. Yet, the dominance of economic thinking makes many people consider the economics of parenthood. Western women time their childbearing around their careers, which have increased the age of first-time mothers in developed countries by nearly a decade over the past 30 years, leading to an explosion of the numbers of 'test tube babies' (Sifferlin 2014). Many young career women now opt out motherhood altogether. A 'rational economic' calculation considering earning potential and career competition no doubt plays a major part in such decisions.

Economic rationality draws its authority from being a derivative of scientific rationality. Just like scientific rationality, it rests on measuring, quantification and calculation. Their crucial common thread is the authority of numbers over words and measuring over judging. Some aspects of economic rationality—devising ways to maximise production—existed in pre-modern societies, but it experienced its detailed articulation only in modern capitalism, with the development of industrial cities, the division of labour, and market competition and exchange. The success of capitalist venture rests on careful calculation.

Economic Science and the Authority of Quantification

Economics as a science developed to explain the complex structure of production and exchange that developed in modern urban society which gradually replaced the common-sense simplicity of subsistence farming. Economic ideas that still govern the Western world today are quite old: they were fully formed in the late eighteenth and early nineteenth centuries, at the time of the Industrial Revolution in Britain. The early economists, nowadays considered 'classic'—Adam Smith, David Ricardo and Thomas R. Malthus—alongside founders of sociology—Max Weber, Karl Marx, Emile Durkheim and Ferdinand Tönnies—were impressed by the great transformation of the closely-knit, face-to-face rural communities into a complex industrial society marked by urban anonymity and individualism. However, there was a price to pay: the premise of the inevitability of mass deprivation and great inequality earned early economics the name of the 'dismal science.'[5]

The English-speaking world where modern capitalism was first fully developed—and Britain specifically as the cradle of industrial capitalism—has also been the leader in economic science from its inception, although significant schools have also existed in Italy, Austria and France (Hobsbawm 1975, 299). Almost all Nobel Prize winners in economics[6] come from the Anglosphere, chiefly the US and UK. Those who come from other countries at the very least studied or worked in the US and UK. Partly due to the global dominance of the Anglosphere, economic rationality, elaborated by economic science, has spread globally and attained nearly universal ideological reign.

The economic rationality of capitalism was first fully articulated in the works of Adam Smith (1723–99), considered the father of modern economics. Adam Smith was one of the prominent figures of the Scottish Enlightenment, a Francophile and an advocate of cultural exchange with continental Europe. In his 1776 classic *The Wealth of Nations,* he described in detail the workings of the market economy embedded in its three main pillars of production—land, capital and labour—whose prices make the component parts of the 'price of commodities.' Smith's articulation of the workings of the market as 'the invisible hand' which turns actions of self-interested individuals into common benefit has been a central tenet of economic science for more than two centuries. According to Smith (1993, 11), the invisible hand 'naturally distributes' the 'Produce of Labour among the different Ranks of the People': 'Wages of Labour; Profits of Stock [capital] and Rent of Land.' Every individual 'intending only his own gain' is frequently 'led by an invisible hand to promote an end which was no part of his intention,' that is in 'the interest of the society' (p. 292). According to Adam Smith, 'not leaving things at perfect liberty' [of the free market] occasions imbalances and inequalities. Non-interference in the 'natural liberty' of the market is therefore best for advancing the wealth of nations, which is the explicit social purpose of capitalist economic rationality. Critics argue, however, that private profit always takes primacy over the interest of society. Stiglitz (2002) noted that 'Adam Smith's invisible hand [...] is invisible, at least in part, because it is not there'.

In another seminal work of social science, *The Protestant Ethic and the Spirit of Capitalism,* coming out of Germany, Max Weber (1958) argued that rational capitalist production was complemented by a 'rational spirit'—the conduct of life in general became increasingly calculative and therefore 'rational.' The 'capitalistic' economic rationality, expressed 'purely numerically,' is, according to Max Weber (1978, 85), uniquely Western. 'Rational capital accounting' is the basis of the functioning of modern capitalism. French historian Fernand Braudel (1992) argued that careful bookkeeping serves to build the reputation of a particular business and legitimised business in general. In a recent reflection on modern accountancy, Alain de Botton (2009, 241) noted that 'levels of commitment that in previous societies were devoted to military adventure and religious intoxication have been channelled into numerical needlework.'

Fig. 2.2 Adam Smith's statue on *Royal Mile*, central Edinburg

During the third quarter of the nineteenth century, the science of economics developed a close and direct link with mathematics. The marginal utility school of economics developed simultaneously in Britain, Austria and France around 1870. W.S. Jevons[7] was one of the pioneers of contemporary neoclassical economic analysis, and the first to propose the concept of marginal utility (Jevons 1866). The marginal utility school was more narrowly focused than the old 'political economy' practised by J.S. Mill[8] in the preceding decades. Hobsbawm (1975, 290–291) argued that the situation where economic progress was obvious was 'unlikely to concentrate the minds of economists on the more profound aspects of their science' and there was a tendency to 'separate economic analysis from its historic social context.'

The economic rationality of the market is indifferent towards social good and ethical postulates. Its argument is quantitative: *more = better*. It's about measuring, not judging. In reality, economic actors cannot fully disregard ethics, but often clash with it, and in these battles the economic argument usually prevails. Yet, society is a broader concept than the economy; the economy is part of society, although the dominance of economic rationality often implies the reverse. Is then the current state of affairs a situation where the tail wags the dog? There are some radical answers to this. One comes from Margaret Thatcher: 'there is no such thing as society,' she declared in 1987. Indeed, society is a vague and complex entity that not even sociologists can agree how to define. What apparently does exist is the individual: ideally a self-reliant, hard-working, competitive and entrepreneurial economic agent—the *homo economicus*, the ideal capitalist citizen.

A Rational Market?

The market is the central concept of economic science. Adam Smith, and his twentieth-century ideological reincarnation Friedrich von Hayek, represented the market as a balancing force that distributes factors of production in a more efficient and fair manner than any individual human mind or carefully crafted policy ever could. Moreover, Hayek argued that policy decisions which interfere with the functioning of the market are likely to make economic problems worse and give much unwarranted power to the government, leading to a loss of liberty. He called it a 'road to serfdom,' the extreme of which was communism.[9] The belief in the indispensability and naturalness of the market has taken some extreme forms: Popper (1973, 136) cited political theorist Edmund Burke: 'The laws of commerce are the laws of nature, and therefore the laws of God.' For Hayek's teacher, Austrian economist Ludwig von Mises, economic theory that has the idea of the 'free market' in its centre is '*a priori*, not empirical. Like logic and mathematics, it is not derived from experience; it is prior to experience' (Mises 1960, 13).

Schumpeter[10] (2009), one of the most influential economists of the twentieth century, saw the capitalist entrepreneur as a heroic figure, forged in the crucible of the competitive market. Entrepreneurs are the elite troops on the capitalist battlefield, the innovators and risk takers. Entrepreneurship generates development, and a lack of it leads to stagnation.

Many respected economists, not to mention social scientists and philosophers, have warned that understanding the market, and creating economic policy to direct inherently complicated and not fully rational human affairs, vastly transcends number-crunching economics. Market exchange is interaction among people and therefore a social relationship closely intertwined and inseparable from other, non-economic aspects of human affairs. Economics is a social science, although it has always attempted to distance itself from 'soft' social sciences through heavy reliance on mathematics.

The two most influential economists of the twentieth century, J.M. Keynes and F. Hayek, fierce opponents on the issue of macroeconomic policy, agreed that economics is a social science and not everything it covers can be fitted into mathematical models. Much of what is happening in the economic sphere is open to interpretation. Economists explore relationships between people—individuals, groups and nations—in competition and cooperation with each other. In this domain, truths are not set in stone but socially constructed and debatable, as well as changing. The real-existing economic transactions never fully match economic models and ideal-types: they are normative, value-laden and often irrational, far from the rational calculative world of neoclassical economics.

This is something behavioural economists have been pointing out for some time (see Kahneman and Tversky 1979; Akerlof and Schiller 2009; Kahneman 2011). The rationality of market participants is bounded by their ability to accumulate and process relevant information and make informed decisions. Fully informed decisions are not really a practical possibility since the amount of information to be processed is overwhelming, as is the number of consumer or investment choices. Even when we make big economic decisions—investing considerable sums or buying a home for example—we rely on our likes, dislikes, hunches, emotions and suggestions of our significant others, often unsolicited and poorly informed. We are often guided by what Keynes (1936, 161–162) called 'animal spirits'[11]: confidence, fairness, corruption, non-monetary values and the contagion of popular opinion. Did the market rationally and justly distribute resources during the 'tulip mania' in seventeenth-century Netherlands, where at its peak in 1636, a single rare tulip bulb was exchanged for 12 acres of residential land (Mackay 1995, 77)? Or during the 'dotcom bubble' at the turn of the millennium where many internet companies with modest revenue and little chance of achieving more reached multi-billion dollar valuations (more on this in Chap. 5)?

The free market, many respected economists argue, is nowadays just a hard-core conservatives' daydream. In spite of its French name, *laissez-faire*—the idea of unregulated free-market capitalism—is a deeply Anglo idea. In the nineteenth century, Germans called the free-market ideology *Manchesterismus*, after the city-leader of the Industrial Revolution. Even if a *laissez-faire* approximation of perfect competition existed between the late eighteenth century and mid-nineteenth century, there has been more than a hundred years over which the market has been dominated by the several hundred largest corporations. Legal regulation of trade practices has had limited success in preventing concentration of ownership that severely limits market competition. Even a cursory look at big business in English-speaking countries and globally—media, supermarket chains, digital and internet moguls such as Apple, Microsoft, Facebook and Google, and much else—shows that the free market is an abstraction with no close equivalent in reality. J.K. Galbraith (1977) argued that the idea of the 'free market' actually serves as an instrument for the implementation of the power of multinational corporations. The influence of big business extends into politics, popular culture and social values: these are messy, multifaceted social processes, and there is nothing clear-cut and mathematical about them.

Since the time of Adam Smith, the world has changed more than in the many millennia beforehand. After more than two centuries of extremely dynamic development, the capitalism of today is much different from its early industrial form in the late eighteenth-century Britain. At the time, the steam engine ushered the first major wave of technological innovation coming out of workshops and factories owned and run by individual businessmen. They employed what Adam Smith called the 'inferior ranks of people'—labourers who worked up to 16 hours a day for sheer survival, often alongside their wives and children. Popper (1973, 140) emphasised that the capitalism of unrestrained '*laissez-faire* has disappeared from the face of the earth' and that it is 'absurd to identify the economic system of the modern democracies with the system Marx called capitalism'—let alone with the time of Adam Smith.

Capitalism Triumphant

> Capitalism is a system where man exploits man. In communism, exactly the reverse is true. (An old Soviet joke)

> Capitalism is teetering on the edge of a precipice. Communism is always one step ahead. (A more recent Soviet joke)

The West became economically and technologically superior to other civilisations in the seventeenth and eighteenth centuries, when capitalism became the established mode of production in north-western Europe. As mentioned, some elements of capitalism existed much earlier: banking started in Florence in the thirteenth century; merchants of Venice and Genoa ran international trade in the fourteenth and fifteenth centuries; double-entry bookkeeping was introduced in Venice in the fifteenth century. The word 'capital' first appears in the Italian language at the end of the fourteenth century (*il capitale*; at that time spelt *il chapitale*). The concept of 'capitalism,' denoting a socio-economic system based on private property, free enterprise and profit-focused production, is much newer.

According to French historian Fernand Braudel (1992, 255–263), the earliest appearance of the concept of capitalism can be traced to French authors of the mid-nineteenth century, but it entered into a more widespread usage at the beginning of the twentieth century. According to Popper (1973, 335), Marx used it first. The notion of capitalism (just like 'communism') had pejorative connotation so it was usually used by critics of the system; its apologists were more prone to refer to it as 'market democracy' or 'industrialised society.' However, with widespread use, the concept acquired value neutrality and now simply denotes a certain type of economic and political system first fully developed in the north-western corner of Europe and then spread far and wide.

What is the best way to define capitalism? Capitalism is a socio-economic system, or a 'mode of production,' where the means of production are privately owned by individuals—the 'capitalists'—who invest capital in an economic enterprise in order to earn profit. For this to happen, the capital needs to be connected with labour that gets the actual work done; capitalists engage workers for a wage. Businesses compete and sell their products, goods or services. In market competition, smaller and less successful firms are eliminated or swallowed by the bigger and more successful ones. More efficient businesses are those that can best cut costs of production, including labour costs, in order to maximise their profits. This is done either by introducing technological innovations and thus increasing productivity, or by finding cheaper workers, for example, by moving the business to poorer countries. This practice, widespread since the 1970s, has turned Western economies into 'service economies' and created 'rust belts' in areas with previous concentrations of manufacturing. It also obliterated a respectable, full-time employed working class that earned a decent living wage and created the casually employed 'precariat' (Standing 2011).

The nineteenth century was a veritable age of capital and a time of spectacular economic progress. Urbanisation and industrialisation of north-western Europe led not only to a dramatic social change but also to the first wave of globalisation: the dynamic capitalist economy sought to expand beyond Europe (Hobsbawm 1975). The British Empire was the most momentous outcome of capitalism's inherent urge to expand, but not the only one. The steam engine, employed in shipping and railways, brought a revolution in transportation. The growing global traffic enabled not only much faster colonisation of extra-European lands but also a multiple increase in the size of capitalist economies. Goods, from gold to opium, were now travelling across vast distances. The invention of the telegraph in the late 1830s was another technological leap that propelled a rapid growth of world trade and, together with the patenting of the telephone, was every bit as revolutionary in connecting the world as the internet was at the end of the twentieth century (Hobsbawm 1975). We often think of globalisation as a recent phenomenon, but in the last quarter of the nineteenth century the capitalist economy was already global (ibid.).

Alongside the north-west of Europe, the nineteenth-century US was also going through an extraordinary growth spurt. Towards the end of the century, many millions of European peasants from the not-yet-industrialised European South and East migrated across the Atlantic, where they became factory fodder in the fast industrialising American cities. The growth was phenomenal: the population of Philadelphia, in 1800 the second largest American city and a major centre of textile, railroad and ship building, grew from around 40,000 at the start of the nineteenth century to nearly 1.3 million by its end. Immigrants from Germany and Ireland, and later Russia, Poland and Italy made up a large part of the growth. The Irish famine of the 1840s brought a great influx of immigrants, and by mid-century a quarter of New Yorkers were Irish. New York's population had risen from around 60,000 in 1800 to 3.4 million by the end of the century (Hobsbawm 1975).

Other English-speaking settler nations—Canada, Australia, New Zealand—also went through rapid economic development based on free-market principles during this period. Due to the scarcity of labour, the working masses enjoyed a better deal in the overseas colonies—later independent countries—so many chose to leave Europe, even its most advanced parts such as Britain and Germany, and try their luck overseas. Gold Rushes in California and Australia in the mid-nineteenth century secured the multiplication of the means of payment, lowered interest rates and enabled the expansion of finance and credit. The discovery of gold placed the US and even the sparsely populated Australia firmly on the map of the global capitalist economy. However, until the end of the First World War, Britain, with its vast colonial empire, was without a serious global competitor (Hobsbawm 1975, 1989).

In contrast to the economic and technological boom, the quality of life in the nineteenth-century slums of London and other growing cities of industrialising Europe was comparable to that in today's slums of the developing world's mega-cities. In 1832, cholera epidemics swept through Paris, claiming 20,000 lives; in 1849 over 14,000 died of cholera in London. It was not until 1854 that its cause was linked to contaminated water. Bubonic plague, which devastated medieval European cities several times, reappeared in 1894, having spread from Canton through Hong Kong and India, killing mostly slum dwellers. A number of limited outbreaks hit Australia in the early twentieth century, especially Sydney where infected rats arrived on ships.

The abject misery of the working classes led not only Adam Smith in the late eighteenth century, but also his nineteenth-century successor economists Malthus, Ricardo, Marx and others, to draw pessimistic conclusions about the prospects of the working masses in capitalism. In spite of the extraordinary industrial progress, there was still not enough material goods to supply the conspicuous consumption of the rich and at the same time secure a decent life for the working masses. In the conditions of mass poverty, the increase in society's wealth—economic growth—was of primary importance.

The pessimistic view of the 'dismal science' started to fade in the theories of the 'second wave' of classical economists (usually called 'neoclassical,' again all British) in the second half of the nineteenth century. John Stuart Mill, William Stanley Jevons and Alfred Marshall started to refer to their country as 'opulent.' J.S. Mill argued that 'the future wellbeing of the labouring classes [was] principally dependent on their own mental cultivation' (Mill 1970 [1848], 123). Britain was already affluent enough to allow him to speculate about the 'stationary state' of the economy, as elaborated below.

Economic Growth: Does 'More=Better' Still Apply?

The maximising logic of economic rationality can be expressed as *more=better*. We need to produce more and consume more. Our individual wealth, our particular business and our national economy, they all need to grow. In capitalism, anything else is a failure. It is an established axiom of economic science that 'stationary capitalism' is a contradiction in terms. Even economists who think about the economy in its social and historical context and may have socialist sympathies, such as one of the most respected twentieth-century economist Joseph Schumpeter (2009), agree with this view.

If a national growth rate drops under an acceptable level, there will be talk about an 'economic downturn.' Experts will be interviewed to analyse the reasons, give their predictions and suggest remedies. They will remind us of the gradient of the slippery slope: stagnation, recession, depression. The public debate will unfold under an unquestioned assumption that there is only one way out of the problem: to try as hard as possible, by all economic and political means, to re-invigorate the economy and speed up growth. Yet, this is ultimately irrational since endless growth is impossible in a finite world; if the goal of pursuing 'endless' growth is not rethought in the foreseeable future, the global consequences will be dire, as many have warned (e.g., to name just a few, Thompson 2010; Smith 2014; Martenson 2015).

Western countries are usually described as 'developed,' as opposed to 'developing,' which may suggest that economic development is finite. A slow-down tendency of economic growth in these countries has been established (Piketty 2014). In a society that starts from a low developmental point and embarks on urbanisation and industrialisation, economic growth is initially steep (e.g., China since the 1970s), but the curve inevitably flattens (Rostow 1960). In the early nineteenth century, England had a similar growth rate to China of the late twentieth century. Many prominent economists forecast the era of slow growth in 'developed' countries. Piketty's (2014, 72–109) projection of an average 1 per cent per capita growth of the global economy in the second half of the twenty-first century and beyond is based on long-term macroeconomic and demographic data. Under prevailing political conditions—the aversion to redistribution of wealth through taxes—the slowing of growth is likely to increase inequality.

Apparently, the developed countries have crossed a threshold: *more* does not necessarily mean *better* any longer. We have left what economists call the 'society of scarcity' and arrived in the 'affluent society.' The latter term entered general (academic) jargon after Galbraith's 1958 bestseller of that name. The difference between the society of scarcity and the affluent society is not just quantitative, but qualitative. It is easy to agree that some countries are poor and some are rich and that because of that they have a different set of issues to deal with. Problems arise when we try to 'objectively' establish the point at which we become affluent and 'have enough.' Clearly, this is a moving target.

To use Oscar Wilde's expression, the 'soul of a man in capitalism' is an insatiable soul, and this is hailed as a systemic virtue. 'Greed is good,' we have been told, and 'consumer confidence'—the readiness to spend rather than save—is an important parameter of the economic health of a society. If I feel an acute lack of a new iPad or an iPhone, that's good, not only for Apple, but also for my local retailer, my country's gross domestic product (GDP), and for the millions of Chinese workers who supply Apple with components, therefore also for the Chinese economy, and by extension for most world economies that trade with China or borrow money from it. Assailed by relentless marketing and driven by status among her peers, a Western teenager may feel in need of a new iPhone as acutely as a teenager from a Third-world slum may feel a need for a second pair of shoes.

The average GDP per capita for the 35 countries in the Organisation for Economic Cooperation and Development (OECD)—consisting of the world's leading economies—was $38,024 in 2016. At this level, we can argue that we can have all our material needs satisfied. But as the forces of production grow, new material needs and wants are created by advertising, and an increasing number of goods and services fall into the perceived realm of necessity. Affluent Western nations regard economic growth as the primary policy goal and a necessary condition of their collective wellbeing. As individuals, we are persuaded to crave things that we do not yet have, and to regularly replace our perfectly good clothes, furniture, cars and electronic gadgets by new, fashionable ones. We live in a 'throw-away' and ever-updating society. In the 'home ownership societies' of the Anglosphere, we are also under systemic pressure to progress our 'housing careers'—move to larger and more expensive houses in 'better' (i.e., more expensive) suburbs as our earnings increase. Dwellings have become larger in spite of declining household size. We need to work hard to service large debt for most of our lives.

GDP vs. Quality of Life

The success and health of national economies, and by extension of our societies, has been conventionally measured by the economic growth rate, that is, by the increase in the GDP.[12] GDP is the sum of the value of all goods and services produced in a country in one year. The simplest method to calculate the GDP is to measure total expenditure: in a market economy, it is assumed that everything that is produced is ultimately sold and bought. In this method, GDP is the sum of private consumption of goods and services, investment in new assets (but not 'investment' in buying shares or existing property, which is classified as 'saving'[13]), government spending (including wages of government employees, but excluding payments such as social security which is merely redistribution) and the net value of exports minus imports.

This traditional measure of economic success is flawed on both technical and substantive grounds. Technically, it does not include the 'grey' or 'cash in hand' economy. Recently, attempts have been made to rectify this deficiency. In the European Union for example, even illegal prostitution and the trade in drugs are to be included in GDP (Alderman 2014). The 'social economy' is not included in the GDP either. For example, if friends and family exchange services and favours but no money is changing hands, from grandparents baby-sitting to neighbours giving each other a helping hand, this is valuable work, but it has no official economic value. Such social economy is considerable in 'middle-income' and poorer countries, but it does not feature in the official GDP measurement, which makes those countries seem poorer than they actually are. For capitalist economic rationality, such social economy constitutes non-systemic, or perhaps even anti-systemic, behaviour: if you drop off a friend at the airport, that's a loss to the GDP—she should have paid for a cab! A substantive flaw of the GDP is that it counts much undesirable expenditure that actually decreases our collective quality of life: if there is more crime, the rising expenditure on law enforcement and prisons increases the GDP; more car accidents mean more expenditure on repairs and so on. Robert Kennedy stated this forcefully in a speech at the University of Kansas in 1968[14]:

> Our gross national product [...] counts air pollution and cigarette advertising, and ambulances to clear our highways of carnage. It counts special locks for our doors and the jails for those who break them. It counts the destruction of our redwoods and the loss of our natural wonder in chaotic sprawl. It counts napalm and the cost of a nuclear warhead, and armoured cars for police who fight riots in our streets.

Perhaps most importantly, GDP measures expenditure and not outcomes. For example, the per capita cost of the health care system in the US is far higher than in Australia or Western Europe, but this does not lead to people being healthier or better cared for. Typically, the reverse is true since poorer Americans cannot afford medical treatment. From Robert Kennedy's speech again:

> Yet the gross national product does not allow for the health of our children, the quality of their education, or the joy of their play. It does not include the beauty of our poetry or the strength of our marriages; the intelligence of our public debate or the integrity of our public officials. It measures neither our wit nor our courage; neither our wisdom nor our learning, neither our compassion nor our devotion to our country; it measures everything, in short, except that which makes life worthwhile.

The main point here is that GDP is a quantitative measure, counting all financial transactions regardless of what they mean to society and people's quality of life. The conventional measure of a nation's economic progress, the GDP per capita, can rise but be concentrated in the hands of a minority due to increasing inequality. For example, the inflation-adjusted median household income in the US fell by 4 per cent between 2000 and 2008 despite impressive economic growth of the US economy as a whole (GDP increased at an average of close to 3 per cent per annum) over that period (Stiglitz 2010, 284). In the post-2009 recovery period, almost all the economic growth in the US has been concentrated in the top 1 per cent of earners. Moreover, the real income (income adjusted for inflation) of the lowest US earners (often referred to as the 'working poor') has fallen since the 1970s, while at the same time the real income of high earners has increased considerably (Stiglitz 2010; Piketty 2014).

The mismatch between the relentless quest for growth and wealth accumulation, at an individual and societal level, and the quality of life, was noted by Oscar Wilde (1912, 18–19) in his pamphlet *The Soul of Man under Socialism*:

> In a community like ours, where property confers immense distinction, honour, respect, titles and other pleasant things of the kind, man, being naturally ambitious, makes it his aim to accumulate this property, and goes on wearily and tediously accumulating it long after he has got more than he wants, or can use, or enjoy, or perhaps even know of. Man will kill himself by overwork in order to secure property, and really, considering the enormous advantages that property brings, one is hardly surprised. One's

> regret is that society should be constructed on such a basis that man has been forced into a groove in which he cannot freely develop what is wonderful, and fascinating, and delightful in him—in which, in fact, he misses the true pleasure and joy of living.

Inevitably, however, in any society at any time, most people are 'forced into a groove.' By definition, a majority conforms to 'systemic behaviour,' which does not mean they necessarily enjoy it most of the time. Given that our social status depends primarily on our earnings, 'net worth' (assets minus debts) and consumption, we conform: we work hard, we buy, we update, we keep up with the Joneses. We have to make sure we get regular promotions and salary increases; if we run a business we have to make sure we keep up with the competition by cutting costs and keeping productivity high.

There are people among us, a brave—or just lazy perhaps?—minority of the 'unconventional' who ignore, or at some stage of their lives started ignoring the economic and consumerist 'imperatives' and 'pressures.' This often exacts high social costs of disapproval, including by one's own children. However, is the conventional cycle of want, overwork, consumption, waste, debt and stress indeed *rational*? In spite of the dominant economic logic, it is not hard to agree with a proposition that enrichment has a very strong non-pecuniary aspect which deserves more time than the rat race normally leaves us in the adult part of our time on Earth. In the words of J.S. Mill (1970 [1848], 113), the most authoritative voice of nineteenth-century British liberalism:

> [...] It is scarcely necessary to remark that a stationary condition of capital and population implies no stationary state of human improvement. There would be as much scope as ever for all kinds of intellectual culture, and moral and social progress; as much room for improving the Art of Living, and much more likelihood of its being improved, when minds ceased to be engrossed by the art of getting on.

Is it possible that the best minds of the nineteenth century were simply wrong? Is there something we now know that they could not know, when we take for granted that growth is not only desirable but also indispensable?

The mounting argument against the relentless policy concentration on economic growth is summarily dismissed by policymakers. Politicians, economic experts and business people repeatedly tell us that without growth 'jobs would be lost' and our economy would stall. It is implied that to argue against maximisation of material wealth is irrational. Indeed, how can one argue against an increase in the 'standard of living'? But if we substitute 'level of material consumption' for 'standard of living'—for this is what it really is—all of a sudden it does not sound as fateful. J.S. Mill, a scholar and a member of the British parliament, and by no means a wild-eyed revolutionary, argued:

> I confess I am not charmed with the ideal of life held out by those who think that the normal state of human beings is that of struggling to get on; the trampling, crushing, elbowing, and treading on each other's heels, which form the existing type of social life, are the most desirable lot of human kind, or anything but the disagreeable symptoms of one of the phases of industrial progress. (ibid., p. 116)

Surely, given the impressive industrial progress in the intervening period of more than 150 years, the possibility of a 'stationary state' warrants even greater consideration today. Without embarking on a difficult argument on whether we 'have enough,' it is obvious that advanced capitalism replaces the problem of scarcity with another set of problems.

This has not escaped the attention of many authors, who queried the dominance of the GDP per capita as the central measure of social progress and wellbeing, and argued against equating economic performance, of individuals and societies, with wellbeing. Over the past decades, a research literature on (other than economic) 'social indicators' have emerged (see Cummins et al. 2003; Stiglitz et al. 2009). A Human Development Index (HDI) was created in 1990 to 'emphasize that people and their capabilities should be the ultimate criteria for assessing the development of a country, not economic growth alone.' It measures three dimensions of human development: longevity and health; education; and a standard of living (UN 2016). Remarkably, in 2009, the French centre-right government commissioned a report on *Measurement of Economic Performance and Social Progress*. The investigation was entrusted to three unorthodox economists, Joseph Stiglitz, Amartya Sen and Jean Paul Fitoussi, two of them Nobel Prize winners (Stiglitz and Sen[15]). A unifying theme of the 2009 report is that 'the time is ripe for our measurement system to *shift emphasis from measuring economic production to measuring people's wellbeing*. And measures of wellbeing should be put in the context of sustainability' (Stiglitz et al. 2009, 12, emphasis in the original).

The policy focus on growth, and the idea this is best achieved by deregulation, may indeed lead to a higher average GDP per capita (for some time), but it also leads to many unintended consequences. These include increased inequality (since the 1970s) and higher incidence of various diseases and conditions brought about by competitive, economically focused 'progress.' For example, an epidemic of mental health issues, drug abuse, obesity (including child obesity, especially in English-speaking countries), diabetes and hypertension has been well documented. Many experts argue that life expectancy in Western countries has peaked and that problems associated with affluence and 'overdevelopment' need serious attention by policymakers. At the same time, developing countries are eager to emulate the Western, economically focused path to prosperity and join the global competition where a country's progress and global importance is measured squarely through its GDP. In the West however, there are recent but clear signs that policymakers are gradually starting to take the non-economic indicators of social progress more seriously.

Notes

1. Usually defined as the period from the fall of the Roman Empire (476 AD) to the Renaissance and the 'Age of Discovery' that started in the fifteenth century.
2. The population of Florence is currently under 400,000. At its largest in 1971, the city was home to 460,000 people.
3. *Cristobal Colon En Las Américas* by Sicilian sculptor Ugo Attardi (1923–2006) was installed in Plazoleta Provincia de Tucumán, at the intersection of Avenida 9 de Julio and Avenida Santa Fé in central Buenos Aires on 12 October 1992.

4. For example, the US prison for terrorism suspects in Guantanamo Bay established in January 2002. In December 2014, the US Senate Select Committee on Intelligence released key findings and the executive summary of the 6000-page 'Committee Study of the Central Intelligence Agency's Detention and Interrogation Program' (covering the period 2001–06) revealing widespread use of torture ('enhanced interrogation techniques') on the detainees. During his presidential campaign, Donald Trump advocated the use of special interrogation techniques where justified. See https://fas.org/irp/congress/2014_rpt/ssci-rdi.pdf. Accessed 18 June 2017.
5. Scottish philosopher and historian Thomas Carlyle (1850) wrote in a pamphlet of 'respectable professors of the Dismal Science.'
6. The prize in economics is actually the 'Sveriges Riksbank (Bank of Sweden) prize in Economic Sciences in Memory of Alfred Nobel,' first awarded in 1969, and it is not directly linked to the Nobel Foundation.
7. Jevons is nowadays best known for the 'Jevons paradox.' Its meaning and contemporary significance can be illustrated by the case of the automobile in the US. The introduction of more energy-efficient cars in the 1970s did not curtail the demand for fuel because decreased costs led to an increase in driving and the number of cars on the road. Similarly, technological improvements in refrigeration led to more and larger refrigerators. In the capitalist context, improvements in technology do not lead to savings but to growth—an ever-larger productive output.
8. John Stuart Mill (1806–73) was a philosopher and economist, and also a member of the British parliament (1865–68), a philanthropist and one of the rare plausible male feminists.
9. *The Road to Serfdom* is the title of Friedrich von Hayek's (1944) book in which he argues against government regulation of economic affairs, and especially against centralised planning, which, according to him, inevitably leads to totalitarianism.
10. Joseph Schumpeter (1883–1950) was an influential Austrian-born economist. He worked in Austria and Germany before becoming a US citizen in 1932. He popularised the term 'creative destruction' to describe the process of continual renewal in capitalism.
11. More recently, Akerlof and Schiller (2009) have written extensively about 'animal spirits' in their book of that name.
12. Although GDP is the most quoted measure, two other measures are preferred by some analysts: per capita gross national income (GNI) and net

national income (NNI). More details at http://www.oecd-ilibrary.org/economics/oecd-factbook-2011-2012/national-income-per-capita_factbook-2011-20-en.

13. Including the purchase of an existing property into GDP would lead to double counting since the property was included in GDP when it was first built.
14. The full speech is available at https://www.jfklibrary.org/Research/Research-Aids/Ready-Reference/RFK Speeches/Remarks-of-Robert-F-Kennedy-at-the-University-of-Kansas-March-18-1968.aspx. Accessed 26 June 2017.
15. The HDI is based in the intellectual legacy of Amartya Sen.

Bibliography

Akerlof, George A., and Robert Schiller. 2009. *Animal Spirits: How Human Psychology Drives the Economy, and Why it Matters for Global Capitalism.* Princeton: Princeton University Press.

Alderman, Liz. 2014. Sizing Up Black Markets and Red-Light Districts for G.D.P. *The New York Times*, 9 July 2014. Accessed 18 June 2017. https://www.nytimes.com/2014/07/10/business/international/eu-nations-counting-sex-and-drug-trades-toward-gdp.html

Appadurai, Arjun. 2003. Illusion of Permanence: Interview with Arjun Appadurai. *Perspecta* 34: 44–52.

Botton, Alan de. 2009. *The Pleasures and Sorrows of Work.* New York: Penguin.

Braudel, Fernand. 1992. *Civilization and Capitalism 15th–18th Century: The Structures of Everyday Life.* Berkley: University of California Press. First published in 1979 as *Civilisation matérielle, économie et capitalism, XVth–XVIIIth siècle.* Paris: Armand Colin.

Brentjes, Sonja, and Robert G. Morrison. 2010. The Sciences in Islamic Societies (750–1800). In *The New Cambridge History of Islam*, ed. Robert Irwin, vol. 4. Cambridge: Cambridge University Press.

Burckhardt, Jacob. 1990 [1867]. *The Civilization of the Renaissance in Italy.* Penguin Classics.

Carlyle, Thomas. 1850. *Latter Day Pamphlets*, No. 1. London: Charles Scribner's, 1901.

Cummins, R.A., R. Eckersley, J. Pallant, J. Van Vugt, and R. Misajon. 2003. Developing a National Index of Subjective Wellbeing: The Australian Unity Wellbeing Index. *Social Indicators Research* 64: 159–190.

Galbraith, John Kenneth. 1977. *The Age of Uncertainty: A History of Economic Ideas and Their Consequences*. New York: Houghton Mifflin.
Hayek, Fredrick von. 2005 [1944]. *The Road to Serfdom*. London: Routledge.
Hobsbawm, Eric. 1962. *The Age of Revolution 1789–1848*. New York: New America Library (Mentor Books).
———. 1975. *The Age of Capital*. London: Weidenfeld and Nicolson Ltd.
———. 1989. *Politics for the Rational Left: Political Writing, 1977–1988*. London: Verso.
Huisinga, Johan. 1996. *The Autumn of the Middle Ages*. Chicago: University of Chicago Press. First published in Dutch in 1919 as *Herfsttij der Middeleeuwen*.
Jevons, William Stanley. 1866. Brief Account of a General Mathematical Theory of Political Economy. *The Journal of the Royal Statistical Society*, London, XXIX (June): 282–287. First presented to the British Association in 1862.
Kahneman, Daniel. 2011. *Thinking Fast and Thinking Slow*. New York: Farrar, Straus and Giroux.
Kahneman, Daniel, and Amos Tversky. 1979. Prospect Theory: An Analysis of Decision under Risk. *Econometrica* 47: 263–291.
Keynes, John Maynard. 1936. *General Theory of Employment, Interest and Money*. London: Macmillan.
Mackay, Charles. 1995 [1841]. *Extraordinary Popular Delusions and the Madness of Crowds*. Ware, UK: Wordsworth Editions Ltd.
Martenson, Chris. 2015. In Denial: We Pursue Endless Growth at Our Peril. *PeakProsperity*. Accessed 18 June 2017. https://www.peakprosperity.com/blog/92776/denial-we-pursue-endless-growth-our-peril
Mill, John Stuart. 1970 [1848]. *Principles of Political Economy with Some of Their Applications to Social Philosophy*, Books IV and V. Edited with and introduction by Donald Winch. Harmondsworth, UK and Baltimore, MA: Penguin Classics.
Mises, Ludwig von. 1960. *Epistemological Problems of Economics*. New York: David Van Nostrand Company. First published in 1933 as *Grundprobleme der Nationalökonomie: Untersuchungen über Verfahren, Aufgaben und Inhalt der Wirtschafts- und Gesellschaftslehre*.
Moore, Barrington. 1966. *Social Origins of Dictatorship and Democracy: Lord and Peasant in the Making of the Modern World*. Boston: Beacon Press.
Piketty, Thomas. 2014. *Capital in the Twenty-first Century*. Cambridge, MA: Harvard University Press. First published as *Le capital au XXI siècle* in 2013 by Éditions du Seuil.
Popper, Karl. 1973 [1945]. *The Open Society and its Enemies*. Vol. II. London: Routledge.

Rostow, W.W. 1960. *The Stages of Economic Growth: A Non-communist Manifesto*. Cambridge: Cambridge University Press.

Schumpeter, Joseph. 2009. *Can Capitalism Survive? Creative Destruction and the Global Economy*. New York: Harper Perennial Modern Classics.

Sifferlin, Alexandra. 2014. IVF Babies Hit Record High. *Time*, 18 February 2014. Accessed 18 June 2017. http://healthland.time.com/2014/02/18/ivf-babies-hit-record-high/

Smith, Adam. 1993 [1776]. *An Inquiry into the Nature and Causes of the Wealth of Nations*. Indianapolis and Cambridge: Hackett Publishing Company.

Smith, Warwick. 2014. Do We Dare Question Economic Growth? *The Guardian*, 13 October 2014. Accessed 18 June 2017. https://www.theguardian.com/commentisfree/2014/oct/13/do-we-dare-to-question-economic-growth

Standing, Guy. 2011. *The Precariat: The New Dangerous Class*. London: Bloomsbury Academic.

Stiglitz, Joseph. 2002. There is No Invisible Hand. *The Guardian*, 20 December 2002. Accessed 18 June 2017. https://www.theguardian.com/education/2002/dec/20/highereducation.uk1

———. 2010. *Freefall: America, Free Markets and the Sinking of the World Economy*. New York and London: W. W. Norton & Company.

Stiglitz, Joseph, Amartya Sen, and Jean-Paul Fitoussi. 2009. *Report by the Commission on the Measurement of Economic Performance and Social Progress*. A report commissioned by the French Government. Available at http://www.stiglitz-sen-fitoussi.fr/documents/rapport_anglais.pdf

Thompson, Clive. 2010. Nothing Grows Forever. *Mother Jones*, May/June 2010. Accessed 18 June 2017. http://www.motherjones.com/politics/2010/07/peter-victor-deficit-growth/

UN. 2016. United Nations (UN) Development Program, Human Development Index (HDI). Accessed 18 June 2017. http://hdr.undp.org/en/content/human-development-index-hdi

Weber, Max. 1958 [1905]. *The Protestant Ethic and the Spirit of Capitalism*. New York: Scribner.

———. 1978 [1921]. *Economy and Society*. Edited by G. Roth and C. Wittich. Berkley: University of California Press.

Wilde, Oscar. 1912 [1891]. *The Soul of Man under Socialism*. London: A.L. Humphreys.

3

The Rationality of Competition

Back in the 1830s John Stuart Mill (1977 [1836], 132) described competitive society in a way that we can recognise as our own twenty-first-century reality: '[The] inevitable fruits of immense competition; of a state of society where any voice, not pitched in an exaggerated key, is lost in the hubbub. Success, in so crowded a field, depends not upon what a person is, but upon what he seems: mere marketable qualities become the object instead of substantial ones [...] [Q]uackery there always was, but it once was a test of an absence of sterling qualities: there was a proverb that good wine needed no bush.'

It is both mildly comforting and alarming to see that the necessity of 'blowing one's trumpet' is an old affliction. Competition is an entrenched feature of capitalist culture and most people have it deeply internalised. The society in which we live is a ceaseless scramble to achieve, advance one's fortunes, make good, better oneself, get ahead (many alternative expressions available!) and, since the appearance of mass media, become famous. Even the most selfless and cooperative individuals cannot avoid comparing themselves with others, consciously or unconsciously, and being compared, formally and informally, individually and in groups.

V. Colic-Peisker, A. Flitney, *The Age of Post-Rationality*,
https://doi.org/10.1007/978-981-10-6259-9_3

Free competition for truth, wealth and power is often cited as the historic contribution of Western civilisation. Based on this principle, capitalism has secured an unprecedented level of technological advancement and consequently global domination. To a Western mind, the idea of competition makes almost immediate sense, and as a social principle, it sounds fair: people reap social rewards on the basis of their skill, hard work and ambition, which can only be measured against other people. If China 'catches up' and in a due course surpasses the West, as many expect or fear, it will be because this ancient and sophisticated civilisation recently adopted Western-style competition.

Time and Money

> Tired of lying in the sunshine, staying home to watch the rain
> You are young and life is long and there is time to kill today
> And then one day you find, ten years have got behind you
> No-one told you when to run, you missed the starting gun
> Lyrics of the song 'Time' by Pink Floyd (*The Dark Side of the Moon* album, 1973)

In capitalism, time and money are the quintessential couple. Equally so on The *Dark Side of the Moon*, one of the top-selling albums of all time. Pink Floyd's *Time* and *Money* are famous songs familiar to several generations of rock music fans. Alongside their deep existential subtext—a meditation on the transience of youth and life itself and the premonition of death—the songs have another, social subtext. They can be understood as a commentary on the rat race. In the race, one should not 'miss the starting gun,' and money is the measure of how well one is doing in the race. Time is money and money is time. Our time is extremely structured, but we are not its masters. In capitalism, time is our master and we are slaves to it. An actual slave may have had a chance to lie about when the master is not watching; the slavery of the modern individual is internalised and therefore impossible to escape. Our mortality adds an existential dimension to the idea of 'limited time.' We feel pressured to compete and achieve something that will last beyond our physical demise, and this quest leads to joining the rat race in some form.

The pithy phrase that depicts the essence of capitalism—'time is money'—originates from Benjamin Franklin (1748). Franklin gives advice to a young tradesman:

> Remember, that *time is money*. He that can earn ten shillings a day by his labor, and goes abroad, or sits idle, one half of that day, though he spends but sixpence during his diversion or idleness, ought not to reckon *that* the only expense; he has really spent, or rather thrown away, five shillings besides [emphasis in the original].

We all have 24 hours available in a day, so this far the time issue seems fair. However, if we have money, we can pay other people—buy their time—to do various things for us and instead of us. In effect, this gains us time to do what we like and perhaps work on something that will make us 'immortal' instead of, say, cleaning the house or looking after young children (even though children are the 'ordinary' people's fall-back on achieving immortality). While some people may use the time buy-out to relax and enjoy themselves, many people buy extra time based on a cost-benefit analysis close to Ben Franklin's advice cited above. They delegate routine tasks to people poorer than themselves and use the time saved to press on with the rat race and make more money. Money buys not only domestic cleaners and babysitters but also status, security, anything we want …or so it seems. Chasing money, or 'wealth accumulation' in standard economic language, is therefore the default, commonly accepted rational goal of our paid work and other exertions, indeed a rational way to spend our limited time on earth. Even if we have enough, we feel compelled to want more. Many people who grew up in developed Western capitalism consider pleasant idleness as an irrational wastage of time, while the right thing to do is turning time into money.

A typical citizen of an affluent country, and especially an English-speaking one, is convinced that it is better to have money than to have time. A respectable person never complains about lack of money, but is always busy and pressed for time, never idle and with some luck, never unemployed. Even if we do not need to be terrifically busy, we will make ourselves that way or at least create an impression that we are busy. Working hard and taking part in the (rat) race is 'normal.' This systemic behaviour—often manifesting as a neurosis of workaholism, and wealth and status accumulation—is internalised by millions of overworked competitive individuals. Time is not to be *enjoyed*, but to be *used* to make money, or something that improves our ability to make money in the future, such as getting an education or schmoosing around important people, thus developing important social networks. We are a highly strung civilisation of anxious individuals, and that's how capitalism likes us to be.

During those couple of weeks a year when busy Westerners turn into carefree tourists somewhere in the Pacific, Caribbean or Mediterranean, they often comment how the pace of life there is (pleasantly) slower and the people are relaxed and generous with their time. These people's time may not be so readily exchangeable for money and social status as is the case with our 'Western' time, so they enjoy the spontaneity of pleasant activities momentarily on offer: chatting with their neighbours, playing music and dancing in the street, or in church, flirting and making love, or sitting on the side of the road and watching the world go by. Once capitalism with its 'economic opportunities' kicks in and the scramble for money and status starts in earnest, the relaxed lifestyle is over; people start using their time 'rationally.' We may wonder whether such 'progress' actually makes much sense: let's rush, work hard and compete for 48 weeks a year so we can have four relaxed weeks—if we're lucky! The rat race leaves little time and energy for such subversive thoughts, however, and the life focused on work and business goes on.

Meritocracy?

The most passionate advocates of unbridled competition, the neo-classical economists and neo-liberal governments, see competitive society as inherently meritocratic. Competent and hardworking entrepreneurs and workers are rewarded, while others, naturally and fairly, are penalised for their ineptitude and sloth (Galbraith 1974, 67). Market competition motivates and indeed forces people to optimise the use of resources, to specialise, to carefully calculate costs and benefits and to improve work organisation, technology and productivity. It is widely accepted that society's dynamism and progress depends on continually churning out winners and losers. The end result of such a capitalist-rational economy is the growth of its productive outputs and winning the battle against scarcity. Therefore, according to this view, competition is a major contributor not only to an affluent, but also to a fair society.

The central feature of the capitalist economy—a 'free' market contest among economic actors—is meant to secure rational allocation of scarce resources. This is what conventional economics, which used to be presented to undergraduate students as the 'science of scarcity,' has argued for over two centuries. Yet, many have criticised this paradigm and argue that the allocation of resources resulting from market competition is not entirely rational, and even less fair: apart from creating large inequalities between individuals and nations, it disregards the wellbeing of other living creatures and damages the natural environment on which we ultimately depend.

To be sure, the material achievements of capitalism are beyond dispute; they have been acknowledged even by its fiercest critics, the best known of whom is Karl Marx and a long line of his disciples. It is usually forgotten that Marx's classic early text, *The Communist Manifesto* (1848, co-authored with Friedrich Engels), paid tribute to the extraordinary success of the 'bourgeois society,' which achieved a 'subjection of the forces of nature to man in barely a century.' If Marx could look down at us from the after-world,[1] he would be impressed by the level that the 'subjection of nature to man' has reached in the twenty-first century—and by the problems it has created.

By producing winners and losers, competition motivates people to work harder, run faster, look better: most people do not want to end up at the bottom of the heap. 'Loser' is one of the nastiest labels in the English language. When another cyclist zooms past Author 1 on her way to work, she automatically presses harder on the pedals. In this particular case, there is nothing palpable to be gained, but she instinctively dislikes being left behind; it must be her 'competitive nature'—an instinct most people develop while growing up in a competitive society. We are social beings and comparison with others tells us how good we are and where we stand in the pecking order. The outcome of this comparison is crucial not only for our self-esteem but also for our status in society. We are constantly assigned a place in various competitive rankings; it starts at school and continues in our working lives. Group comparisons are pervasive. A myriad of human collectives are constantly compared: suburbs, nations, ethnic groups, universities, banks, restaurants, airlines, retailers, fashion labels—you name it. Competition turns people on: sporting league tables and politicians' standings in opinion polls are major ingredients of daily news. Sporting contests make us scream and cheer, celebrate and mourn, and occasionally run amok and kill each other. We may have our private doubts about the value of the rankings, but publicly they count as a key method of meritocracy, its vital tool. The winners who top the rankings are invariably rewarded in more or less tangible ways. Being able to assert one's winning status is a great pleasure in itself for many people. Author 2 used to play a rather obscure, but fiercely competitive, sport called canoe polo. A few years ago, an A-grade team had, in a clichéd style, come from behind in the grand finals to dramatically snatch victory from his team. Needless to say, he wasn't too happy. It did not make him feel any better when the formidably built captain of the winning team collected his gold medal wearing a T-shirt with the slogan 'Second place is the first loser.'

The popularity of rankings is hardly diminished by the fact that cheating to win is endemic in many, if not most, domains of social life. There must be some honest winners, because there are areas where it is impossible to cheat, for example, being a great comedian. But as a rule, the higher the rewards of winning, the more likely it is that there will be cheating. The widespread corrosion of the meritocratic ideal may be seen as, in a large degree, a consequence of what we often refer to as 'competitive pressure.' The pressure is manifold: we pressure ourselves to protect our self-concept and call it ambition or 'drive to succeed'; our significant others (typically parents) have expectations of our success that we do not want to disappoint. The motive for the latter may vary from noble ones like a sense of duty (e.g., a dutiful son) to rather more selfish ones like vanity and 'ego'—although a combination of motives is always the most likely scenario.

Our present argument is that a competitive society creates competitive people and, under high pressure, also dishonest cheats, but personal factors are not entirely irrelevant. The so-called 10-80-10 rule is a plausible simplification of many psychological experiments on conformity and the influence of social milieu on the individual (Cialdini and Goldstein 2004). The rule states that a large majority of about 80 per cent of people adjust to their surroundings and act as others do. If people around them are honest, they will also be honest; if cheating is widespread, they will jump on the bandwagon. The top 10 per cent (the principled) will always be honest regardless of what others do. It is likely that these honest people are more rarely found at the top of various ranking tables. The bottom 10 per cent (the devious) will always cheat regardless of their environment; these people will be frequently found among winners if their core ability comes even close to their level of deceit.

There are three examples of widespread cheating close to our hearts. Both authors of this book are/were keen cyclists and follow the world's premier cycling competition, the Tour de France. The case of Lance Armstrong, a celebrity cyclist who turned out to be a ruthless cheat, is illustrative. Armstrong overcame cancer and proceeded to win the Tour de France seven times, and was therefore a miracle of determination and physical form, many people's ultimate sporting hero. In 2013, an amazing twist to this story revealed he was gorging on banned performance-enhancing substances and consequently he was stripped of his titles. Still, he was merely within the 80 per cent of conformists and was better at cheating than others. He enjoyed fame, fortune and the admiration of millions for many years. Nathan Page, an Australian cyclist-turned actor, may serve as a much needed contrast to this story. He abandoned the idea of competing in the Tour de France when he reached the level at which taking banned substances was a necessary condition of success—since everyone else was doing it. His motives may be honesty itself or not being prepared to take health risks, likely both, but he nonetheless falls into the principled top 10 per cent. He's doing very well as an actor, and we wish him further success—although we suspect he'll never reach the planetary fame and riches afforded to Lance the Top Cheat. Most people realise that drugs have been widespread among top athletes for decades, just like cosmetic surgery is among Hollywood actors. This does not change the fact that cheating was not meant to be an integral part of meritocracy.

Another example comes from the world of finance (see Chap. 5). In Geraint Anderson's (2008) astonishing account of his life as a financial analyst in London's 'Square Mile,'[2] he makes it clear that the cheats are the most successful and likely to earn the highest among the generally mind-boggling salaries. Those prepared to engage in 'insider trading' (acting on price-sensitive information before it is publically released) and those who spread rumours in order to influence the share price of specific firms can make huge profits. In Anderson's accounts, hedge fund managers are virtually unbeatable in this game. Their cheating is much harder to intercept and prove than the cheating of athletes buzzing with steroids. Therefore, according to Anderson (2008, 73–74), 'greed, luck and having the morals of a hyena were clearly the principal determinants of one's financial success' in the Square Mile. This is quite different from ability and hard work determining success, as defined by the ideology of meritocracy.

The third example comes from our own working lives. Over the past couple of decades, university life has become more competitive. The nominally public universities are increasingly similar to private corporations that compete for students as 'customers.' They advertise their wares just like any other business. In addition, university academics have to be highly competitive in order to win research grants and get promoted. A large part of the competitiveness is about their publication record. Over the past decade, all manner of low-quality refereed journals have stepped in to meet the desperation of academics to get published. Most belong to the so-called open access category where authors pay a publication fee, often a considerable sum. The academic authors have therefore become the journals' 'valued customers,' and in consequence their work is reviewed less rigorously, if at all. The mushrooming of academic journals makes it hard to distinguish respectable journals from the shoddy and outright fake. In such an environment, those who value quality over quantity simply cannot compete, that is, produce as long a list of publications as their 'less fussy' colleagues. An overall effect is that the volume of academic publishing is ballooning, while quality is decreasing. There are other examples where quantification, comparison and competition have produced perverse outcomes—a poor quality of products or services and a 'race to the bottom' in an industry. Clearly, in such an environment, meritocracy is compromised.

Free Competition?

The ideology of competition has a powerful hold on the contemporary Western mind. According to Galbraith (1974, 34), as 'competitive society was developed and idealized, it was a thing of precision and symmetry, almost of beauty.' American, and Anglo-Saxon thought more generally, has always been prone to naturalise market competition. On the [European] continent, says Galbraith, 'men did talk about socialism [which treats cooperation rather than competition as the core principle of social interaction] but in the Anglo-Saxon tradition, they took the market [competition] very nearly for granted' (ibid., p. 27). Indeed, 'socialism' is a dirty word in the American political vocabulary—it is seen as a corruption of a 'normal' competitive state of being. The ideology of liberalism, centred on free-competing individuals, is an Anglo-Saxon invention, while socialism, with its emphasis on cooperation, redistribution and social justice, originated in continental Europe, initially championed by German and French thinkers.

Conventional capitalist wisdom maintains that a high personal motivation to compete requires the private ownership of productive resources—land, industrial and financial capital and lately also 'intellectual property'—and freedom from 'red tape.' Therefore, government should steer clear of stifling competition and dampening people's motivation by too much regulation; the role of government should be limited to establishing and enforcing the essential rules of competition. Yet, the complexity of competition requires a rather elaborate system of regulation. Ostensibly, this is to ensure that the competition is fair. In Australia, for example, the main regulating authority is the Australian Competition and Consumer Commission (ACCC) which can intervene if it notices instances of 'anti-competitive behaviour' banned by the 2010 Competition and Consumers Act (previously the 1965 Trade Practices Act and even earlier the 1906 Australian Industries Preservation Act). Its mantra is: competition is beneficial and protected by the ACCC because it provides the incentives or pressures for business to improve efficiency and the quality of their products or service, which ultimately benefits consumers, that is, everyone.

As discussed in Chap. 2, market competition is seldom fully 'free' because larger players gradually swallow smaller ones and a few large companies come to dominate the market. The ideal of free and fair competition in the labour market is distorted by well-networked individuals who profit by 'who they know'; conversely, some people are discriminated against based on economically irrelevant characteristics such as gender, age or race. Even if the system of competition is relatively efficient in its overall economic effect, it tends to make some individuals rich and some poor. To prevent the most negative social consequences of competition, such as extreme inequality, governments intervene. They introduce progressive taxes, publicly funded health services and welfare rights for the unemployed and those unable to work, such as mothers of young children, the elderly and the disabled. Governments also try to limit the economic power of the largest corporations (the 1984 split of the near-monopoly telephone provider in the US and Canada, Bell Systems, into a number of 'Baby Bells' is a prime example), regulate international trade, restrict unfair and false advertising, control and police unsafe products, prevent 'insider trading' in financial markets and legislate against discriminatory practices in employment. Most governments also choose to subsidise certain industries, often agriculture for the purpose of national 'food security,' and to support traditional industries important for local culture, 'character' and tourist attractiveness—think of French vignerons and cheese makers. Therefore, overall, 'free competition' is in fact heavily regulated. The level of freedom varies somewhat, with the Anglosphere earning higher scores than continental Europe. Americans seem especially allergic to 'government intervention.'

Competitive Individualism

The ideology of competitive individualism has deep roots in the Western history of ideas. The idea of the autonomous individual is central to Western culture and considered one of the core values of Western modernity (Lukes 1971). The liberal-democratic societies assign supreme value to the individual, above any collective the individual may belong to and draw support from; it is understood that a collective is likely to place a range of restraints on his (and especially her) individual freedom. Some key modern Western political ideals, such as human rights and civil liberties, rest on the central moral and legal position granted to the individual. Many have argued that this is also one of the key differences between the West—upholding principles of individual rights and liberties—and the Rest that gives primacy to community and authority over the individual. Non-Western cultures are purported to be less squeamish about limiting individual freedoms for the sake of various collective goals. For example, the family or the nation may assume primacy over the individual, and therefore s/he may not be allowed to divorce or may be obliged to serve in the army. Some Asian cultures seem to have successfully reconciled collective loyalties with competition. Examples include the Japanese loyal 'company man' with his life-long employment and readiness to work long hours for his company and not just personal promotion, and the tightly knit Chinese family where familial obligations often take primacy over the quest for individual freedom or success.

Fig. 3.1 John Brack, *Collins St, 5pm* (1955)

Christianity, the religion that represents a key cultural foundation of the West, is credited with the early establishment of the idea of the individual as a unique carrier of moral worth and the bearer of rights and responsibilities. This position is derived from the Christian postulate that a human being is a unique creature possessing an eternal soul. The secular Enlightenment took over the view which privileges the human individual over a collective, but shifted the core of the individual from the Soul to the Reason. Therefore, a human being—or more precisely a 'human person'[3]—is a special, unique creature endowed with reason, and therefore also of unique moral value. Philosophers gave rational humans a special status among living creatures, although, until relatively recently, 'she' was seen as less of a person than 'he,' because women were considered 'closer to nature,' more emotional and impulsive, and not as reasonable as men. In recent times, we started to reconsider the special status of humans. However, we have a vested interest in upholding this self-proclaimed exceptionalism from which we derive our right to exploit animals and the natural environment, while continuing to claim the high moral ground (Singer 1986).

Capitalism developed the Christian basis of individualism for its own purposes. The ideology of individualism—free people competing for social rewards—developed as an important part of capitalist culture and was gradually inscribed in Western legal systems. According to Max Weber (1958), the sixteenth-century Church Reformation and Protestantism which developed from it were important cultural factors in the development of capitalism and individualism in north-west Europe and its overseas colonies. In his *Protestant Ethic and the Spirit of Capitalism*, Weber argued that the work ethic and the high value placed on worldly success—primarily accumulating wealth—were peculiar to the reformed versions of Christianity. The increasingly well-educated and well-off burghers, the middle classes of northern German cities, were eager to run their businesses free of traditional barriers. They were catalysts of social and cultural change towards the rationalisation and secularisation of capitalism, which was also reflected in the re-articulation of Christian dogma during the sixteenth-century Reformation (Weber 1958).

The Protestant ethic presupposes a competitive society and personal responsibility for one's salvation. In general, a deeply felt religious devotion is likely to discourage activism and interest in worldly affairs, including the pursuit of wealth, and lead to a fatalistic surrender to God's will. However, in the Protestant interpretation of the Christian dogma, God's grace shines on an entrepreneurial person whose hard work, wealth accumulation and success in his chosen occupation ('calling,' with its religious overtones) indicate he had been chosen for salvation. Women's primary task remained to produce children while being pious and obedient to men. Christian piety, which kept a person righteous and therefore led to salvation, now took a form of a capitalist virtue: one had to shun hedonism and embrace asceticism, self-discipline and an unwavering work ethic, leading to wealth accumulation. Protestantism endowed work, even its humble manual varieties, with moral and spiritual significance, while sloth was likened to a failure to glorify God. This ascetic Calvinist/Puritan version of virtue was well suited to the pre-affluent stages of capitalism such as the eighteenth-century New England of Benjamin Franklin and Adam Smith's Britain. Today's version of capitalist virtue still requires not only hard work but also lavish consumption and 'consumer confidence' in order to keep the wheels of capitalism turning.

The Christian doctrine of equal value of human individuals found its political expression in universal suffrage: the 'one person one vote' rule. This required the abolition of various electoral censuses—limitations to vote—where only certain categories of people had full citizenship, normally property-owning white men. The idea that every person endowed with reason should have full voting rights prevailed quite late however. Restrictions to voting and holding public office based on gender, race, social status and wealth persisted in some of the most advanced societies until relatively recently. In the UK, it was not until 1928 that both men and women without property could vote at the age of 21. Ladies of the rich and conservative Switzerland voted for the first time in federal elections in 1971.

Of course, reality is always only an approximation of lofty ideals. Our everyday experience tells us that the democratic principle of parity of individuals is a tall order. The principle is corrupted daily in many small as well as significant ways. Individuals do not have equal clout—their ability to voice their views and exercise influence over others is extremely variable. As a compensation for inequality and the consequent corruption of the democratic ideal, in modern democracies individuals do not have a permanently allocated place in various hierarchies and are free to compete and advance their position. According to Napoleon Bonaparte, who became a general at the age of 24 and an emperor at 35, 'every soldier carries a marshal's baton in his knapsack.' These days we are regularly encouraged to believe that everyone who is ready to work hard and compete can become a Prime Minister or a President, or at least a millionaire.

The concept of individualism was first scrutinised by French historian Alexis de Tocqueville in his acclaimed 1835–1840 study *Democracy in America*. He starts a chapter titled 'Of individualism in democratic countries' by defining 'individualism' in contrast to 'selfishness,' though individualism does not get much better press:

> [...] *Individualism* is a novel expression, to which a novel idea has given birth. Our fathers were only acquainted with *égoïsme* (selfishness). Selfishness is a passionate and exaggerated love of self, which leads a man to connect everything with himself and to prefer himself to everything in the world. Individualism is a mature and calm feeling, which disposes each member of the community to sever himself from the mass of his fellows and to draw apart with his family and his friends, so that after he has thus formed a little circle of his own, he willingly leaves society at large to itself. [...]. Selfishness blights the germ of all virtue; individualism, at first, only saps the virtues of public life; but in the long run it attacks and destroys all others and is at length absorbed in downright selfishness. Selfishness is a vice as old as the world, which does not belong to one form of society more than to another; individualism is of democratic origin, and it threatens to spread in the same ratio as the equality of condition. (Tocqueville 2014, Ch. 2)

The contemporary understanding of individualism is focused on a person's autonomy, a necessary counterpart to free competition. Citizens of Western democracies keep a close watch over their governments lest they impinged on individual liberties. Competitive individualism could be considered a key foundational narrative of Anglo-Saxon capitalism, particularly its American variety. In his book *Community and Purpose in America*, Drukman (1971) argued that individualism, particularly economic individualism, had been the 'dominant national purpose both in actuality and in rhetoric.' Drukman seemed to regret the absence of 'society' and argued that the absence of a sense of national community was a massive consequence of the unfortunate predominance of 'negative liberty' (to compete) over 'fraternal sentiments' (to collaborate).

Americans, inhabiting the 'land of the free,' are especially vigilant about their government's reach. The defence of the constitutional right to 'bear arms' is an expression of such vigilance and the 'every man for himself' individualism borne in the days of the 'Wild West'—and one that seemingly cannot be shaken by a relentless frequency of mass shootings. Americans seem to cling to an old-fashioned version of the *laissez-faire* competitive individualism persisting from the romanticised version of the Wild West, and America is often seen as a country of intense and brutal competition. Paradoxically, the individualism-worshipping Americans are often also described as highly conformist (Fisher 2010).

The ideology of individualism has many positive social implications and applications, among them personal liberties, democratic rights and equality before the law. However, Western individualism has also been criticised as excessive, especially in its American version (Ketcham 1987; Keller 1988). American communitarian sociologist Amitai Etzioni (2004) described individualism as an 'explosion of a sense of entitlement': taking but not giving back to the community. According to communitarians, globalisation coupled with neo-liberalism has given a boost to a selfish, competitive conception of society, where people are concerned about their rights and anxious about their privacy, but suspicious about calls for social and moral responsibility. It should be noted that Tocqueville (2014), critical of American individualism on these same grounds, was positive about American democracy and its then 'egalitarianism.'

While communitarianism appeared as a reaction to the neo-liberal surge of the 1980s, competitive individualism was criticised much earlier by thinkers on the left who argued that Western society was 'atomised' and people alienated from each other. Although competition as a macro-structural principle may lead to innovation and higher productivity, thus maximising the total economic output, micro instances of competition are always a 'zero-sum game'—if one person is to win, another must lose. If you are elated by that great phone call offering you a desired job, other shortlisted hopefuls are sure to feel miserable because they have received rejection letters. If you made money by share trading last year, someone else's loss mirrored your gain.

The idea of the American dream glorifies the self-made entrepreneur in a relentless quest for success expressed in their financial 'net worth.' Billionaire financier George Soros (1998), the epitome of the American dream, is also a fierce critic of market fundamentalism. He argued that untrammelled individualism represented a danger to what he considered an essential value: the open society. Soros's biography reveals an unexpected mindset. He talks down individualism and argues that the promotion of self-interest to the status of the supreme moral principle has corrupted politics, making leaders concerned primarily with their hold on power—being re-elected—rather than with the public interest. Ironically, such a failure of politics and distrust of politicians have become important arguments in favour of giving markets, as 'spontaneous order' (see Chap. 2), primacy in regulating social affairs, instead of allowing self-interested politicians, assembled in potentially corrupt government bodies, to exercise their power over the people.

Conditions of Competition

Full-blown competition can only take place under certain conditions. The most important of these is the absence of formal limitations to social mobility. A rigid system of social stratification prevents people from moving up or down the social ladder. The best-known contemporary example of a system blocking social mobility, and therefore also competition, is the Hindu caste system, still existing in rural areas of India in spite of being officially banned in 1950. The caste system prescribes segregation between groups and strict endogamy. People are categorised in five major castes defined primarily by their hereditary occupations: Brahmins, Kshatriya, Vaisyas, Shudras and Dalits ('Untouchables'). Brahmins, the priestly caste, are at the top of the social hierarchy. Dalits are at the bottom, living on the outskirts of villages, strictly segregated from others—not unlike Gypsies in parts of Eastern Europe. In spite of traditional barriers, some Dalits experienced social mobility during British colonial rule, but even today stories of people being cruelly punished for disobeying traditional hierarchies appear in the news. Untouchables are still expected not to aspire to climb up from their bottom rank (BBC 2012).

A similar situation existed in European feudal society, where a peasant or a serf could not become a nobleman no matter how able he was or how hard he worked. The barrier was absolute because a person's status was determined by birth. A man may have gained higher status within his village community by virtue of his wisdom and skill in his trade, but that was the limit of his achievement. Christian clergy sometimes adopted exceptionally talented sons of the working classes and some of them rose to positions of prominence and power, but these were rare exceptions. Women could only move up in the hierarchy of pre-modern society through marriage, but the story of Cinderella marrying a prince most certainly was *not* based on a true story. A nobleman (or noblewoman), on the other hand, could never lose hereditary status, although s/he could lose wealth and even respect of peers and subordinates; the romantic nineteenth-century novels are littered with impoverished Russian princes and French counts. In European feudal society, competition and social mobility were limited to the upper classes: the contest for land and political power was endemic and included royal families, landed nobility and clergy. Others, a vast majority of the population, laboured in order to provide food and other necessities for themselves and their masters. Slaves, serfs and free peasants get individual mention in history books only as leaders of major rebellions.

Urbanisation, economic progress and the appearance of entrepreneurial burghers—bourgeoisie—have gradually dissolved this rigid system. The French Revolution in 1789 was a dramatic point in asserting rights for the common people (the 'Third Estate') to climb to powerful positions in society.

From the point of view of modern capitalism, any rigid hierarchy is irrational because it prevents the full use of the available pool of talent. By implication, any ideology that supports a rigid stratification discourages critical thinking and free expression. Socially immobile societies do not motivate people to give their best effort and are doomed to economic sluggishness in the long term. Pre-capitalist societies were stagnant for centuries. The excitement and change started with the elimination of the barriers to freedom of thought and entrepreneurship, as discussed in Chap. 2.

There is another necessary structural condition for a competitive society: there has to be a surplus over which to compete. For example, if food supply is precarious, cooperation and sharing is a survival imperative. For hunter-gatherers or subsistence farmers toiling their land in order to produce enough food for mere survival, competing and progressing through social ranks is not a consideration. Until recently, a majority of humans lived in such conditions and a sizeable portion still does. In modern societies, circumstances of acute scarcity appear only in emergencies such as wars or natural disasters, and this is when competitive behaviour is suspended. In emergencies, people share generously with their neighbours, help each other without calculation and expect help from others 'for free' (though deviant or disgruntled individuals may resort to looting instead). But once the emergency is over, we are back to our rational calculations, splitting the lunch bill and yielding to competitive pressures.

Contemporary capitalism has far surpassed scarcity. We live in a society where nearly everyone's income exceeds bare necessities. We could choose to work less, have less disposable income but more free time. But in a society where pathways to social advancement are clearly defined and relatively open, most people want to 'get ahead.' The space beyond survival necessity is the space of competition and, perhaps paradoxically, the competition tends to intensify as society grows richer. At the same time, competition is a game of diminishing returns. Past a certain point, climbing the social ladder does little in terms of advancing our physical and emotional comfort, improving our quality of life or enhancing our happiness (Wilkinson and Pickett 2009). Psychologists say that winning in a competition is only likely to produce a short spike in one's happiness and self-esteem. For example, winning a lottery—although used as a metaphor for the ultimate luck and ecstasy that follows it—has in fact ruined the lives of many winners (Carbone 2012).

Apart from social-structural, there are psychological conditions of competition: people must be motivated to compete. Some people are clearly more motivated than others. What are the factors determining this difference? Are people from 'humble backgrounds' more motivated by the prospect of intergenerational social mobility than the children born into well-off families? Immigrants are seen as having a special drive to achieve in their host society which offers better opportunities than the one they left. There is no empirical evidence for either, however. Social research has consistently shown that middle-class children are more likely to become middle-class adults than their working-class counterparts; and that the native-born individuals are on average much better off than immigrants from poorer countries (Colic-Peisker 2011; Ho and Alcorso 2004). A competitive drive may not suffice in a situation when one's competitors have a head start. Of course, the examples of people from modest and/or foreign origins rising to prominence are memorable, and the perception of their numbers is therefore exaggerated creating an unrealistic picture of an egalitarian society, or at least a society of 'equal opportunity.'

The Psychology of Competition

We are often told, explicitly or implicitly, that we need to perform and 'sell ourselves' on the labour, marital and other 'markets.' We must show our best side at all times and never show weakness to our competitors, who are, potentially, everyone, including one's siblings and spouse. From an early age, we are conditioned to crave success in its different guises: school and sport success, a good job, public office, a desirable sexual mate, an impressive home, personal good looks. Even happiness can be a symbol of success, rather than something we enjoy intrinsically, regardless of whether anyone is watching; other people's envy validates our success. Given the intrusion of mass media in our lives, fame and celebrity seem to be the ultimate marker of success and status, in spite of being many times proven hollow and even detrimental to the famous person. We are bombarded by images of 'successful people,' which may motivate some of us and frustrate others. The blessed are those who are indifferent, but they are rare. Desiring one's 'fifteen minutes of fame' is now a mainstream part of the popular culture (Van Krieken 2012).

The psychology of the competitive society infuses our deepest selves and transforms all into diffuse competitors. We compete even when we do not have to, when the game is not 'zero-sum.' Who is the best dressed woman at the party? Which man takes the tacit prize for the best looking blonde hanging off his elbow? Is the host's home imposing enough? The culture of hyper-competition spreads from the sphere of economics to all life's domains. The competitive capitalist individual (the identical twin to *homo economicus*) tends to apply a cost/benefit calculus across the board, including in domains considered most intimate and least economic.

An example is a 'marital market' where people aim to secure the best possible partner: good genetic material represented by youth and good looks in women and sound earning potential in men are the most valued features. Given that we can normally only secure an equal worth partner on the marital market, people go to impressive lengths to increase their personal 'exchange value.' Competitiveness and advanced medicine combine to produce cosmetic surgery procedures that leave the less adventurous among us flabbergasted—the old-fashioned nose job and 'boob job' are now complemented by the quest for perfect private parts: think labiaplasty or anal bleaching. Traditional gender roles still represent dominant psychological conditioning for most people, preparing them for 'proper' gender-determined areas of competition: personal attractiveness and youth for women versus money making, sport prowess and political power for men. No-one is surprised that rich and powerful Donald Trump is married to an attractive, much younger model Melania; this is a common transaction on the marital market. The fact that the French President Emmanuel Macron has a much older (which equals unattractive in the marital market) wife is an anomaly picked up by the media as soon as he appeared in the public arena. However, as more women earn good incomes and become economically independent, sexual attractiveness is becoming less absolute as the requirement for their marriage value. As women enter the previously male-only sphere of economic and professional competition, men enter competition for sexual attractiveness, submitting themselves to procedures such as penile extension and muscle implants.

There are outsiders unaffected by the psychology of competition, 'egoless' individuals who seemingly have no vanity and are able to effortlessly resist competitive pressures. These 'eccentrics,' who do not play by the mainstream rulebook, may still have their own, less conventional peer group pressures, that is, those imposed by other eccentrics. Their competitive pressures may take a different guise, as they may compete over 'goods' not conventionally desired, such as chess prowess or sophisticated knowledge of medieval poetry. There have been peer groups and subcultures within society that did not conform to the imperative of wealth accumulation. Take a group of talented but more or less penniless young artists meeting in a *belle époque* Parisian café. In their society, being impecunious was not a sign of being low in the pecking order, as other criteria determined their status among the peers: daring, originality, obsessive dedication to their art and possibly the number of young beauties ready to model for them. In such cases, competition appears in alternative forms. The hippy subculture that emerged in the 1960s denounced competition altogether and emphasised togetherness and sharing. In mainstream society which prescribes competitive behaviour, such subcultures are subversive. Usually, they are co-opted into the mainstream through commercialisation of their symbols, ideals and products.

The Emotional Cost of Competitive Society

While competition and 'rational economic' thinking seems good for the economy, is it also good for people? How does the constant pressure to compete affect the individual? How does competitive society shape our relationships? How does it make us feel? Ex-financial analyst Geraint Anderson (2008, 101) described his first experience at a big bank's 'corporate retreat' thus: 'In this kind of pseudo-friendly event aggressive one-upmanship was not only tolerated but was actually the norm; however, only within certain parameters. Hostile put downs and catty comments were *de rigueur*, but only if done subtly and with a smile on the face.' Drilling deep into the mores of London's financial district, Anderson (2008, 108–109) described it as a 'hideously competitive environment,' and brokers, traders and analysts inhabiting the 'Square Mile' as selfish, ruthless individuals participating in a 'continual cockfight with their peers.' The finance industry may be among the most competitive, but the discomfort of constant competition is ubiquitous—in this war, there is no truce.

Yet, some degree of cooperation is necessary in any social context. We forge alliances to better compete; we cooperate with some people in order to compete against others. Sport teams, political parties, commercial firms, professional 'fraternities,' work teams, families, criminal gangs, nations and 'houses,' in which schools organise their pupils in order to incite competition, all work on this principle. We are encouraged to develop loyalty and form our identities around our competitive 'units.' Do these collectives which cooperate internally in order to compete externally provide comfort and an emotional respite? This is dubious. Political parties are beset by bitter internal rivalries and back-stabbing; workmates engage in ceaseless, albeit usually quiet and discrete, battles for leadership positions and promotions; sibling rivalries extend from toddlers' fights over toys to feuds over inheritance.

Competitive society is dynamic, always in flux, requiring constant effort. If we are on top, we need to work hard to keep ourselves there; if we are not doing very well, we need to try harder. By preventing people from being able to relax and trust other people, a relentless pressure to compete can damage our psychological wellbeing. The adverse health effects of work stress, long work hours and tense work relationships with colleagues (i.e., potential rivals) detract from our enjoyment of life (Botton 2004). Unremitting competition is likely to cause considerable discomfort and status anxiety: in nearly all people some of the time, in many people quite often, and in some people all the time. Of course, a calculus of pleasure and pain is complex, and the variables are hard to define and measure. In consequence, most of us (about 80 per cent, as discussed previously) feel that the safest, and at some level also the easiest, thing to do is to behave like those around us: compete for conventionally defined success.

It is possible that in the Anglosphere, and in some professions in particular, the rat race has reached such a speed that 'competitive pressures' indeed impinge on people's mental and physical health. Lawyers, especially 'article clerks' fresh out of law school, often work under incredible pressure to prove themselves, accounting for every 15 minutes (or even less!) of their working time. The start of a medical career seems no easier, with long shifts, night work and a burden of responsibility requiring an extreme physical fitness and mental resilience from young interns and registrars. This is also the case in finance and many other industries. Recently, investment bank Goldman Sachs placed a daily work limit of 17 *hours* on its junior employees (Neate 2015).

Fig. 3.2 The *karoshi*-land: corporate headquarters at the Yokohama waterfront

Surviving the knock-out initial competition usually leads to a career as a well-paid high-status professional—and to a working life of continued competition and stress.

Many novels and films feature status-conscious people exposed to the cold winds of competitive society and suffering from anxiety about securing their place in the winners' camp. Marriageable young ladies compete for the most eligible (rich and handsome) bachelor in Jane Austin's novels; Balzac's Eugene de Rastignac, the central character of his 1835 novel *Le Père Goriot*, is an epitome of an ambitious social climber; in Joseph Heller's 1974 novel *Something Happened*, the anti-hero Bob Slocum obsesses about work promotion. There are many movies about ambition, power struggle and greed, where happy-endings which reward nice and altruistic people may induce a sort of collective catharsis. But in reality, ruthless competitive conduct is more likely to be rewarded than niceness.

We are often warned about the health effects of stress and overwork and encouraged to relax and have a good time—during our socially

Karoshi!

Workaholism is a serious capitalist affliction. At the level of the individual, it can also be seen as an addiction. Long working hours cause stress and lead to poor life-work balance, lack of exercise, neglecting one's children and relationship problems. In most developed countries, there has been no formal reduction in working hours since the 1970s, in spite of computerisation. Well-known examples of burning midnight oil come from the Anglosphere (especially UK, US and Australia) and Japan. Somewhat unexpectedly, the most extreme example of long working hours comes from Mexico, where the working week is legally limited to 48 hours and annual leave to only 5 working days (Lee et al. 2007, 20). One important exception to the pattern is France where the working week was reduced to 35 hours in the mid-1990s (Lee et al., p. 26). In news stories coming out of Japan, deaths of young and fit people have been linked to overwork.

When the authors first heard of *karoshi*, a Japanese concept meaning 'death from overwork,' we were slightly incredulous. We asked a Japanese colleague over lunch in order to verify the story. When asked, she vigorously shook her head up-and-down—yes, she said, *karoshi* is quite a long-standing concept. Mitsuko[4] volunteered a story of near-*karoshi* in her own family. At one stage her husband, an IT engineer, used to typically work until 3–4 am, so that travelling home across Tokyo, where all train services stop at midnight, made little sense. Luckily, his company was paying for hotel accommodation, so he didn't have to take his all-too-short night's rest in a 'capsule hotel' (affordable accommodation specialising in hosting office slaves, where one's bed is covered by a hard shell, becoming a 'capsule'—a kind of hard-cover tent). 'This was when our son was just a baby. My husband used to only come home on the weekends, usually on the first 5 am train on Saturday. I would have become suspicious ...perhaps he had a mistress, you know ...? But the state he was in on Saturday mornings—exhausted, unshaven and bleary-eyed, looking like a homeless person—dispelled my doubts. No woman would want a man like that, and I didn't either! We had six months of this crazy life and I was worried he'd die and I'd end up as a *karoshi* widow. So I gave him an ultimatum: you need to find work closer to home, like, within 2 km diameter, so you can, at the very least, sleep at home—or else! Practically, I forced him to quit. He found work closer to home. Needless to say, he loves it here in Australia—he's home before dark!'

approved and precisely allocated leisure time, weekends and annual holidays. However, it is often hard to switch from a sober, highly strung participant in the rat race to an idle, carefree person. Our relaxed moments often have to be chemically induced, fuelling a massive trade in alcohol and drugs. The large entertainment industry has the task of providing mental relaxation to the anxious masses.

Ways to relax are highly structured and prescribed for each social group and subculture. Often, it may feel like more hard work. An example of this is holiday travel. Whether you're camping down the coast, embarking on an adventure holiday or boarding a flight to Paris, the amount of organisation, actual hours of travelling and effort at the destination is far from relaxing. You may even decide to join thousands climbing Mt. Everest[5] or some other challenging mountain—another high-status holiday to report over dinner with friends. A relaxing holiday? Not at all. We compete again. For the global middle classes, holiday travel is a widespread form of conspicuous consumption—an opportunity to flaunt one's money, cultured taste, sport prowess, bravery and a sense of adventure—earning us some status brownie points. Some people spend their annual leave on renovating the house. Popular TV programmes emphasise the meaningful element of 'self-realisation' among the renovators. One can certainly indulge one's hobbies and creativity in making one's house a dream home, but 'keeping up with the Joneses' is never far from the renovators' daydreams.

Is Competition Good for Education?

Increasingly, competition and rankings penetrate school education. The following is a 2012 exchange between the UK Secretary of State for Education Michael Gove and the House of Commons Education Committee:

> Chair: "[…] if 'good' requires pupil performance to exceed the national average, and if all schools must be good, how is this mathematically possible?"
> Gove: "By getting better all the time."
> Chair: "So it is possible, is it?"
> Gove: "It is possible to get better all the time."
> Chair: "Were you better at literacy than numeracy, Secretary of State?"
> (UK Parliament 2012).

Worryingly, Gove overlooks the obvious fact that in every hierarchy or ranking someone has to be at the bottom, and that there is exactly the same number of people in last place as in first: precisely one. But does education have to be competitive?

The school system of Finland dispensed with competition altogether and is widely regarded as one of the best in the world (Burridge 2010). How did this educational utopia take place? In 1970, Finland created *peruskoulu*, merging the existing primary, grammar and government secondary schools into nine-year comprehensive municipal schools. All students, regardless of their background or socio-economic status, enrol in the same basic schools, with running of the schools devolved to local municipal authorities that enjoy considerable autonomy. One of the key differences from other developed countries is that, in Finland, teaching is a well-paid, elite profession and therefore there is no problem in attracting the best young people into teaching careers. Teachers are required to have Master's level education. Classes are small and the classroom is highly interactive and relaxed. Ninety-three per cent of students graduate from high school, a proportion greater than that in the US, Australia or any other European country.

There are no rankings, no comparisons or competition between students, schools or regions. There is only one standardised test at age 16; prior to that, most students never sit a test or exam. Despite this, Finnish students excel in the international rankings of high school performance in the Organisation of Economic Cooperation and Development's (OECD) Programme for International Student Assessment (PISA) tests (PISA 2015).[6] Pasi Sahlberg (2010, 39), one of the architects of the Finnish system, wrote:

> The ultimate success of a high-stakes testing policy is whether it positively affects students learning, not whether it increases student scores on a particular test. If student learning remains unaffected, or if testing leads to biased teaching, the validity of such high-stakes tests must be questioned.

Initially, critics of the new Finnish school system were concerned that it was not possible to have the same educational expectations of students from very different backgrounds and that the whole system would have to be 'dumbed down.' However, the results now speak for themselves, and administrators of more competitive models of education have trouble explaining why Finland's obvious success could not translate to their country.

A. Kohn (1986, 1987) cited a large review of psychological studies on competition that concluded competition did not help children learn and was in fact more likely to stifle their learning. On the topic of competition as children's formative experience, he argued that 'competition is to self-esteem as sugar is to teeth' and that it 'leads children to envy winners, to dismiss losers and to be suspicious of just about everyone.' According to Kohn, 'the reason our workplaces and schools are in trouble is that they value competitiveness instead of excellence.' A more rational approach to learning would be to encourage students to do their best and to compare themselves to their earlier selves rather than to others. The success of the Finnish education system that produces top educational outcomes in numeracy and literacy seems to be an important piece of evidence for Kohn's thesis. One could ask, of course, how do we define 'excellence' if not through a comparison of individual results? Strictly speaking, comparison (by necessity in a quantified form) is not yet competition, but it is a closely related notion.

It should be mentioned that Shanghai also regularly tops the PISA league table, and its school system is the epitome of competition: even young primary school students regularly attend supplementary holiday and weekend classes for fear of falling behind. However, a growing number of well-off Chinese send their children to be educated in the West to ensure that their children have a less stressful transition to fully 'credentialised' adulthood.

Competition Versus Cooperation

Is competition for status, prestige and power a primal, biological urge, and competitive society the only context that can motivate us to be productive? While free marketeers tend to consider the competitive urge an essential part of 'human nature,' according to psychologists and their less empirical-research-based colleagues, the evolutionary psychologists, human beings are as much creatures of cooperation as they are of competition. Social scientists have long argued that it is impossible to discuss human nature as competitive or cooperative in an abstract sense; human beings are largely products of the society in which they live. If the society emphasises cooperation, they cooperate; if competition is prescribed, they compete.

Adam Smith, hailed as the patron saint of the free market, wrote an elaborate treatise on cooperation and compassion between people. In *The Theory of Moral Sentiments* (1790), he argued that people relentlessly seek 'gains from trade' in all social transactions, but this was by no means limited to economic gain. Unfortunately, this point has been largely forgotten, in a process which Eric Hobsbawm (2010) called the *reductio ad absurdum* of Adam Smith's economic science.

If people could be 'unconditioned' and able to freely and rationally choose, it is reasonable to argue that most people would prefer cooperation over competition at the individual, national and global levels. Cooperation is a more pleasant and peace-inducing way of life; we are in fact more likely to achieve the most important and lasting life goals if others around us also enjoy them; peace is better than war. Tranquillity, social harmony and camaraderie are more likely to be by-products of cooperation and equality than competition and inequality. If there's anything natural, biological and inevitable about our competitive urges, we could always vent them through sporting competition, trivia nights in the pub, or just overtaking other cyclists on the way home from work.

If we try to test the 'naturalness of competition hypothesis' by looking at our relatives in the animal kingdom, examples of both competition and cooperation abound. While noting that human communities are infinitely more complex that those of bees, lions and chimpanzees, we will for a moment succumb to the line of enquiry pursued by sociobiology and evolutionary psychology in order to tell you about our cousins the bonobos.

Get in Touch with Your Inner Bonobo

Ask people what our closest animal relative is and most will nominate the chimpanzee. Chimpanzees are generally territorial and aggressive and have a strongly hierarchical social structure. Males fight and often kill other males. However, we have an equally close but lesser-known cousin, the bonobo (or *Pan paniscus*). We share 98.6 per cent of our genes with both species. The ancestors of modern-day chimpanzees and bonobos separated from the ancestors of *homo sapiens* 6–7 million years ago. In contrast, chimpanzees and bonobos only became distinct species about 2 million years ago when the formation of the Congo River created a natural barrier between two primate communities. Bonobos are the 1960s, hippy-beatnik, make-love-not-war primates. They live in a highly cooperative and peaceful matriarchal society, with no known examples of deliberate bonobocide. Conflict or tension is usually resolved by sexual contact, which does not appear to discriminate by age or gender. Among mammals, only female bonobos and humans have sex throughout their reproductive cycle—that is, for non-reproductive purposes such as pair-bonding, the formation of alliances, stress relief or simply for pleasure (Ryan and Jethá 2010, 61–78 and 101–104).

What lessons does this hold for us? Human beings are without doubt the most broadly cooperative species on the planet. The social insects—ants, bees and wasps—cooperate strongly but only with their close relatives; carnivores often cooperate in hunting packs and herbivores in herds; but only humans cooperate in groups of millions (cities), tens of millions (countries) and even globally (although quite shakily at this level). The Hobbesian view of the natural state of human life as 'solitary, poor, nasty, brutish, and short' (Hobbes 1911, Ch. XIII) is more a reflection of the society he experienced in seventeenth-century Europe than a reflection of some ontologically fixed 'human nature.' Our 'natural' competitiveness is more socially conditioned than genetically determined. Instead of emphasising competition and our close resemblance to aggressive chimpanzees, we may be better off getting in touch with our 'inner bonobo.'

A thought-provoking take on competition, cooperation and their psychological as well as economic impact comes from ex-communism. In a 2009 BBC radio documentary on the 1990 German unification, an academic commentator observed that East Germans did not necessarily like every aspect of the Western lifestyle. Westerners have to be upbeat and selling themselves at all times, he commented. An 'ordinary' East German woman argued that 'West Germans' were not free because there was nothing but pressure from morning to night—pressure to buy this or that, pressure to keep their job or get the next one. A 2009 opinion poll found that 57 per cent of East Germans think life was better in the old system than in the reunified Germany (Bonstein 2009). In the more egalitarian and less competitive communist system, Eastern Europeans were largely free from the pressure to compete. However, according to many analysts, this was a central reason why communist economies stalled in the 1980s and collapsed into a heap at the end of the decade (Huntington 1991).[7]

The absence of 'competition anxiety' in communist societies was matched by a relative poverty and a lack of political and individual freedoms when compared to the capitalist West. Yet, in the post-communist decades, a considerable nostalgia for the old system has developed in Eastern Europe. The nostalgia for the past seems to be focused on the loss of existential security: guaranteed jobs and housing for everyone, although at a modest level, as well as free education and healthcare.

Is there anything to be learnt from the failed social experiment of communism that outlawed inequality and placed emphasis on cooperation instead of competition? In the 1960s, a system of industrial democracy called 'worker's self-management' was introduced in Yugoslavia, attracting considerable interest and also praise from Western social scientists. The economic units, from 1974 called 'Organisations of united labour' (locally known as 'OURs'), were 'socially' rather than privately owned. In spite of the progressive ideology and possibly also best intentions, it soon became clear that the one-person-one-vote rule in 'worker's councils,' formally ruling every OUR, could not prevent managers and directors from usurping power. A big positive for the workers was that virtually no-one was ever fired. The bad side of the full employment and low wages was the absence of either carrot or stick, which led to low productivity, a problem affecting all communist countries. The absence of monetary motivation was especially problematic given that most jobs in the at the time prevailing manufacturing and construction sectors offered little potential for intrinsic motivation. The total wage differential between workers and managers was limited to 1:3, which did not motivate management to their best work either.

Worker-run cooperatives have also existed within capitalist economies. These cooperatives do not fit into the capitalist logic of profit maximisation, where minimising cost of production often happens at the expense of workers' wages and, when technology can replace them, also their jobs. 'Utopian socialist' attempts to sustain cooperative production stretch from Robert Owen, a Welsh manufacturer and reformer who started experimental 'utopian' communities in Scotland and the US in the early nineteenth century[8] to the contemporary Argentinean 'Barter network' or *Red del Trueque* (Powell 2002). In most cases, the alternative projects did not last long; the logic of the surrounding social context prevailed after the initial idealism, and funds, wore out.

A noteworthy contemporary example of industrial democracy is the Mondragón Corporation (*Mondragón Corporacion Cooperativa*), a federation of worker-owned cooperatives in the Basque region of Spain (Thomas and Logan 1982; Macleod 1997; Whyte and Whyte 1991; Wolff 2012). It has been widely studied as an example of a third way between capitalism and socialism. The first cooperative was founded in 1956 in the city of Mondragón by a group of enterprising graduate students from a local technical college. The corporation has grown into a network of companies operating across the areas of finance, manufacturing, retail and education, and training and innovation. Only employees are allowed to own equity in the companies, with around 80–85 per cent of workers being shareholders. The businesses are democratically managed, and workers elect, hire and fire management and directors, rather than the other way around; all employees, from the lowest paid worker to top managers, have the same voting rights in the General Assembly. The cooperatives have a shared business culture embodied in a set of rules passed by the Cooperate Congress and consistent with a philosophy of cooperation, social responsibility, participation and innovation. The wage structure is far more egalitarian than in most conventional businesses, with managers limited to 6.5 times the wage of the lowest paid worker—compared to the US where a CEO can expect to earn 400 times the wage of the *average* worker, a figure that has multiplied 20-fold since 1965. The system has its own social security co-op to provide pensions and health care, and its own schools from primary to Master's degree level. Over the decades, the Mondragón Corporation has grown into one of Spain's largest conglomerates.

The businesses have to profitable in their own right since they compete in the 'real world' of capitalist enterprises, but since the workers are also owners, their rights get much higher consideration than they would in a traditional capitalist-owned company. For example, when one business needs to shed workers, they are relocated to other firms within the cooperative, rather than thrown onto their own resources or to the not-so-tender mercies of a government social security system.

However, a utopia has not necessary been achieved. Kasmir (1996) criticised the 'myth of Mondragón' and argued that class structure has not been eliminated in the supposedly fully democratic and egalitarian workplaces. In addition, Mondragón is not immune to the political culture of radical Basque nationalism that has called for both independence from Spain and socialism for the Basque nation. However, it provides an example of an alternative to both the failed experiment of centrally planned communism and the hyper-competitive 'free market' capitalism.

Although competition is an essential part of the success story of the modern Western industrialised societies, the time has passed when it was necessary to compete our way out of a society of scarcity. It may be time to re-examine competition as a core constituent of our culture which has become all pervasive, permeating into all aspects of our lives. Technically, humans remain the most cooperative species on the planet; competition is more about ideology than destiny.

Notes

1. A witty description of Marx doing just that, while chatting to John Stuart Mill, can be found in the epilogue of Ginsborg (2008). Marx made it to heaven via purgatory, while Mill was granted direct access.
2. The 'Square Mile' is the nickname of the City of London's financial district. The book caused a stir—and not just because it should definitely be R-rated and supplied with a 'coarse language' warning. Anderson set out to 'break the code of silence that governs everyone in the Square Mile.'
3. Eminent Australian moral philosopher, Peter Singer (1986) makes the distinction between 'human being' and 'human person,' the latter being in full possession of his/her exclusively human faculties: self-awareness and reason.

4. The name has been changed to preserve confidentiality.
5. By the end of 2016, there had been 7646 successful summit attempts by 4469 different climbers (Alan Arnette 2017).
6. Finland was third overall in 2009, but the gap with the rest of the OECD has closed somewhat since then.
7. Communism was beneficial for backward rural societies. Its early successes in industrialisation were due to what Samuel Huntington (1991) called the 'advantages of backwardness'—that is, the ability to prosper quickly starting from a low base. Once the industrialisation was over, the advantage was lost.
8. For an overview of Owen's ideas and activism, see https://www.britannica.com/biography/Robert-Owen

Bibliography

Alan Arnette. 2017. Everest by Numbers. The Blog on alanarnette.com. Accessed 14 June 2017. http://www.alanarnette.com/blog/2016/12/30/everest-by-the-numbers-2017-edition/

Anderson, Geraint. 2008. *Cityboy: Beer and Loathing in the Square Mile*. London: Headline Publishing Group.

BBC. 2012. India's Dalits Still Fighting Untouchability. *British Broadcasting Commission (BBC) News*, 27 June 2012 (by Natalia Antelava). Accessed 19 June 2017. http://www.bbc.com/news/world-asia-india-18394914

Bonstein, Julia. 2009. Majority of Eastern Germans Feel Life Better under Communism. *Der Spiegel*, 3 July 2009. Accessed 19 June 2017. http://www.spiegel.de/international/germany/homesick-for-a-dictatorship-majority-of-eastern-germans-feel-life-better-under-communism-a-634122.html

Botton, Alain de. 2004. *Status Anxiety*. London: Hamish Hamilton.

Burridge, Tom. 2010. Why do Finland's Schools Get the Best Results? *BBC World News America*, 7 April 2010. Accessed 19 June 2017. http://news.bbc.co.uk/2/hi/8601207.stm

Carbone, Nick. 2012. The Tragic Stories of the Lottery's Unluckiest Winners. *Time*, 27 November 2012. Accessed 19 June 2017. http://newsfeed.time.com/2012/11/28/500-million-powerball-jackpot-the-tragic-stories-of-the-lotterys-unluckiest-winners/slide/

Cialdini, Robert B., and Noah J. Goldstein. 2004. Social Influence: Compliance and Conformity. *Annual Review of Psychology* 55: 591–621.

Colic-Peisker, Val. 2011. 'Ethnics' and 'Anglos' in the Australian Labour Market: Advancing Australia Fair? *Journal of Intercultural Studies* 32: 639–656.

Drukman, Mason. 1971. *Community and Purpose in America: An Analysis of American Political Theory*. Ty Crowell Co.

Etzioni, Amitai. 2004. *The Common Good*. Cambridge, UK; Malden, MA: Polity Press.

Fisher, Claude. 2010. Sweet Land of…Conformity? Americans aren't the Rugged Individuals We Think We are. *Boston Globe*, 6 June 2010. Accessed 19 June 2017. http://www.boston.com/bostonglobe/ideas/articles/2010/06/06/sweet_land_of_conformity/

Franklin, Benjamin. 1748. *Advice to a Young Tradesman, Written by an Old One*, cited by Max Weber (1958, p. 48).

Galbraith, John Kenneth. 1974 [1958]. *The Affluent Society*. Boston; New York: Houghton Mifflin.

Ginsborg, Paul. 2008. *Democracy: Crisis and Renewal*. London: Profile Books.

Ho, C., and C. Alcorso. 2004. Migrants and Employment: Challenging the Success Story. *Journal of Sociology* 40: 237–259.

Hobbes, Thomas. 1911 [1651]. *Leviathan, Or the Matter, Form and Power of a Commonwealth Ecclesiastical and Civil*. London: Routledge.

Hobsbawm, Eric. 2010. *How to Change the World: Reflections on Marx and Marxism*. New Haven and London: Yale University Press.

Huntington, Samuel. 1991. Democracy's Third Wave. *Journal of Democracy* 2: 12–34.

Kasmir, Sharryn. 1996. *The Myth of Mondragón: Cooperatives, Politics, and Working-Class Life in a Basque Town*. New York: State University of New York Press.

Keller, Suzanne. 1988. The American Dream of Community: An Unfinished Agenda. *Sociological Forum* 3: 167–183.

Ketcham, Ralph. 1987. *Individualism and Public Life: A Modern Dilemma*. New York: Basil.

Kohn, Alfie. 1986. *No Contest: The Case Against Competition*. Boston: Houghton Mifflin.

———. 1987 The Case Against Competition. Accessed 19 June 2017. http://www.alfiekohn.org/article/case-competition/

Lee, S, D. McCann, and J. C. Messenger. 2007. *Working Time Around the World: Trends in Working Hours, Laws and Policies in a Global Comparative Perspective*. London and New York: Routledge. Also published by International Labour Organisation (ILO), Geneva. Accessed 19 June 2017. www.ilo.org/wcmsp5/

groups/public/@dgreports/@dcomm/@publ/documents/publication/wcms_104895.pdf

Lukes, Steven. 1971. The Meaning of 'Individualism'. *Journal of History of Ideas* 32: 45–66.

Macleod, Greg. 1997. *From Mondragon to America: Experiments in Community Economic Development*. Sydney, Nova Scotia: University College of Cape Breton Press.

Mill, John Stuart. 1977 [1836]. Civilization. In *The Collected Works of John Stuart Mill, Vol. XVIII: Essays on Politics and Society, Part I*, ed. John M Robson. London: Routledge and Kegan Paul.

Neate, Rupert. 2015. Goldman Sachs Restricts Intern Workday to 17 Hours in Wake of Burnout Death. *The Guardian*, 18 June 2015. Accessed 18 June 2017. https://www.theguardian.com/business/2015/jun/17/goldman-sachs-interns-work-hours

PISA. 2015. Programme for International Student Assessment (PISA), OECD, 2015. Accessed 19 June 2017. http://www.compareyourcountry.org/pisa/country/oecd?lg=en

Powell, Jeff. 2002. Perfecting Capitalism or Post-capitalism? Lessons from the Argentinean Barter Experiments. *Review of International Political Economy* 9: 619–649.

Ryan, Christopher, and Cacilda Jethá. 2010. *Sex at Dawn: The Prehistoric Origins of Modern Sexuality*. New York: Harper Collins.

Sahlberg, Pasi. 2010. *Finnish Lessons: What Can the World Learn from Educational Change in Finland*. New York and London: Teachers College Press.

Singer, Peter, ed. 1986. *Applied Ethics*. New York: Oxford University Press.

Smith, Adam. 1790 [1759]. *The Theory of Moral Sentiment*. London: A. Millar.

Soros, George. 1998. *The Crisis of Global Capitalism: Open Society Endangered*. New York: Perseus Books Group.

Thomas, Henk, and Chris Logan. 1982. *Mondragon: An Economic Analysis*. Allen & Unwin.

Tocqueville, Alexis de. 2014 [1840]. *Democracy in America*, vol. II. Translated by Henry Reeve, 1899. ebooks@Adelaide, University of Adelaide Library. Accessed 19 June 2017. https://ebooks.adelaide.edu.au/t/tocqueville/alexis/democracy/complete.html

UK Parliament. 2012. Uncorrected Transcript of Oral Evidence. 31 January 2012. Accessed 19 June 2017. https://www.publications.parliament.uk/pa/cm201012/cmselect/cmeduc/uc1786-i/uc178601.htm

Van Krieken, Robert. 2012. *Celebrity Society*. London and New York: Routledge.

Weber, Max. 1958 [1905]. *The Protestant Ethic and the Spirit of Capitalism*. New York: Scribner.

Whyte, William Foote, and Kathleen King Whyte. 1991. *Making Mondragón: The Growth and Dynamics of the Worker Cooperative Complex*. New York: Cornell University Press.

Wilkinson, Richard, and Kate Pickett. 2009. *The Spirit Level: Why More Equal Societies Almost Always Do Better*. London: Allen Lane.

Wolff, Richard. 2012. Yes, There is an Alternative to Capitalism: Mondragon Shows the Way. *The Guardian*, 25 June 2012. Accessed 19 June 2017. https://www.theguardian.com/commentisfree/2012/jun/24/alternative-capitalism-mondragon

4

Hyper-consumption and Inequality

Describing an achievement, but also a problem of the affluent Western society, the concept of 'consumer society' started its life in the 1950s (Schor and Holt 2011). Alongside the Marxist philosophers of the Frankfurt School, Adorno, Horkheimer, Marcuse and others, critical economists such as our old friend J. K. Galbraith (1974), took interest and provided a mid-century critique of the new way of being in the West, focused on shopping and material abundance. The Oxford English Dictionary defines 'consumer society' as 'derogatory noun' meaning 'a society in which the buying and selling of goods and services is the most important social and economic activity.' The Collins English Dictionary defines it as 'a capitalist society in which the consumption of goods and services is promoted as a public good.' Other definitions also mention 'mass-produced good,' 'mass media advertising' and 'the ideology of consumerism.' People from less affluent societies cannot help being dazzled when they first encounter a shopping precinct of a Western city with its shiny, glossy plenty.

In comparison with twenty-first-century consumption, the early years of the consumer society, the 1950s, were rather innocent times. For a start, fridges and television sets were tiny compared to today's. The mass

V. Colic-Peisker, A. Flitney, *The Age of Post-Rationality*,
https://doi.org/10.1007/978-981-10-6259-9_4

ownership of cars that materialised in the post-war decades was an important milestone which enabled a host of other phenomena, including the suburban sprawl, which in turn enabled people to have bigger and bigger houses where they could accumulate more and more things—especially in the 'New World' part of the Anglosphere, where a self-standing house with a garden became a normal way to live for the expanding suburban middle class. At the time, babies were also in abundance—it was the time of the post-war 'baby boom.' The nuclear family was the norm, consisting of a full-time employed father, a stay-at-home mother and three to four children.

Of the many current forms of increasing consumption that we like to term 'hyper-consumption,' we shall mention just two: fast food and fast fashion. Once upon a time in the British Isles or Australia, fast food meant a local fish-and-chips shop, and later on perhaps a Chinese takeaway. Now that we are likely to be time-poor but have some extra cash (see *Time and money*, Chap. 3), fast food outlets of many varieties and ethnic origins have sprung up in every shopping precinct. For example, a study by the University of Cambridge showed that the number of takeaway food outlets in Norfolk county, UK, had risen by 45 per cent between 1990 and 2008, from 2.6 to 3.8 per 10,000 residents, with the greatest increases in poorer areas (Maguire et al. 2015). Most takeaway outlets offer energy-dense, high-calorie food, while the sedentary civilised life offers less and less need for physical energy expenditure (car dependency has lot to answer for), and this unfortunate combination of factors has led to a high prevalence of obesity. Again, the English-speaking countries lead the trend. For example, in the US the per capita calorie consumption increased by around a quarter between 1970 and 2000 (USDA 2004), a trend that almost certainly has continued in this century.

We hyper-consume clothes as well. When the Duchess of Cambridge, the next in line British queen, had the temerity to wear the same dress twice within a relatively short period, the tabloid headlines screamed: 'Kate wears same dress twice in 11 days' (*People* 2012). Why was such an event considered newsworthy? Because even 'ordinary' people are not supposed to wear the same clothes twice if they are being watched, let alone the royals! In the 1950s and 1960s, clothing was generally made of natural fibres such as cotton, linen and wool, and we owned a moderate amount of items which we wore repeatedly. Winter coats were worn for several seasons. If we look even deeper in the past, at the first half of the twentieth century, a majority of working people had two outfits, one for 'every day' and one for Sunday. The rise of synthetic clothing, garments made out of petroleum-derived materials such as nylon or polyester, meant that clothing could be produced more cheaply and hence we could update our wardrobes more often. The fact that almost all of our clothes are produced by low-paid workers in developing countries brings the price down further.

In *Deluxe: How Luxury Lost Its Lustre*, Dana Thomas (2007) writes of the epiphany that leading fashion designers had in the 1980s: they decided to 'democratise fashion,' to make it 'accessible' to the masses by introducing cheaper versions of their luxury items. Although it was meant to sound egalitarian, their real aim '[…] was as capitalist as could be: the goal, plain and simple, was to make as much money as heavenly possible' (p. 8). Cheaper prices and the promotion of 'luxury' brands to the middle class resulted in the advent of 'fast fashion': instead of clothing stores updating their fashions each season, some now offer weekly fashion updates. According to *the Wall Street Journal*, the average American bought 63 garments in 2013. Even schoolgirls are not ready to be seen in the same outfit twice (ABC). Most of the synthetic garments are not meant to last and make a rapid transition to landfill—or clog the ever-bigger wardrobes of those who feel guilty about the short lives of the clothes they loved, briefly, only a little while ago. Ironically, once in landfill, these garments are virtually indestructible.

Conspicuous Consumption

In the consumer society, the ascetic norms that guided early capitalism no longer apply. It is the opposite: the duty of the righteous is to spend, even waste. Keeping fit by running in the park or swimming in the ocean is not good consumer behaviour; better to run on a treadmill in a gym or pay for the use of a swimming pool (or have one's own). To have a personal trainer is even better! Spending money on unnecessary things is not wasting, however. We compete with other consumers, where our consumption signals our status; we also keep the wheels of the capitalist economy turning.

Consuming for status has long been known as 'conspicuous consumption.' The concept was formulated by American economist and sociologist Thorsten Veblen (1857–1929), best known for his 1899 book *Theory of the Leisure Class*. Veblen (1899) defined conspicuous consumption as consumption of 'goods of a higher quality or in greater quantity than might be considered necessary in practical terms.' In his 1931 *Essays in Persuasion*, J. M. Keynes (1931, 365) argued that '[T]he needs of human beings fall into two classes—those needs that are absolute in the sense that we feel them regardless of circumstances; and those which are relative only in that their satisfaction lifts us above and makes us superior to, our fellow human beings.' The significance of conspicuous consumption led some contemporary sociologists to declare that our identities and status are no longer determined by the type of work we do and the level of income we earn but by what we consume (see Pakulski and Waters 1996). This may be a debatable claim, but certainly worth a thought.

In Eastern European communist countries of the second half of the twentieth century, the choice of consumer goods was more or less severely limited, compared to the West. During the Cold War, the West used its fast-rising consumption and affluence to belittle its ideological competitor. The response from the authorities in the East was to remind their citizens about the shallow and mindless consumerism of the West, and both the exploitation and bribing of the working class by 'capitalists.' While many citizens of communist countries craved the glitzy, fashionable Western products, such as blue jeans, rock music and cars, in their countries, money was considered the root of all evil. This meant that modestly paid people could not and did not have to plot how to earn their first million dollars and were not tempted to get into debt in order to own a snazzier car or a more impressive house than their friends. With the absence of consumer goods, they were spared from consumer pressures. They lived much more frugally but also worked less than Westerners. Since shopping did not take much time, they could spend more time with their families, friends and hobbies. Perhaps they played chess instead![1] Westerners were under pressure to work harder and buy harder in order to achieve the elusive lasting satisfaction—because one is always 'one Rolex short of contentment' (Monbiot 2013).

Status anxiety, coupled with an easy availability of credit, has contributed to a steep increase in conspicuous consumption over the past decades. It started in earnest in the 1950s, when 'consumer goods' became available to nearly everyone. There were only about 20 years between the wartime (and immediate post-war) food rationing to supermarkets offering 90 types of ice cream and 70 types of tomato sauce. During the 1950s and 1960s, suburban living focused on material consumption became the norm in the Anglosphere. A happy housewife showing off her new refrigerator or television (always in a pretty dress and high heels), and her handsome husband sporting a new family car featured in commercials as consumer symbols of the era. The conspicuous consumption of the twenty-first century shifted towards 'smart' portable electronic gadgets, but cars are still a common way to conspicuously consume. Their advantage as status symbols is that they move and display our wealth and taste wherever we go. Bulky, petrol-guzzling SUVs are the latest in the conspicuous consumption on four wheels. There is no practical advantage in driving such cars in large cities where the average speed of traffic does not exceed 20 km/h, and there is no wilderness in sight to be conquered. The advantage of showing off one's financial prowess in this way comes packaged with endangering other participants in traffic by blocking their view. As to fridges and TVs, they are now several times their 1950s size, but TV sets may have peaked. Giant flat-screen TVs are a conspicuous consumption of the middle-aged; you are not going to find them in homes of the under-40s.

Technological and social changes go hand in hand with changing styles of conspicuous consumption, but middle-class households, representing a majority of Western populations, remain the core of conspicuous consumers, with a small number of exceptions who instead choose to work less and spend less. Middle-class conspicuous consumption is a central pillar of the capitalist status quo and a key contributor to environmental woes. No amount of recycling and progressive petitions-signing can change this fact.

In popular jokes still circulating in social media in these post-feminist times, wives are often portrayed as insatiable consumers and careless spenders of their husbands' hard-earned money. According to Galbraith (1992), they are in fact doing the hard work of spending. In his book

Economics and Public Purpose, he proposed that the suburban lifestyle of middle-class America required an elaborate 'administration of consumption'—a role allocated to the housewife. The very word 'housewife' may strike as somewhat old fashioned these days, as a majority of women are employed and the nuclear family is increasingly a lifestyle choice rather than the norm, so we can translate 'wives' into 'homemakers.' Yet, the gender dimension remains. According to Galbraith (1992), affluence turned most wives into a 'crypto-servant class' whose role is critical for the expansion of consumption. The maintenance of ever-larger dwellings, garden and vehicles, care for children, from feeding to chauffeuring, 'heavy demands of social intercourse involving competitive display of housewifely competence' (p. 256), and administration and outsourcing of some of these functions (engaging tilers, cleaners, babysitters, etc.) require constant efforts to which a life of the homemaker is devoted. Through such conspicuous household consumption, housewives are not only custodians of their family's social status, but they also grease the wheels of capitalism in significant ways.

More than a century ago, Veblen deplored the wastefulness of consumption for status. Today, as we discuss in Chap. 5, we choke the planet with our rubbish, pollute the last pristine areas and warm the globe to dangerous levels, so there are further serious reasons to deplore it. But the call of consumption for status remains irresistible for most of us: it is part of our conventional wisdom which is in need of reform, in the name of reason.

The Bonfire of Vanity

To be sure, conspicuous consumption is much older than modern-day middle-class suburbia. Privileged members of society showed off their wealth throughout recorded history. A dramatic story of conspicuous consumption comes from Florence, one of the richest cities of late medieval Europe and the birthplace of the European Renaissance (see Chap. 2). In the fourteenth century, Florentine financiers and artisans were the core of the emerging European urban middle class, the bourgeoisie, which would become the architect of capitalist modernity. Industries that Italy is famous for to this day—textiles, clothing design, shoemaking, home furnishing, decorative and visual art—flourished at that time.

The burghers of Florence, growing in numbers and wealth, were keen to show off their success through beautiful clothes, shoes, jewellery and intricately built and furnished stately residences where finely crafted household items and exquisite works of art were on display. The Florentine bourgeoisie sponsored artists to build churches, town halls and other public buildings that have enchanted visitors ever since. Under the onslaught of profane pleasures and bourgeois immodesty, the church was losing its influence. While most popes in the nearby Vatican were all too happy to join in the pleasurable hedonism, the forceful march of conspicuous consumption stirred up ire on the part of the Catholic clergy. It was obvious that material riches and creature comforts had a stronger pull on those who could afford them than the spiritual life and religiously inspired modesty. The battle of material versus spiritual was, in historical and political terms, the war of modern secular leaders and the new powerful class of bourgeoisie against the traditional power of the church.

A famous battle in this war was the 'bonfire of vanity,' staged by Girolamo Savonarola (1452–1498), a Dominican friar whose calling was to advocate modesty and righteously rage against clerical corruption and secular excess; these days we would probably call him a 'whistle-blower.' The immodest 'objects of vanity'—luxury clothes, personal accessories, jewellery, furniture, books, painting and other objects of desire likely to lead people to sin—were to burned at the central city square. Those fearful of eternal fires of hell, described vividly in the work of the Italian poet laureate Dante Alighieri a couple of centuries earlier, contributed their sinful goods. The beautiful things went up in flames in Florence's central Piazza di Signoria in February 1497, marking an unusual finale to the traditional Mardi Grass festival.

'Sumptuary laws' introduced against conspicuous consumption were meant to restrain luxury and extravagance and maintain the traditional social hierarchy and religion-based morals against the onslaught of a new social class that unashamedly transgressed both. The increasingly assertive bourgeoisie was building its power on trade, commerce and banking and challenging the traditional power of the nobility and clergy. Along the way, they were building a more open society where, at least in theory, anyone could have a 'rags to riches' experience. It is not surprising that they encountered significant opposition from the forces of the old regime, personified in Savonarola, who also advocated democratic rights for the poor against despotic rule. However, Savonarola lost popular support in the war against the powerful Florentine burghers and was subsequently tried and executed. He disobeyed the pope and annoyed the powerful de Medici family, the rulers of Florence at the time. Too much power was stacked against his cause. We could also say that he fought against the unstoppable march of modernity.

Judging by the example of Florence, today the top destinations for the lovers of visual arts and architecture, the tradition of conspicuous consumption, status-seeking and vanity can leave behind impressive achievements. Without the vanity of the rich and powerful, there would be no magnificent artefacts that became proud symbols of human civilisation(s): there would be no Egyptian pyramids, no medieval cathedrals, no Taj Mahal, no Empire State Building. The SUVs mentioned earlier may be admired in a museum of petrol-fuelled cars in a 100-years' time. The small town of Prato next to Florence is still the centre of the Italian textile

Fig. 4.1 'Street of beautiful women' in the centre of Florence. Beauty has been an important female asset for millennia, and not just in Italy. It has enticed competition and fed conspicuous consumption much before someone came with the idea of a beauty contest

Fig. 4.2 'Street of Shoemakers' in Florence, (all four vowels in a row should be pronounced)

industry with deep roots in centuries of tradition[2] and home to a unique *Museo dei Tesuti* (Textile Museum). A multimedia *Museo Salvatore Ferragamo* in the heart of the city of Florence, named after a celebrity shoemaker for Hollywood divas, celebrates centuries of artisan Florentine shoemaking but is also a museum of top-end stylish conspicuous consumption. The museum offers an exclusive shoe-shopping experience to visitors with such inclinations and deep pockets.

So what is the moral of this story about the lost battle against conspicuous consumption? Perhaps that the battle is even less likely to achieve any success today when conspicuous consumption is not a province of a tiny proportion of the rich, but is enjoyed by the middle classes. Religious and spiritual reasons for the pursuit of material modesty are largely ignored in the secular West; ignoring the environmental cost, however, is a sign of a civilisation slipping into the era of post-rationality, hyper-consuming its way to perdition, on the finite planet that hosts it, as discussed in more detail in Chap. 5.

Marketing

As society grew richer and people had more disposable income, the battle for consumers' attention became big business. Prior to the nineteenth century, economies mostly consisted of regional producers who sold goods on local markets. As transportation improved, the idea of 'marketing,' promoting goods to a wider audience became accepted. After the post-war boom created the 'affluent society,' marketing accounted for an ever-growing proportion of production cost. We are constantly lured into 'retail therapy': buying new stuff is supposed to provide a momentary pleasure and relief from our anxieties. If we are not keen consumers, informed about the latest trends and fashions, we may fall behind our peers. Conversely, acquiring the right stuff makes us cool and improves our status.

The more we earn, the more we are able to spend following our tastes and whims. This makes us persons of interest to marketing experts: these are people who know a great deal about relative deprivation (see following section). On a daily—in the era of social media perhaps hourly—basis, advertising reinforces the idea that consumption is the greatest source of pleasure and the main source of our personal attractiveness, popularity and, by extension, happiness. Back in the 1960s, Galbraith (2001/1964, 103–104) was critical of the emotional manipulation by marketing experts: '[…] Social distinction must be associated with a house, sexual fulfilment with a particular automobile, social acceptance with a mouth wash. We live surrounded by a systematic appeal to a dream world […]'

In the consumer society, everything is on the market in a myriad of brands: the objects of personal and visceral consumption, such as food and clothing, but also the objects that clutter our homes, entertainment, education, music, tourist destinations, ideas, ideologies, policies and finally political candidates, are all there for us to choose from. In most instances, the amount of choice is mind-boggling. How can we ever be confident we are making a good, if not the best, choice? A few years ago, the thoughtful cousin of Author 1, a precisely minded engineer, bought her a subscription to *Choice* magazine for her birthday. She read the first issue enthusiastically, but soon realised that regularly heeding good advice on what to buy is just too much work, even if it is pre-chewed for quicker consumption. In a glut of choice and confronted with information overload, choosing rationally—that is, by methodically comparing all that is on offer—becomes impossibly time-consuming. Not even Google can save us: too much choice is simply counter-productive. Due to the size of the advertising industry—the cacophony of voices and the excess of images competing for our attention—it is expensive not just for producers to advertise their wares but also for consumers to decide what to buy.

A survival response is to choose on a whim or rely on the word of mouth coming from our peers. Given the way we choose, marketing experts are more interested in the deep psychology of our whims than in appealing to our rational selves. Therefore, they do not bother trying to explain the brilliance and indispensability of various products. Advertising consumer products or services works on the same principle as marketing political ideas and policies during election campaigns: none is meant to be subject to our rational and critical judgement, but to simply become imprinted on our brains by ceaseless repetition or associated with pleasant and desirable things. Marketing also uses subliminal messages about things that matter to us most: for example, how our sexual attractiveness

The World Without Advertising

Advertising works primarily on the idea of making people feel inadequate and then offering a remedy. We rush to buy things in order to feel better and appropriate some of the magic contained in a certain brand of car, shoes or drink. What would the world be like without advertising? Would our lives be better or worse? For a start, there would be no free-to-air television apart from public television paid for by our taxes; there would be no huge billboards on the side of roads and no bright, blinking signs above shops and on roofs of tall buildings. Without this visual pollution, we may be compelled to notice the architecture, and if we aim even higher, the often fascinating cloud formations and the stars at night. The Brazilian megalopolis of Sao Paolo recently banned advertising in public spaces, and many other cities around the world have partial bans and restrictions (Lawson 2012). Despite warnings of dramatic job losses and millions in lost revenue, most residents of Sao Paolo have found the ban beneficial.

Without advertising we would not feel the urge to buy new furniture or clothes just because today is the last chance to catch the 'sale of the decade.' We would not be bombarded with nonsense such as 'the more you buy the more you save.' Shopping would occupy less time in our lives and less space in our minds. We would be more likely to buy what we need and therefore we would waste less. Most things would be cheaper because the cost of advertising is a considerable portion of the price of most items. Fewer women would stand in front of their bulging wardrobes in the morning thinking 'I have nothing to wear.' Middle-aged men would not think it reasonable to crawl through a city traffic jam in a red sports car routinely overtaken by cyclists. Children would not pester their parents to buy them the newest super-cool soft drink or super-sour crisps that every self-respecting youngster must love to devour.[3] We would spend much less on unnecessary electronic gadgets. Without constant food advertising, there would be less obesity. Sport would not be a billion-dollar business, and it would be played by amateurs for the enjoyment of the game and its health and social benefits.

But as our desire for things diminished, so would the sales of various products. Shops would close. Advertising, retail and some other industries would shrink, and many jobs would be lost. Marketing as a profession would cease to exist. Businesses that heavily rely on marketing would go bust. It is likely that our GDP and economic growth would fall, at least initially. What would the army of unemployed shop assistants do? All this is anathema to economists—but would a society emerging from this scenario really be worse off than what we have now? Clearly, a redeployment of human resources would be necessary and a significant social change would be likely to follow. It could be done gradually. Marketing professionals could take jobs as art educators and psychologists.

If we shopped less and spent less, we would apparently need to produce less, and therefore work less. All of us. Deep down, many people are sick of the rat race by their middle age. You can no doubt imagine working a 30-hour week? Or even 20? Would you agonise to find something else to do? Or conversely, would you enjoy some free time for creative, social or sport pursuits of your own choice? What if the competitive pressure eased and people kind of chilled out? If they had time to talk to each other when they met in the street, or stop and have a coffee together as people do in some slower-living societies? Sit on a park bench and relax, admire the trees, smell the real and proverbial roses? Read a book? Take time to cook food rather than grabbing a takeaway or a frozen lasagne on your way home? Cinemas, theatres, galleries and public parks would have more visitors, like in times past.

In fact, not so long ago we had a world without advertising. Advertising only started in earnest with mass media, especially television, in the 1950s. It existed in magazines and newspapers before electronic media entered our homes, but at that time it only reached a minority of people. It may be hard to imagine the disappearance of something so ubiquitous. Any social change inevitably triggers many other changes. We invite you to give it a thought!

or prowess will be improved by buying a certain product—an alcoholic drink, a red sport car or a new miraculous cosmetic product that will erase our wrinkles in 90 days (KLM 2017, 14). The marketeers appeal to our immediate impulses and hidden desires as well as fears, bypassing our rational brain. At some point, this thought might have occurred to you: could the world go on without advertising?

Relative Deprivation

In spite of living in safety and material comfort, twenty-first-century Westerners still find many reasons to be unhappy. This includes those who can be described as conventionally successful. The obesity epidemic, depression and anxiety disorders, and addictions of various kinds, from shopping to gambling, alcohol and drugs, to mention just the most widespread, are rather serious 'First World problems.' Often, commentators refer to the 'pressures of modern life.' The 'rat race' seems to be the best, if somewhat informal, way to summarise these pressures: chasing money, status and success. These, however, are all moving targets: whatever level we achieve, we always seem to want at least a little more.

In a consumer society, those who have only a little less may feel like losers. We therefore make undue sacrifices in order to be successful. For example, if moving to another town for a better job will jeopardise a close friendship, or even a relationship, not to mention parting with some good colleagues, then too bad, it will! Financial and status considerations usually win over other considerations. Many explicit as well as subliminal messages constantly point us in that direction.

Therefore, in an affluent society where most people have more than they need for a safe and comfortable life, people still feel deprived. Our life satisfaction is a subjective feeling which may not have much to do with our 'objective circumstances'; it depends how our achievements measure up to our aspirations. The latter are largely defined by our peer group. When conventionally measuring our individual success, we compare and rank ourselves within our relatively narrow circle. People who form our familial, social and professional networks have roughly comparable social status to our own. This inner circle determines our aspirations, the sense of entitlement and the reach of our ambition, that is, a status to which we could realistically aspire.

A successful middle-aged financier may feel entitled to become a millionaire, or even a billionaire, and feel deprived and unhappy if this does not come true. He ('she' is much rarer in this group) may look up to George Soros or Warren Buffett as his role models. A primary school teacher may entertain more modest ambitions, for example, to own a home in a middle-class suburb and send her children to a respectable university. The reason why a majority of refugees recently resettled in Western countries report being satisfied with their low income is because they compare themselves to other refugees or their compatriots back in their unsettled homeland, rather than with the much richer native population (Colic-Peisker 2009). A recent book described slum dwellers of Mumbai as 'happy in spite of their wretchedness' (Boo 2013). We can safely assume that their aspirations are likely to be low by First World standards, not least because the wider society imposes strict boundaries on what they can achieve. This limit may, paradoxically, increase their happiness by freeing them from nagging ambition and status anxiety. They may not feel 'wretched' at all. In contrast, many frustrated Westerners live in an environment where a presumed equality of opportunity constantly goads them to aspire for more. We hasten to add that we do not mean to romanticise poverty in a Mumbai slum.

Therefore, our feeling of deprivation, or contentment, is relative; not a result of what we have, or have achieved in itself, but only in comparison with our significant others. This is what social psychologists and other social scientists have called 'relative deprivation' (Runciman 1966; Panning 1983; D'Ambrosio and Frick 2007). It also works on a larger plane: poverty is relative and its definition in America is different from its definition in India. In America, being poor still means having more than enough food and a private toilet with plumbing—not so in India where the poorer half of the population (more than 600 million people) still do not have one (Anand 2014). The relative deprivation theory suggests that this does not mean it is easier to be poor in America. It is actually likely to be the other way around: being poor in a rich society can be relatively more painful than being poor in a society where this is nothing exceptional. One can live happily on very little if others around them do the same. Some special circumstances have proven this point. Britons did not complain about food rationing during the Second World War because it was clear that everyone was in the same boat. Everyone was deprived of meat and sugar, but no-one was relatively deprived of status because of this. Ironically, the enforced wartime diet based on potatoes and oats cooked in many imaginative ways was healthier than the twenty-first-

A Stagnant Income Scenario

Given you are reading this book, you are likely to be over 35 and live in a Western country. As such, you are likely to have had a decent income for a number of years, allowing you to have a comfortable life and a hope for a financially stable future. You probably own a fully furnished home (what this means depends on your peer group), clothes for every occasion including those you haven't worn for years or never worn yet, a number of electronic gadgets keeping you super-connected, a car or two or three, a regular holiday away from home and a budget for out-of-home entertainment such as restaurant meals, concerts, and so on.

Now imagine you will never again receive a pay increase—apart from a rise compensating for inflation. Although your income will not rise, this does not exclude the possibility of having a more interesting or higher status job in the future. If you own your own business, imagine it will never again be more profitable that it is now—but not less so either. It will neither grow nor shrink. Your income will be stagnant, but you will be able to pay off your mortgage and secure decent education for your children, if you have them. It is just that you won't get any richer than you are right now.

How does that make you feel? You may instinctively dislike this idea. If so, what exactly worries you? If this 'frozen income' scenario concerns you in spite of the guarantees provided, you are, according to the relative deprivation theory, concerned about being left behind by your peers. With your income stagnant, you may feel something is wrong with you in spite of being comfortably off. If your peers—long-term friends and close work colleagues—continue to get pay increases and in few years earn considerably more than you, this may affect your self-esteem and your life satisfaction—you may start feeling like a loser. They would be able to travel to more exotic locations for their overseas holidays, drive more expensive cars, live in a more salubrious home and tell you about their fabulous dining experience at a fashionable restaurant you cannot afford. This would not mean they would have a better time on holidays, or be safer in traffic, or enjoy a better home, or eat better food; their higher income would not mean their children respect them more or their spouses are fonder of them.

Once we reach a certain level of earnings, the benefit of a rising income is purely psychological. For better or for worse, most people's contentment and happiness are in a large measure determined by a comparison with other people. Therefore, if others' income rises, we are compelled to want the same. We must keep up with the Joneses.

In an opposite scenario, if your peers were happy to remain on their current income level indefinitely, then this would most likely be okay for you too. This no-growth scenario could be applied to nations too. We ask you to consider: can we dismount the hamster's wheel of consumption as individuals and save the planet as nations?

century British diet dripping with sugar and fat. While relative deprivation is depressing, some absolute deprivation may be good for us all.

The consumer society and the issue of relative deprivation are responsible for a general expectation that our disposable income will rise indefinitely, at least until we retire. No-one wants to have a stagnant income amidst people with rising incomes. However, life satisfaction surveys show that after a certain level of income, a further increase has no substantive impact on our wellbeing (Wilkinson and Picket 2009). If it makes us happier, it is only because we get ahead of, or are able to at least keep up with, our significant others. Many of us would be happy to swap some of our earnings for more free time. What stops us is not a concern about any real deprivation but the fear of feeling relatively deprived—losing our hard-earned status and career progression, our place in the rat race. Since it is logically and economically impossible for everyone to get richer relative to everyone else, on a group level, the effort to get ahead of the pack is wasted and irrational. Moreover, as we all get richer in our never-ending quest for more, this inevitably leads to overwork and hyperconsumption. On a national level, the claim about the rationality of

Fig. 4.3 The West defined by Christianity + consumerism? Or is it just that good French Catholics like to smell nice?

competition stipulates that only competition can keep us productive and that, if we are not (increasingly) productive, we are doomed to fall behind in the global economic competition. Is there any salvation from this relentless circular logic?

Inequality

In the very first sentence of the introduction to his famous 1835–1840 study *Democracy in America*, Alexis de Tocqueville 2014 [1840] stated: 'Amongst the novel objects that attracted my attention during my stay in the United States, nothing struck me more forcibly than the general equality of conditions.' Unlike today, the nineteenth-century US was seen as a land of equality and opportunity, at least in comparison to Europe dominated by 'old money' and riddled by insurmountable class barriers. In his *Capital in the Twenty-first Century*, Piketty (2014) documents an American transition from being the most egalitarian

Western country in the nineteenth and the first half of the twentieth centuries, including going further than Europe with progressive taxation after the Second World War (pp. 152–153), to being the most unequal.

Over past centuries, many reformers have argued that society should aim to eliminate extremes of inequality; they often used religious argument and made it a moral issue. Society's moral standards and its degree of civilisation are often measured against its treatment of its weakest members: the disabled, the sick, the mentally ill, the old, the poor, the homeless, all of whom need a social welfare net. Such a net, the modern 'welfare state,' was born out of the Great Depression and presupposed a degree of redistribution between the rich and the poor in order to avoid extremes of poverty and disadvantage. Yet, redistribution has never been a universally popular policy; it is 'socialist' and it contravenes the dominant tenets of capitalism, that of economic rationality, as well as competition and the 'meritocracy' that is supposed to be its result. In addition, the understanding of equality differs across the political spectrum. For conservatives, the central moral and political issue is the equality of opportunity, not the equality of outcomes. From the left of the political spectrum, the response is that the equality of opportunity has never been achieved.

In consequence, a major purpose of economic growth is to serve as an alternative to redistribution, easing the tensions associated with inequality by making the poor (a little) better off. Economic growth also keeps the problem of economic insecurity at bay by keeping unemployment at a relatively low level despite there being little redistribution of income or employment (Galbraith 1974). However, Galbraith (1974, 80–81), and others in his wake, argued that whatever its distribution, economic growth would never end poverty: 'increasing aggregate output leaves a self-perpetuating margin of poverty at the very base of the income pyramid,' which goes largely unnoticed. Contrary to the conventional wisdom that 'a rising tide lifts all boats,' and that if the cake is bigger, everyone will get a bigger slice, it has been well documented that the gap between the rich and the poor in Western societies has widened, after reaching its minimum in the early 1970s.

Piketty (2014) put an end to a decades-long debate about whether the gap between the rich and the poor in affluent societies has increased. He showed that the return on capital (after adjusting for inflation) in the West is greater than the rate of economic growth. In other words, a greater share of the spoils of economic growth has gone to profits over wages, therefore to the propertied class rather than to income earners. This leads to an increasing concentration of capital because those with equity increase their wealth faster than society as a whole and faster than those who earn their living as employees. Low capital gains tax (in US it currently sits on 14 per cent; in Australia at 15–23 per cent) contributes to the rise in inequality. Levels of inequality are now similar to those of the 1910s, retracing all the gains made in the intervening decades (Piketty 2014). The share of US national income of the top 1 per cent of earners rose from 9 per cent in 1970 to 20 per cent in the 2000s (Reich 2008, 107). They absorbed nearly 60 per cent of the growth in incomes over the period 1977–2007 (Piketty 2014, 294–303).

During and after the Great Depression (1929–1933), the stark reality of massive unemployment and poverty made the welfare state a necessity to preserve the stability of the system. The 'New Deal' was introduced in the US under Roosevelt's administration (Hobsbawm 1995). Rather than a sudden emergence of a sense of social solidarity, the welfare state was an admission that the capitalist market is far from a self-balancing system and that the state needs to intervene when the system gets seriously out of kilter. When inequality reaches intolerable proportions, social peace must be secured by providing a public safety net for the jobless, homeless and others in need. The argument is not just moral (from the left) and political (from the right) but also economic. In order for capitalism to function, Keynes argued, there must be demand for goods and services; most people must have purchasing power and therefore must have employment and earnings, or at the very least a government-provided minimum of income (Hobsbawm 1995).

The strong welfare state and so-called Keynesian economics lasted until the 1970s, through the 'golden era' of equality in the West in the 1950s and 1960s (Reich 2008; Piketty 2014). After the wounds of the Great Depression healed and economic growth started to falter, the pendulum of economic thinking swung again, this time towards advocating the free market. The leading voice belonged to Fredrick Hayek who argued that redistribution through the welfare state was a 'hodgepodge of ill-assembled and often inconsistent ideals which under the name of the Welfare State has largely replaced socialism as the goal of the reformers' (Hayek 1944). A host of neo-liberal economists concurred: free market competition, however cruel and unpleasant its outcomes may be for some people, should be supported because it secures the optimal allocation of resources. The free marketers found a receptive ear on both sides of the Atlantic, where trimming down the welfare state and giving the market as free rein as possible was called 'Thatcherism' and 'Reaganomics.' The main goal was to revive economic growth as a cure for all social ills.

In their book *The Spirit Level: Why More Equal Societies Almost Always Do Better*, sociologists Wilkinson and Pickett (2009) argue that an egalitarian society is better not only for the poor but also for the rich. From many different angles and through a review of existing quantitative research, they show that more equal societies have lower crime rates, higher life satisfaction, lower rates of illicit drug use, less mental illness and even less obesity. By extension, decreasing global disparities would make the world a safer and more stable place. In 2016, GDP per capita (excluding tax havens and other anomalous cases) varied from Norway's US$69,000 to Somalia's US$400[4]—hardly egalitarian (CIA 2016).

In the US, the median wealth of a white household is twelve times the median wealth of a black household (2013 data, EPI 2017). The gap between black and white wages has been growing since 1979. To this centuries-old endemic inequality residentially concentrated in 'black ghettos' of American cities, a large post-1965 influx of non-white immigrants contributed pockets of disadvantage on an ethnic basis (Sullivan et al. 2015). In some countries, the situation of the 'ethnic' underclass is rather explosive. French cities provide a stark contrast between the rich, historic, architecturally stunning city centres attracting millions of tourists and the 'other France' featuring nondescript *banlieues* populated mostly by North African *Les Arabs* (Packer 2015). Apart from this deep rift, there are more subtle class distinctions and inequalities in French society. In his monumental work *Distinction: A Social Critique of the Judgment of Taste*, Pierre Bourdieu (1984) analysed the class patterns of consumption and posited that not only economic but also cultural capital determines what and how we consume, and in turn our place in the social pyramid.

In the settler countries of the Anglosphere—Canada, Australia and the US—the most confronting aspect of inequality is the intractable problem of the indigenous underclass that showcases an impressive selection of social ills. Disturbing reports from Australian rural and remote indigenous communities illustrate the yawning gap of social inequality and the depth of indigenous disadvantage: Australian reports on alcoholism, family violence and sniffing glue and petrol among indigenous youth are matched by Canadian reports on the 'first nations' killing themselves slowly with 'Oxy,' a prescription drug sold on the black market (Ubelacker 2012; CBS 2016).[5] A rather dramatic illustration of the pernicious effect of rising inequality can be found in Eastern European post-communist countries, where the gap between the rich and the poor exploded after the abrupt, uncontrolled and corrupt privatisation of the 1990s, which led to general anomie—a situation where old norms were thrown to the rubbish tip of history but replaced only by corruption and lawlessness. In Russia, for example, life expectancy for men dropped dramatically in early post-communism due primarily to extraordinary levels of vodka consumption, and then improved somewhat after controls on alcohol sales were introduced, but still sits at a low 64 years (Zaridze et al. 2014).

There seem to be good reasons for trying to make society more equal using the policy tools of taxation and redistribution. However, these are two among the most unpopular words in the policy lexicon of the Anglosphere. The Scandinavian version of social democracy, the 'Nordic model,' provides a reasonable blueprint for a fairer and more compassionate society, but the Anglosphere has not been willing to take this direction, considering the market a better judge of fairness than democratic deliberation. Interestingly, Swedish economist Gunnar Myrdal, an advocate of the welfare state as a mid-way between capitalism and socialism, shared the 1974 Nobel Prize for economics with his ideological antagonist, the free market advocate Friedrich Hayek. This was an admission, by the Nobel Prize committee at least, that both sides of the argument should be heard. Yet, since then, the free market argument has been much louder, at least in the main English-speaking countries.

'Masters of the Universe' Versus the Working Poor

As elaborated in the next chapter, financial markets are supposed to have a central role in the efficient allocation of capital. Does this mean that financial traders who shift around millions of dollars belonging to other people should have astronomical salaries and bonuses? Should they be entitled to feel like 'the masters of the universe,' as they are sometimes referred to?[6] They certainly seem to be the winners of capitalism, earning much more than other professionals with demanding and responsible jobs. If we indeed live in a meritocracy, does this mean that financial decision makers—financial traders, fund managers and CEOs of large companies—possess skills so extremely rare, and hold jobs so much more complex and riskier than anyone else's? The usual insider response to the question is that six-, seven- or even eight-digit annual remuneration is essential for attracting the best people to risky and stressful jobs.

In his book *Cityboy: Beer and Loathing in the Square Mile*, British financial analyst-turned-writer Geraint Anderson (2008) 'tells all' and confesses that in his first year in the City, which he entered as a complete ignoramus, he earned 'nearly as much as his father, who had been a successful public servant for nearly thirty years' (p. 67). In a few years, alongside many of his colleagues, he was earning more than the British Prime minister. Anderson (2008, 154) pours scorn on the risk justification for vast salaries and argues that the large bonuses finance professionals receive are in many cases guaranteed by their contracts and not dependent on performance. It is easy to agree with him that the job of a policeman, a fireman or a nurse involves more stress and risk, while their salaries are a pathetic fraction of the salaries commanded by financial professionals in London's famous financial district, the 'Square Mile.'

In many cases, high-ranking finance professionals and CEOs make rules that suit them, and fragmented shareholder assemblies do not have the power to stop them. Piketty (2014, 334) calls it 'pay for luck,' arguing that there is no 'rational productivity justification for extremely high executive pay.'[7] Stern (2012) found no correlation between CEO pay and company performance in the UK. Similar results were found for leading Swiss, German and US firms. Anderson (2008, 46–47) described the feelings about his huge salary: 'Clearly, impostor syndrome affects people in many different careers but because the salaries in the City are so absurdly large I believe it is particularly prevalent among us stockbrokers. How can we possibly be worth the cash these mugs are throwing at us?'

Adding to the weight of evidence about the Anglosphere being the most capitalistic section of the affluent West, and the most tolerant of capitalist excesses and the resulting inequality, Piketty (2014, 315) considers the regally remunerated 'supermanagers'—people with 'historically unprecedented compensation packages for their labor' (p. 302)—a 'largely Anglo-Saxon phenomenon.' The great income inequality has given rise to an ideology he terms 'meritocratic extremism,' which is especially prevalent in the US (p. 334). Supermanagers are concentrated in the top 1 per cent of the income distribution, whose rise is a major reason for increased income inequality in the Anglosphere in recent decades. A large drop in the top marginal income tax rate is responsible for 'an explosion of very high incomes' and also a considerable political influence of their beneficiaries through the financing of political parties, pressure groups and think tanks (Piketty 2014, 335).

Recently, BBC reported Reuters' comparison of wages paid by 13 leading investment banks based or working in London. They found that Royal Bank of Scotland paid its risk-taking and senior staff an average of £600,000 per year at the time when they recorded the largest loss in UK history (Griffiths 2009). The data showed that in 2013, 2600 City employees were paid a total of more than £3.4 billion (an average of £1.3 million each). This was an annual pay almost 50 times higher than the British average income (Lynam 2015). In the US, the average income of the top 25 hedge fund managers was a hyperbolic $657 million in 2006, topping out at over $1 billion just prior to the onset of the Global Financial Crisis (GFC) in 2007 (Lenzer 2013). The British Trade Union Congress General Secretary suggested it was time that the pay of the financial class 'came out of the stratosphere and back to planet earth' (Lynam 2015).

With its promise of quick riches, speculative trading not only sucks money out of the real economy, but also diverts talent, mainly young and highly educated professionals, out of more socially constructive pursuits. In recent years, highly intelligent 'quants,' often with doctorates in mathematics, statistics or physics, have been recruited by financial institutions to do the mathematical analysis of patterns in financial markets. In

Britain, large finance firms organise an annual fair, in financial circles known as the 'milk round,' to attract the brightest students by the prospect of overblown salaries (Anderson 2008, 14).

One of the earliest and most famous quants, maths genius Jim Simons, founded his own hedge fund, 'Renaissance Technologies' in 1982. The fund has been astonishingly successful, and a third of its 200 employees have PhDs in physics, mathematics or statistics. Simon Jones, who until recently ran the 'quant' desk for a major London bank, puts the brain-drain most explicitly: 'My bank employed the brightest engineers, chemists and scientists—and we were all working together to get richer. The chemical and physics and health industries are worse off because of what we do' (Manzoor 2013). In his book titled *The Quants*, Scott Patterson (2010), a staff writer for the *Wall Street Journal*, described how a number of very smart people used the tools of advanced mathematics and physics to create sophisticated financial products with the purpose of siphoning billions into their pockets, and that of their clients.

It is sign of post-rational times when large incentives are created for people to put short-term personal gain ahead of the longer-term interests of society, while they bear none of the risk if their optimistic, or delusional, vision of the future fails to come to fruition. This is exactly what led to the GFC: an unjustified and reckless expectation that US house prices would continue to rise indefinitely (see Chap. 5). In 1972, a Yale professor and economics Nobel laureate James Tobin suggested that taxes should be used to deter financial speculation. This idea gained increasing recognition after the GFC (Krugman 2009), but the power of the finance industry is such that none of the proposals have gone beyond the discussion stage.

In contrast to the incredibly lavish salaries of top CEOs and finance professionals, there are people whose incomes from full-time jobs can barely cover their essential cost of living. After having thrown off the shackles of the hereditary stratified societies of the 'Old World,' the US has recreated class distinctions through the excessive salaries at the top of the income distribution and the low minimum wages of the 'labouring poor.' The latter work all hours, often in multiple jobs, and still fail to earn enough to support themselves and their children. In 1998, reporter Barbara Ehrenreich went undercover to impersonate a woman desperate for a job to pay the week's rent and put food on the table. She worked in menial, poorly paid jobs: a waitress, a cleaner and an assistant in an aged-care home. She writes passionately about her experiences in *Nickel and Dimed* (2002): 'Janitors, cleaning-ladies, ditch diggers, changers of adult diapers—these are the untouchables of a supposedly caste-free and democratic society.' These are the people who clean the 'McMansions' of the well-off but are largely invisible to them. They live in the trailer parks of America, in cheap motels or in the back of their cars. At one point, Ehrenreich felt compelled to break her oath of secrecy in order to arrange for a pregnant and malnourished co-worker to get medical attention for a broken ankle. Not only could the woman not afford to see a doctor, she insisted on continuing her cleaning work, desperate to maintain her meagre income.

In Australia, the welfare safety net and minimum wage are superior to that of the US, yet still more than a million people, 5 per cent of the population, live in severe poverty[8] (BCEC 2014; CEDA 2015). Having a full-time wage does not exclude one from this group. One fifth of households in severe poverty were supported by wages and salary; 6.4 per cent of single-person, waged households were in the poorest group (BCEC, 34–37). The minimum wage jobs are typically physically demanding such as picking fruit or vegetables, or unpleasant and unhealthy such as meat packing. They usually fall on recent immigrants. In a fairer society, those doing the disagreeable tasks would be financially compensated.

In the UK, the divide between the rich and the poor was thrown into stark relief by the tragic June 2017 Grenfell Tower fire. Seventy-nine people (confirmed or presumed dead as we write these lines) were incinerated in a 24-story public housing tower with inadequate fire safety[9] while just blocks away the most expensive London townhouses—many left vacant as 'investments'—sell for £2 million.

The well-documented rise in equality since its nadir in the early 1970s is placing the cohesion of society at risk. After the Great Depression, there was a rise in populism and nationalism from which terrible consequences flowed, culminating in the Second World War. Ten years after the GFC, there is an ominous echo of the past signalled by the rise of nationalist parties in Europe, Brexit in Britain and the success of Donald

Trump in the US. The current problems of the 'First World' do not seem as acute as those facing our forebears in the 1930s, yet Western democracy is at its low point and the global order is riddled by antagonisms and risks. The economic rationalist neo-liberal policies of the past decades have led us to the age of post-rationality. A more caring and sharing world beyond hyper-consumption and yawning internal as well as global inequality seems to be not just a moral issue—a right thing to strive for—but also a matter of political peace and economic prosperity.

Notes

1. Chess was championed by the Soviet Union as a way of demonstrating the superiority of communism in the intellectual sphere. Apart from the brief reign of American Bobby Fischer, all world chess champions from 1948 until the dissolution of the Soviet Union were Soviets.
2. The tradition is now endangered by the forces of globalisation and increasingly unable to compete with cheaper products. In the past 20 years, the textile industry is increasingly owned and staffed by Chinese immigrants, who may transform it and keep it alive in some hybrid form.
3. Sweden bans advertising to children under the age of 12 for just this reason.
4. Figures quoted are on the basis of purchasing power parity.
5. 'Oxy' stands for Oxycodone, a strong opiate prescription painkiller.
6. From the Tom Wolfe (1987) novel *The Bonfires of the Vanities*.
7. For example, in October 2014, the main Australian airline, Qantas, posted a record \$2.8 billion loss, but the share price subsequently doubled mostly on the back of falling oil prices—fuel is airlines' largest single cost. This share price increase triggered generous, fully unearned performance bonuses for top staff (Freed 2015).
8. Severe poverty is defined as having a disposable income, after housing costs, below 30 per cent of the median.
9. Investigations into the cause of the fire are ongoing, but given the speed with which the fire spread and the large death toll, 'inadequate' is clearly an inadequate term to describe the fire safety measures of the building.

Bibliography

ABC (Australian Broadcasting Corporation). 2017. ABC TV *War on Waste*, episode three, first screened 30 May 2017.

Anand, Anu. 2014. Lack of Toilets Puts India's Health and Rural Women's Safety at Risk. *The Guardian*, 29 August 2014. Accessed 15 June 2017. https://www.theguardian.com/global-development/2014/aug/28/toilets-india-health-rural-women-safety

Anderson, Geraint. 2008. *Cityboy: Beer and Loathing in the Square Mile*. London: Headline Publishing Group.

BCEC. 2014. Falling Through the Cracks: Poverty and Disadvantage in Australia. Report by Bankwest and Curtin Economics Centre (BCEC). October 2014. Accessed 17 June 2017. http://business.curtin.edu.au/wp-content/uploads/sites/5/2015/09/BCEC-Falling-through-the-cracks-Report.pdf

Boo, Katherine. 2013. *Behind the Beautiful Forevers: Life, Death, and Hope in a Mumbai Undercity*. Melbourne: Scribe.

Bourdieu, Pierre. 1984. *Distinction: A Social Critique of the Judgment of Taste*. Abingdon, UK: Routledge. First published in France in 1979 as *La Distinction: Critique sociale du jugement*.

CBS News. 2016. Native Americans Hit Hard by Opioid Epidemic. 21 September 2016. Accessed 17 June 2017. http://www.cbsnews.com/news/native-americans-hit-hard-by-opioid-epidemic/

CEDA. 2015. Addressing Entrenched Disadvantage in Australia. Report by the Committee for Economic Development of Australia (CEDA). April 2015. Accessed 17 June 2017. http://adminpanel.ceda.com.au/FOLDERS/Service/Files/Documents/26005~CEDAAddressingentrencheddisadvantageinAustraliaApril2015.pdf

CIA. 2016. *The World Factbook*. CIA.

Colic-Peisker, Val. 2009. Visibility, Settlement Success and Life Satisfaction in Three Refugee Communities in Australia. *Ethnicities* 9: 175–199.

D'Ambrosio, Conchita, and Joachim R. Frick. 2007. Income Satisfaction and Relative Deprivation: An Empirical Link. *Social Indicators Research* 81: 497–519.

Ehrenreich, Barbara. 2002. *Nickel and Dimed: On (Not) Getting by in America*. New York: Henry Holt and Company.

EPI (Economic Policy Institute). 2017. The Racial Wealth Gap: How African Americans have been Short-changed Out of the Materials to Build Wealth.

Accessed 16 June 2017. http://www.epi.org/blog/the-racial-wealth-gap-how-african-americans-have-been-shortchanged-out-of-the-materials-to-build-wealth/

Freed, Jamie. 2015. Qantas Airways to Pay Staff $90m in Bonuses Amid Financial Turnaround. *Australian Financial Review*, 3 July 2015. Accessed 16 June 2017. http://www.afr.com/business/transport/aviation/qantas-airways-to-pay-staff-90m-in-bonuses-amid-financial-turnaround-20150702-gi45gf

Galbraith, John Kenneth. 1974 [1958]. *The Affluent Society*. New York: Houghton Mifflin.

———. 1992. *Economics and Public Purpose*. Boston: Houghton Mifflin.

———. 2001. Economics and the Quality of Life. In *The Essential Galbraith*. New York: Houghton Mifflin. Originally published in 1964 in *Science* 145: 117–123.

Griffiths, Katherine. 2009. RBS Suffers Biggest Loss in UK History. *The Telegraph*, 18 January 2009. Accessed 16 June 2017. http://www.telegraph.co.uk/finance/newsbysector/banksandfinance/4285892/RBS-suffers-biggest-loss-in-UK-history.html

Hayek, Fredrick von. 1944. *The Road to Serfdom*. London: Routledge.

Hobsbawm, Eric. 1995. *The Age of Extremes: A History of the World 1914–1995*. New York: Vintage.

Keynes, John Maynard. 1931. Economic Possibilities for Our Grandchildren. In *Essays in Persuasion*. London: Mcmillan.

KLM. 2017. *Sky High Collection* (KLM Royal Dutch Airlines inflight duty free shopping magazine), July.

Krugman, Paul. 2009. Taxing the Speculator. *The New York Times*, 26 November 2009. Accessed 17 June 2017. http://www.nytimes.com/2009/11/27/opinion/27krugman.html

Lawson, Neal. 2012. Ban Outdoor Advertising. *The Guardian*, 20 April 2012. Accessed 15 June 2017. https://www.theguardian.com/commentisfree/2012/apr/20/ban-outdoor-advertising

Lenzer, Robert. 2013. The Top 25 Hedge Fund Managers Earn More than All the Top 500 CEOs Together. *Forbes*, 8 June 2013. Accessed 16 June 2017. https://www.forbes.com/sites/robertlenzner/2013/08/06/the-top-25-hedge-fund-managers-earn-more-than-all-the-500-top-ceos-together/#7f41b7f4285e

Lynam, Joe. 2015. Goldman Sachs Paid Highest Bonuses to Staff in 2013. *BBC News*, 1 January 2015. Accessed 16 June 2017. http://www.bbc.com/news/uk-30648333

Maguire, Eva R., Thomas Burgoine, and Pablo Monsivais. 2015. Area Deprivation and the Food Environment over Time: A Repeated Cross-sectional Study on Takeaway Outlet Density and Supermarket Presence in Norfolk, UK, 1990–2008. *Health and Place* 33: 142–147.

Manzoor, Sarfraz. 2013. Quants: The Maths Geniuses Running Wall Street. *The Telegraph*, 23 July 2013. Accessed 16 July 2017. http://www.telegraph.co.uk/finance/10188335/Quants-the-maths-geniuses-running-Wall-Street.html

Monbiot, George. 2013. One Rolex Short of Contentment. *The Guardian*, 10 December 2013. Accessed 17 June 2017. http://www.monbiot.com/2013/12/09/one-rolex-short-of-contentment/

Packer, George. 2015. The Other France. *The New Yorker*, 31 August 2015. Accessed 29 June 2017. http://www.newyorker.com/magazine/2015/08/31/the-other-france

Pakulski, Jan, and Malcolm Waters. 1996. *The Death of Class*. London: Sage.

Panning, William H. 1983. Inequality, Social Comparison, and Relative Deprivation. *The American Political Science Review* 77: 323–329.

Patterson, Scott. 2010. *The Quants: How a New Breed of Math Whizzes Conquered Wall Street and Nearly Destroyed it*. New York: Random House.

People: Royals. 2012. Kate Wears Same Dress Twice in 11 Days, by Jennifer Cress, 29 May 2012. Accessed 15 June 2015. http://people.com/royals/kate-middleton-style-emilia-wickstead-dress/

Piketty, Thomas. 2014. *Capital in the Twenty-first Century*. Cambridge, MA: Harvard University Press. First published as *Le capital au XXI siècle*, 2013 by Éditions du Seuil.

Reich, Robert. 2008. *Supercapitalism: The Transformation of Business, Democracy and Everyday Life*. Melbourne: Scribe.

Runciman, Garry W. 1966. *Relative Deprivation and Social Justice: A Study of Attitudes to Social Inequality in Twentieth-Century England*. Berkley, CA: University of California Press.

Schor, J., and Douglas B. Holt. 2011. *Consumer Society Reader*. New York: The New Press.

Stern, H. J. 2012. UK Pay-for-Performance Analysis FTSE100 Companies, 2008–2010. Report by investment company Obermatt. 10 May 2012. Accessed 16 June 2017. http://ssrn.com/abstract=2055747

Sullivan, Laura, Tatjana Meschede, Lars Dietrich, Thomas Shapiro, Amy Traub, Catherine Ruetschlin, and Tamara Draut. 2015. The Racial Wealth Gap: Why Policy Matters. Report by Demos and the Institute for Assets and Social Policy, Brandeis University. Accessed 17 June 2017. http://www.demos.org/sites/default/files/publications/RacialWealthGap_1.pdf

Thomas, Dana. 2007. *Deluxe: How Luxury Lost Its Lustre*. New York: Penguin.
Tocqueville, Alexis de. 2014 [1840]. *Democracy in America*, vol. II. Translated by Henry Reeve, 1899. ebooks@Adelaide, University of Adelaide Library. Accessed 19 June 2017. https://ebooks.adelaide.edu.au/t/tocqueville/alexis/democracy/complete.html
Ubelacker, Sheryl. 2012. First Nations Oxycontin Addiction Represent Looming Health Crisis, Chief Says. *Huffington Post*, 16 February 2012. Accessed 17 June 2017. http://www.huffingtonpost.ca/2012/02/16/first-nations-oxycontin-addiction_n_1283211.html
USDA. 2004. Profiling Food Consumption in America. Report by the United States Department of Agriculture (USDA). Accessed 17 June 2017. https://assets.documentcloud.org/documents/2461300/usda-chapter2.pdf
Veblen, Thomas. 1899. *The Theory of the Leisure Class: An Economic Study of Institutions*. London: Macmillan.
Wilkinson, Richard, and Kate Pickett. 2009. *The Spirit Level: Why More Equal Societies Almost Always do Better*. London: Allen Lane.
Wolfe, Tom. 1987. *The Bonfires of the Vanities*. New York: Farrar Straus Giroux.
Zaridze, David, et al. 2014. Alcohol and Mortality in Russia: Prospective Observational Study of 151,000 Adults. *The Lancet* 383: 1465–1473.

5

Flickering $creens of Global Finance

The 2007–2008 Global Financial Crisis (GFC) provided sobering evidence that we live in a post-rational era. During the GFC and in its aftermath, we heard a great deal about high-risk moves of irresponsible bankers that brought the global financial system to the brink of collapse. But was the GFC really about bad people? Can it be rational to have society at the mercy of a complex system that no-one fully understands and which has no unified regulations or controls? Such a system is likely to be volatile and present a risk to its environment—in this case, the 'real economy' at a global scale, and by extension, all of us. As we attempt to show below, the finance industry has moved well beyond its remit of financial intermediation and efficient capital allocation to become the prevailing force in capitalist economies. Financial markets can be irrational, and even when they are 'rational' by their own narrow definition—maximising of monetary gains—they often harm the real economy.

Banks, stock markets, currencies, derivatives, securities: for most people, even many of those who own shares, this is a rather arcane world of small-print numbers and puzzling graphs. In movies about the 1929 'Great Crash' on Wall Street, we can see an excited mass of men in suits yelling out in a large hall. Today the trading floor is virtual: men in suits

V. Colic-Peisker, A. Flitney, *The Age of Post-Rationality*,
https://doi.org/10.1007/978-981-10-6259-9_5

clutching their laptops with tense expressions on their faces. What is this all about? During the Great Depression (1929–1933), Bertrand Russell (1935, 79–80) suggested people should know more about the world of finance:

> It will be necessary, if this state of affairs is to be remedied, to make the democracies of the world aware of the importance of finance, and to find ways of simplifying its principles so that they can be widely understood. It must be admitted that this is not easy, but I do not believe that it is impossible.

Contrary to the wise man's suggestion, since the 1930s, the financial system has become only more complex and opaque. The system of global capitalism now rests on a fragile web of finance dominated by reckless corporate climbers chasing fictional money in cyberspace. The problem with this is that, as shown in the wake of GFC, we all suffer consequences when the system slips out of balance and we all pay for the losses of the corporate money shifters who run our banks and other financial institutions, and whom we have no way of avoiding. Russell (ibid.) again:

> There are some activities in which the private profit leads, on the whole, to the promotion of the general interest, and others in which this is not so. Finance is now definitely in the latter class [...] Finance, like war, suffers from the fact that almost all those who have technical competence also have a bias which is contrary to the interest of the community.

Indeed, little seems to have changed since the 1930s!

The Mystique of Unreal Money

> Remember, that money is of the prolific, generating nature. Money can beget money, and its offspring can beget more, and so on. Five shillings turned is six, turned again it is seven and threepence, and so on, till it becomes a hundred pounds. The more there is of it, the more it produces every turning, so that the profits rise quicker and quicker. He that kills a

> breeding-sow, destroys all her offspring to the thousandth generation. He that murders a crown, destroys all that it might have produced, even scores of pounds.
>
> Benjamin Franklin (1748)

> It is natural for certain natural riches to multiply, like grains of corn… But it is monstrous and unnatural that an unfruitful thing, a thing specifically sterile, such as money, should bear fruit and multiply of itself …
>
> Nicholas Oresme (1355)

It is thought-provoking that a fourteenth-century philosopher could see the 'unnaturalness' of finance and 'sterility' of money, but at the dawn of the industrial era, when the intense primitive accumulation of capital made greed a virtue, Benjamin Franklin argued exactly the opposite: that money is alive has 'prolific, generating nature' and not investing it is equivalent to 'murder.' His *Advice to a Young Tradesmen* spells out the role of money in the framework of economic rationality: to generate more money.

It was the need to trade goods that engendered the clever idea of money as a medium of exchange. In the simple pre-modern economic system consisting of self-sustaining villages with stationary populations, economic exchange was not a central social practice. A person could occasionally exchange a bag of beetroot from her farm for a hoe made by a village blacksmith. However, bartering is impractical on a regular basis, and this is why a standardised medium of exchange—money—came into existence.

Money is a very special thing. On the one hand, it is not a 'real thing'; on the other hand, it is loaded with potential reality because it can be exchanged for (almost) any 'real thing.' Real things have a use value: a bed provides comfortable rest and a car enables us to travel independently, faster than our natural bipedal mobility allows (well, most of the time!). Money, however, has no specific use value; it only has exchange value, and that only as long as the system of trust that supports its existence holds up. For a money-mediated exchange to happen, real things need to have a price expressed in units of money, which is their exchange value.

Originally, however, money was also 'real,' usually in the form of gold or silver coins which were valuable because of the precious metals' rarity and durability. Gold and silver coins made their first appearance around 700 BC, in the civilisations of the Mediterranean, and at a similar time in India and China. In the fifteenth century, in renaissance Florence, the birthplace of European banking, the golden *fiorino* ('florin') issued by the Medici Bank emerged as the first European common currency. The first form of printed money appeared in twelfth-century China during the Tang dynasty in order to ease the burden of carrying heavy coins. Venetian explorer Marco Polo brought the idea over to Europe and before long the use of promissory notes or 'banknotes' became accepted. These notes, issued by private banks, symbolised the deposit of precious gold or silver coins and were a 'promise to pay' the bearer the stated amount in coins. Their redemption was usually limited to the issuing bank. The banking system rested then, as it does today, on the confidence of savers and lenders. Lenders must trust that their loans will be repaid during a specified time, and savers must have confidence that they can call upon the bank for their savings when they want them. In early banking, the confidence was a local issue and paper money did not travel very far.

It was not until the early eighteenth century that a fully fledged paper currency backed by the power of nation-states appeared in Europe. John Law, a Scotsman fleeing from justice after having the lucky misfortune of killing his opponent in a duel, was instrumental in this development. In 1694, he escaped to Amsterdam and subsequently travelled across Europe, becoming acquainted with the finance, trade and gambling houses in a number of countries. His success at gambling and his graciousness with the ladies made him a popular guest in the salons of Paris where he befriended many influential members of the royal court. After the death of Louis XIV in 1715, Law proposed a new scheme to his friend the Duke of Orleans, now the most powerful man in France. He suggested that a form of printed currency issued by a government-owned bank, that he would himself administer, would be a solution to the crown's massive debt problem[1] (Mackay 1995, 8–9). Unfortunately, the new currency was linked to the Louisiana property bubble—speculations over parcels of a New World swamp that was being touted as a new El Dorado. The government soon discovered one of the flaws of printed money: if you print too much, confidence in the currency evaporates as soon as it becomes apparent that there is not nearly enough real stuff—gold and silver—for the 'promise to pay' to be fulfilled (Mackay 1995, 1–38; Ferguson 2008, 138–155).

The last link to money's physical backing was lost when the Gold Standard was abandoned in the 1970s. Nowadays money generally takes an electronic form, and the main mechanism for creating new money is by commercial banks making loans (McLeay et al. 2014). Both government regulation and financial prudence stipulate how much new money they can create. Governments do get it wrong, of course, as many cases of high inflation have shown throughout modern history.

The first institution resembling a modern bank was created in Venice in 1171 (Hildreth 1837). Keen to fund a military campaign, the Republic ordered its prosperous citizens to lend money to the state through an institution named *Camera di Prestiti* (the Chamber of Loans). These loans were the first appearance of what we know as government bonds. The chamber quickly established most of the functions of banking: accepting deposits, lending money at interest and the creation and circulation of banknotes.

Since the early eighteenth-century Louisiana bubble, the finance industry has matured with diverse and complex financial instruments. The original *reason d'être* for its creation was for it to be an intermediary between people who lacked capital to buy a house or run a business, and people who had savings, that is, more money than they immediately needed. In the early 'mercantile capitalism,' loans were almost exclusively given for the purpose of trade. Merchants borrowed money in order to transport goods—often exotic goods such as pepper from faraway places such as Thailand.[2] The lender was entitled to an 'interest,' part of the profit from the venture upon its completion. To compensate for the vagaries of storms, pirates and other misfortunes, the interest was often as much as 30 per cent of the trader's profit. In order to obtain capital for a venture, a hopeful entrepreneur usually had to solicit support from nobility. The most famous such story is that of Christopher Columbus, who in the late 1480s persuaded Spanish royal couple Ferdinand and Isabella to fund his travel for the purpose of establishing a direct trade route with India. He expected to avail himself of fame, fortune and aristocratic status (he was to be granted the hereditary governorship of the new lands), and to repay in style the confidence of his sponsors. The royals did not seem to have much faith in the success of his voyage and asked for nine-tenths of his profits.

Financial Markets Versus Real Economy

Even those who know very little about modern finance have a sense that the system of shifting money around in order to make more money has far outgrown simple retail banking. The epicentre of modern capitalist finance is the stock market. In the media, movements of various indices are shown in pretty graphs the news junkies can admire, aware of their importance but without necessarily fully understanding their meaning. The short-term movements of stock market indices are largely an outcome of speculative trading, which sucks money out of long-term investors' pockets, and by extension out of the real economy—the firms that produce goods or provide services we all need. In other words, financial trading is not a source of wealth creation, but a source of wealth redistribution, usually making the already rich even wealthier.

Capitalism made a leap into its next developmental stage when money trading advanced and stock exchanges became command centres of the capitalist economy. The central purpose of stock markets is to connect productive enterprises with investors. That is, financiers secure funds for entrepreneurs who need it for their economic activity in the 'real economy' where goods and services and produced. A 'share' (or 'stock') is nothing else than a share in ownership of the company and a right to a portion of its future profits. The stock market allows the shares to be bought and sold, creating flexibility for investors. As a side effect, stock markets have been fabulous playgrounds for speculators.

The first known financial hub, trading government bonds and promissory notes, appeared in Antwerp (now in Belgium) in 1531. In England, a building known as the *Royal Exchange* was established as a financial trading centre by Elizabeth the First in 1571. However, trading of company stocks generally occurred in a number of London coffee houses.

The world's first stock exchange was created in Amsterdam in 1602 to facilitate trading in shares of the burgeoning Dutch East India Company,[3] the world's first publicly owned, limited liability ('Ltd.') company. *Bewindhebbers*, the managing partners, and *participanten*, who we now call shareholders, contributed funds to the company, thus spreading both the capital base and the risk of the venture. Prior to this time, companies were almost always family-owned ventures. If a company was unable to repay its debts, creditors would come after the assets of the family, so there was ample motivation to exercise caution. The fact that managers and shareholders of publicly owned companies only put their initial investment at risk and were not liable for debts of the company meant that the business could take more risk in an effort to expand.

In return for investing their capital in an economic enterprise, the shareholders were rewarded with a pro rata proportion of the profit, the dividend. Having a large number of individuals contributing capital enabled a great expansion of the business. The Dutch East India Company not only monopolised trade between the Netherlands and Asia but also had its own army to protect its interests. The first official British stock exchange was established in London in 1773, followed soon after by the first one in the New World, in Philadelphia in 1790. As capitalism marched on, private ownership became increasingly social through shareholding of publicly listed 'corporations.'

The most important financial centres we hear about nowadays are 'Wall Street'[4] (formal home of the New York Stock Exchange), London, Tokyo, Hong Kong and Frankfurt. Each stock exchange has its characteristic index, a weighted measure of the prices of the most important or largest (by market capitalisation) companies listed on that exchange. The New York Stock Exchange is characterised by the Dow Jones Index, comprising the 30 most important companies in the US. In 1971, the US-based NASDAQ[5] became the world's first electronic exchange, though initially only quotations were displayed by computer while trading was still done manually. The NASDAQ Composite Index is a broader US index dominated by high-tech companies. London is represented by the Financial Times Stock Exchange 100 Index ('FTSE 100,' colloquially the 'Footsie') which includes the 100 largest companies listed in London. Tokyo has its Nikkei Index, Hong Kong has the Hang Seng and Frankfurt the DAX (*Deutscher Aktienindex*) consisting of the 30 largest German companies. The Australian stock market is usually represented by the ASX 200 index, comprising the largest 200 companies listed in Australia.[6]

While stock exchanges are still named after key financial centres, computerisation made their physical location largely irrelevant. The brain of the New York Stock Exchange, its 'data centre,' is no longer on Wall Street in lower Manhattan, but tucked away in Mahwah, a small town in New Jersey. This is a large, and no doubt carefully guarded, computer that processes all transactions to do with close to 2000 publicly listed companies, mainly but not exclusively US-based.[7]

The vast majority of money trading today is done by speculators who follow a trend or bet against it, trying to outdo one another and pull money out of the market and into their bank accounts, or that of their clients. Even without understanding the financial markets' intricate numbers games, most people choose to believe that simply shifting money around creates more of it. Such a claim is rationally unsustainable, but the faith persists because the evidence seems to be there: some people 'made millions' on the stock market. However, some others went bankrupt as a consequence: no niceties, no mercy and no mutual benefit at a stock exchange!

Fig. 5.1 The Paris Stock Exchange

Trading in shares used to be done by specialists in purpose-designed venues. Shareholders had to talk to their broker about placing an order to buy or sell shares. The late-1990s advent of computerised stock exchanges has enabled people to trade from the comfort of their home computer and, more recently, their smartphone. With computerisation of financial markets, the volume of speculative trades has increased dramatically: the value of shares traded daily on the world stock markets now exceeds the value of goods and services exchanged in the real economy (Fig. 5.2).

Over the past quarter-century, the value of stocks traded relative to GDP increased in all countries. Until recently, the US convincingly topped the list, but speculative trading in China took off hyperbolically in late 2014.[8] In all countries, there was a huge spike in trading just before the 2008 GFC, while the dotcom bubble of 2000 produced the biggest upswing in trading in the US, where most high-tech companies are listed.

Let us say once again that the function of markets is to most efficiently assign funds to productive enterprises. However, financial markets have grown exceedingly large and powerful relative to the real economy. Examples abound of cases where financial markets, particularly in bonds or currencies, have been drivers rather than servants of the real economy—

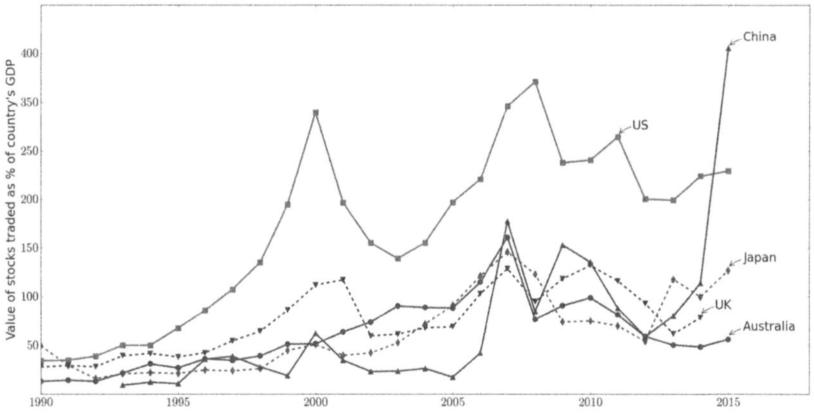

Fig. 5.2 The value of traded stocks on a selection of major stock markets relative to the GDP

usually with detrimental effects. A contemporary example is the earthquake-like ruction in the value of the Swiss Franc. Post GFC, funds fleeing a shaky Eurozone found a safe haven in Swiss bank accounts, and the combined action of investors trying to minimise their risk drove up the value of the Swiss Franc relative to the Euro. This was damaging Swiss exports (making that indispensable Rolex more expensive!) and tourism. In 2011, the Swiss National Bank (SNB) announced that they would act to prevent the further appreciation of their currency. That is, they would sell Francs and buy Euros to keep the value of the Franc down to a set level. The next move came without warning. On 15 January 2015, the SNB announced they would no longer attempt to stem the rising tide of money flowing to Swiss banks (what a problem to have!) and removed the 'peg' on the Franc. Within minutes the currency had jumped up by 40 per cent, settling back to be 18 per cent higher by the end of the day, as traders bet on investment rushing into Switzerland. This has serious ramifications for the Swiss economy—their stock market tumbled on the same day, as traders anticipated the drop in exports that would come from the sharp jump in the price of Swiss products. The Asian financial crisis of 1997 has some parallels: the removal of a peg on the Thai Baht precipitated a collapse in the currency and a stampede of investor funds out of South East Asian economies. This in turn had a serious effect on otherwise healthy, well-functioning economies. The real-life consequences of financial speculation include bankruptcies, loss of jobs and loss of confidence in government institutions.

Financial markets and financial reporting have become so ubiquitous in our lives that we tend to see them as a legitimate part of the real economy and therefore part of general wealth creation. Satyajit Das, a former banker-turned-financial commentator and author, is critical of such perception: '[M]odern economies have long ceased to make anything. The major activity is money: investing it, borrowing it, trading it, making it, and spending it' (Das 2011, 9). Of course, this is somewhat exaggerated—we still make some things, and some developed countries, Germany and Japan, for example, maintained a considerable manufacturing sector and have large trade surpluses. Yet, his point is a valid one: the main game of twenty-first-century Western capitalism is not making real things that people need or want but controlling global money flows happening on flickering computer screens all over the world.

In the last century, the finance industry has grown much faster than the global economy. The total compensation that financial intermediaries receive (profits, wages and salary) as a proportion of the whole economy has moved from 4 per cent of GDP in 1950 to 9 per cent in 2010 (Philippon 2012). However, there is no evidence that it actually performs the tasks for which it is remunerated so handsomely any better than it did in 1910. The finance industry used to claim that financial innovation provided greater stability to markets, but post-GFC this claim is hard to take seriously. In fact, such innovation is providing investors with imaginative but often unsafe substitutes for traditional assets like bank deposits or government bonds. Innovative financial products helped both to inflate the US housing bubble of the mid-2000s and to spread the effects of its demise throughout the world.

A Global Super-casino

Trading goods—cars, furniture, food—and various services, from hotel room accommodation to education, is much different from trading money. In contrast to trading 'real things' which is of mutual benefit to both sellers and buyers, financial trading is a zero-sum game. The iron law of financial trading is that one person's gain is another's loss. In effect, speculative trading is a glamorous, and to most people rather mysterious, form of gambling.

In October 2012, Roger Montgomery (2012), an independent Australian investment analyst blogged: 'The stock market can be approached in two ways. The first and hitherto more popular path is to bet on price action, unwittingly reducing the stock market's role to that of a casino facilitating bets [...]. The other more boring but infinitely more rewarding path, is to approach the stock market as a venue through which portions of business can be acquired.' In other words, choosing wisely and sticking to your plan is likely to make you more money in the long run than frantically trading on a daily basis, hoping to correctly guess where prices are going and make a quick buck. However, many individual players on the stock market are seduced by this possibility and therefore prefer the casino version of the stock market. Christopher Joyce (2013), writing for the Australian Financial Review, put it thus: 'every day trillions of dollars of capital maniacally tries to correctly "price" the future.'

In consequence, the global financial market is nowadays a giant super-casino. This is most explicitly the case in China, where the daily oscillations of the Shanghai share market, limited largely to local traders due to restrictions on foreign investors, would satisfy the wildest roller-coaster addict. Traditionally, the Chinese love gambling and believe in 'luck.' Given that straightforward gambling is illegal in China, they seem to indulge their gambling passion at the stock exchange. According to Nigel Davis, a specialist in financial regulation, corporate finance and company law in Hong Kong University's law department, Chinese share trading is as unpredictable as a casino, with little correlation between fundamentals and share price. In a single week in December 2014, investors in Shanghai and Shenzhen (the two largest stock exchanges in China) opened nearly 900,000 new trading accounts, most of these by ordinary people largely clueless of how it all really happens (SCMP 2015).

Instances of cheating and corruption in the financial world are not rare. The best-known and the most widely practised misdeed is so-called insider trading—trading using information that is not publicly available. Although this is illegal, the law is difficult to enforce, so the offenders often get away with it. A notable exception is Steven Xiao, the unlucky managing director of Hanlong Mining, who was extradited from China to Australia in October 2014 to face numerous charges in Australia's biggest insider trading case. He received an eight year jail term in 2016 (Danckert 2016).

Given that financial markets are meant to enable correct pricing of commodities, the 'price discovery' involves necessary fluctuations as traders adjust to new information and, by the uncoordinated action of many (another appearance of Adam Smith's 'invisible hand'?), arrive at a revised 'correct' price. Having the 'correct price' for things we all need and value enables the most efficient allocation of funds to worthwhile enterprises, according to classical and neo-classical economic theory. The efficient market, as defined by Eugene Fama, a professor in Chicago's Business School, is a 'market in which prices always "fully reflect" available information' (Fama 1970). That is, in an efficient market, prices are 'right'—a correct reflection of all current information, as well as the probabilities of future events. Future price moves are unpredictable since they are driven by unforeseen events. If this was the whole story, there would be much less financial trading and certainly no financial bubbles.

The efficient market hypothesis dominated the theory of financial markets until recently despite ample evidence of its flaws. American economist Robert Schiller (1984) called the logical leap from observing that the price moves were unpredictable to concluding that prices were right 'one of the most remarkable errors in the history of economic thought.' The sheer volume of financial trading often works against price discovery by accentuating price moves in either direction as traders are swayed by the momentum of the market. This herd mentality of traders means that trends always continue further than initially expected.

Over the past centuries and especially in recent decades, money trading has taken increasingly diverse forms. With the proliferation of 'financial instruments' that represent new forms of money—alongside classic forms such as shares and bonds, there are also futures, exchange traded funds, options, warrants, swaps, and more—the financial industry has descended into murky waters that only a chosen few can understand and navigate with confidence. For example, Irving Fisher, a professor of economics at Yale University, is credited with many of the important ideas behind the 'efficient market' hypothesis elaborated above; yet, he is best known for his statement made in October 1929, mere moments before the Great Crash: 'Stock prices have reached what looks like a permanently high plateau' (Fisher 1929). He paid for his poor prediction not just in lost reputation but also suffered a large financial loss in the market collapse.

One of the most mysterious financial instruments to assume importance in modern finance is derivatives. Derivatives are essentially bets between two financial players, individual or institutional, about the future price of some commodity, such as a company's share price, a stock market index, an interest rate or the price of oil. Most derivatives are sold 'over the counter,' that is, they are private contracts between the parties, and not subject to regulatory oversight. Importantly, they involve a degree of financial leverage, which presents an opportunity to control a large financial position with a small amount of capital, therefore magnifying profits if the bet is successful. The flipside is that losses can greatly exceed the initial capital outlay if things go sour. By the end of 2013, the face value of all outstanding derivatives was estimated to be $710 trillion[9] (CME 2014), more than 10 times the size of the entire world economy. That certainly seems strange, or would 'crazy' be a more accurate description? Hopefully these derivatives are nothing consequential, just a strange money game for grown-ups …? To be fair, no event would trigger the payment of more than a small fraction of their notional value, but what can be said with certainty is that derivatives create a web of financial connections which increases the fragility of the global financial system. Derivatives were a major factor in the GFC assuming a global reach rather than remaining confined to the US where it was triggered by the collapse of the local housing market. The increasing vulnerability of the financial system created by derivatives prompted the investment guru Warren Buffett[10] (2002, 16) to call them 'financial weapons of mass destruction.'

When Lehman Brothers, the fourth-largest investment bank in the US, collapsed in 2008, the US government stepped in to prevent the collapse of other major Wall Street financial institutions, all of whom had sustained huge losses by choosing to believe their own misinformation about the US housing market. Rather than just protecting a few troubled, and troublesome, financial institutions, the government was trying to prevent 'financial contagion': the spreading of the losses to the entire financial industry, and by extension, to the real economy. It is impossible to know what effect further collapse would have had or where the losses would have ultimately been sustained (The Economist 2008). As it is, your local council or your pension fund may have been affected by the ripples caused by Lehman Brothers' collapse.[11]

Describing the fallout from the collapse of the US housing market in 2007, Michael Lewis (2011, 223), a bestselling American author on finance, observed: 'How do you explain to an innocent citizen of the free world the importance of a credit default swap on a double-A tranche of a subprime-backed collateralized debt obligation?' We will not try to explain this either because we doubt many people would be interested. We also doubt that the 'citizen of the free world' is 'innocent,' but let's leave the philosophical and political quibbles aside for the moment. Lewis certainly provided a good example of how impenetrable financial language has become, reflecting the state of affairs in contemporary finance.

Currency trading is another form of money games. It has its roots in the need of corporations to buy or sell goods in a country other than the one in which they are based. There is also transnational investment money looking for a more profitable, or less risky, home. Finally, tourists and travellers need foreign currencies, but their needs are rather modest in comparison. A giant edifice of foreign exchange trading, commonly known as FOREX, is built upon this base. Around $5 trillion changes hands due to speculation on foreign currency markets every day, more than 20 times the value of goods and services traded in the real economy (Reuters 2016)! There is *some* method in this madness. Put simply, the 'correct' exchange rate between countries helps to smooth out the international economy. When a country's economy is doing poorly, its currency falls, making its exports cheaper and thus more competitive. At the same time, imports become more expensive and less competitive in the local market. The net result is that the local economy receives a boost in exports compared to those trading partners with stronger currencies. While the volume of FOREX trading is absurd, the market appears to get the relative value of currencies correct much of the time. However, there are occasional major dislocations.

The most famous hero, or villain, of currency trading, depending on how you look at it, is Hungarian-American billionaire financier George Soros, who made his initial fortune by trading currencies in the 1970s. He is also known as the 'man who broke the Bank of England' by betting that Britain would be forced from the European exchange mechanism in 1992. Soros netted around £1 billion from this trade (Litterick 2002). He became persona non grata in Asia when the then Malaysian Prime Minister accused him of damaging Malaysia's economy with massive currency speculation and causing the 1997 'Asian crisis,' during which the economies of a number of Asian countries were seriously destabilised. More recently, Soros was blasted by Chinese authorities when he suggested the Chinese currency would be under pressure due to the slowing Chinese economy (Yan 2016).

Perhaps to atone for his global financial sins, Soros funded the *Open Society Fund* in a number of Eastern European countries after the fall of the Berlin Wall, in order to support their transition from communism to democracy.[12] Somewhat ironically, these countries could join the global super-casino much sooner than achieve a semblance of functioning democracy. Even more ironically, Soros is a fierce critic of global capitalism and what he calls 'market fundamentalism' (Soros 1998).

Okay, I Admit It: I Am a Share Trader

Since the end of the last century, my working days start by logging onto my internet share trading account. Then for several tense hours I stare at a couple of computer screens beside each other on my desk. The screens are crammed with tables of numbers showing prices and volumes of trade, minute-by-minute share price graphs and the latest announcements of stock exchange-listed companies (Fig. 5.3). The screens have a hypnotic quality: my stomach demanding lunch usually wakes me up from this numbers/money-shifting trance.

It all started when a student of mine—at the time I lived just above the poverty line as a university tutor—gave me the idea to buy shares in the initial 1998 (Australian) Telstra float.[13] Back then I was a financial simpleton and all I knew was that people buy shares to get dividends. I had some beginner's luck when on the crest of the incoming dotcom bubble Telstra shares more than doubled in price. I thought this could not last forever (and I was right), so I had better sell while I had a profit. Consequently, I opened an account with an online stockbroker and sold my shares. But I got hooked: I started watching the short-term behaviour of stock prices. I thought I could predict patterns. It turned out I couldn't, at least not very well. I soon lost the money I had made on Telstra and decided I should do some more observation before trading again. During the peak of the dotcom bubble at the end of 1999 and early 2000, I resumed trading and quickly recouped my losses by day trading the shares of high-tech companies.

By this stage I was already a little bit wiser and I knew the market would soon crash, given that dotcom companies were not making any profits and most were never likely to do so. Being down-under was in this case advantageous: the crash was bound to start in the US while Australians were asleep, so each day I sold my shares before the Australian market closed. I would like to be able to say 'and the rest is history' while sipping a martini on my yacht in the Bahamas… but I am still in Melbourne logging onto my computer around nine every morning in order to be ready by ten, the opening time of the Australian market.

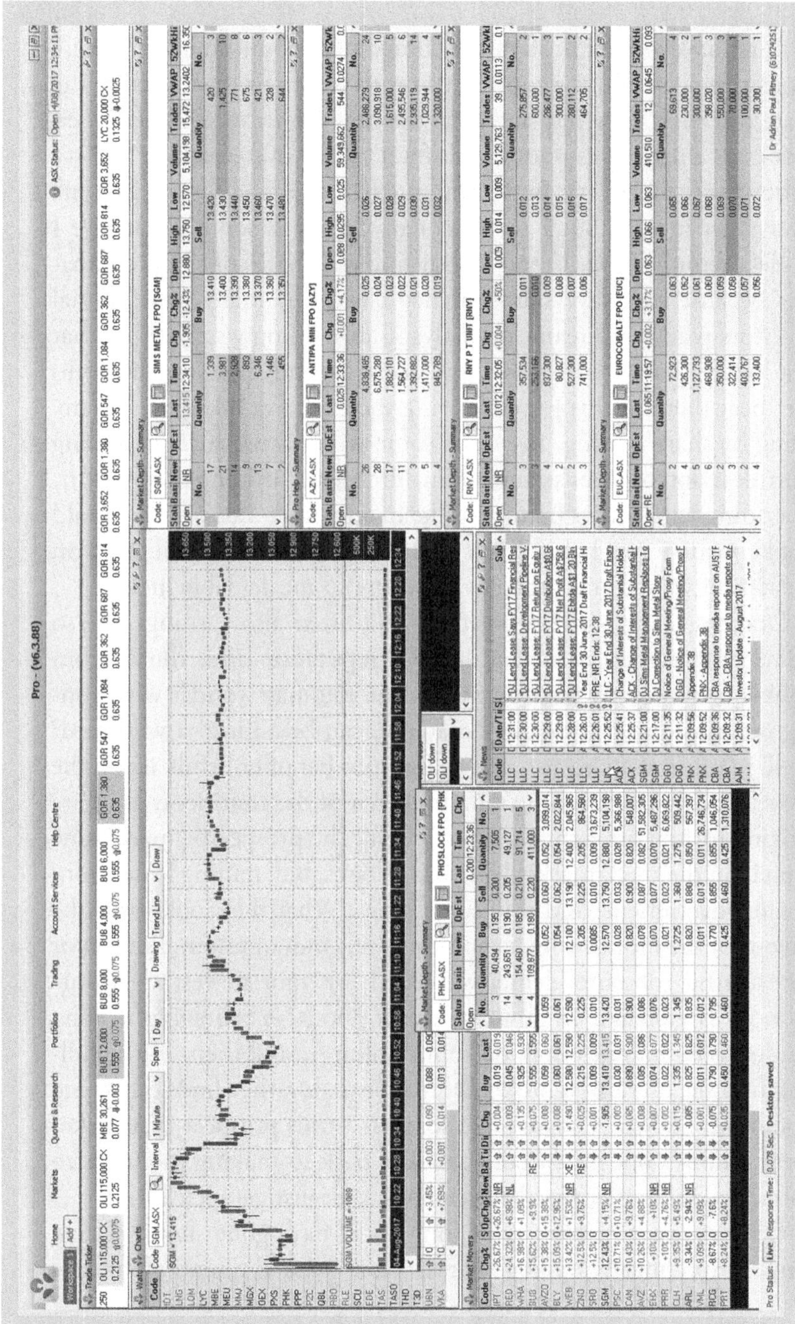

Fig. 5.3 A professional share trading screen for the Australian Stock Exchange

I first have a flick through the company announcements. If there is positive news about a company I try to buy their shares before the share price has fully responded to the news so I can sell later when it does. If the news is poor I wait for a selling over-reaction and try to buy for the recovery. By 11 am, much of the action is over. I don't always get it right but I try to cut my losses as soon as I realise I made a wrong move. I tend to buy and sell shares of small companies because big players are watched closely by many institutional investors who, with teams of analysts, always know something that I, a lonely share trading cowboy, do not—and I am not likely to ever beat them in this game. During the time I've been earning my living by share trading, I've done some wild things, such as trading worthless dotcom stocks and 'penny dreadful'[14] mining prospectors. But doing wild things here, just like in any other area of life, should not be made into a habit. Most of the time I keep a careful grasp on the risks involved and limit my exposure to incalculable luck.

Dotcom stocks, whose business, and often also earnings, are so immaterial, rightly earned a dubious reputation after the dotcom bubble spectacularly burst in 2000. But you may wonder why mining exploration, so ultimately material, can be a bit of a wild card? Well, in mineral-rich Australia, a large number of hopefuls are on the move, ready to dig in some remote corner of the continent. They are looking for the proverbial treasure chest. The prospectors raise some capital on the stock market by issuing shares, buy mining leases from a state government, and drill some holes. What they look for is the flavour of the month which can be nickel, gold, uranium, lithium or 'rare earths' (obscure elements needed for your newest electronic gizmo). They make an announcement about 'encouraging drilling results,' raise more capital, do more drilling…and then, in the fullness of time, usually go broke. Or maybe, rarely, they find something significant and their share price soars. It is this prospect that makes them a honey pot for speculators. The trick to making money is to correctly anticipate others' anticipation…or just get lucky.

Over the years, I have gone long and I have gone short. 'Going long' simply means buying shares. 'Going short' essentially means selling a stock before buying it. At a later time I buy the stock to cover my (negative) holding, hoping that in the meantime the stock price has fallen. In this way I can profit from falling prices.

From about 2008, the life of small-fish share traders became more difficult due to the rise of so-called high frequency trading. This means I now have to battle against superfast computer algorithms whose moves are specifically designed to confuse ordinary human logic. Yet, overall I make enough to live off my flickering screens. I often have pangs of guilty conscience and ask myself how can the profession of financial trading exist at all? My guilt is somewhat dampened by the thought that the people I make money off are generally richer than I am but maybe I should start an STA (Share Traders Anonymous) movement to help financial traders such as myself re-integrate into the real world and do something more useful?

High-Frequency Trading

In the world of high-tech internet-connected computers, things happen extremely quickly. Extreme speed was introduced to finance by so-called high frequency trading (HFT) which these days contains a large proportion of share trading. Many companies now employ computers that trade automatically; the so-called algorithmic trading is commonly known as *bots* (short for 'robots'). HFT *bots* work at incredible speeds: to say that they can buy or sell 1000 times in the blink of an eye is an understatement. Some stock exchanges now allow share trading firms (for a fee) to co-locate their computers with that of the exchange in order to shave off some of those crucial microseconds of the time it takes for an electrical signal (moving at the speed of light!) to travel between the firm's computers and that of the exchange.

As a consequence of the extreme speed, during the 'flash crash' in May 2010, the Dow Jones Index fell more than 5 per cent in a few minutes and then almost as frantically recovered the lost capital. The official investigation by US authorities (CFTC-SEC 2010) concluded that a sudden sale of a large number of futures contracts, whose price was dependent on that of the leading US stocks,[15] led to share price falls that triggered HFTs to begin trading a number of major stocks amongst themselves at blinding speed. In April 2015, it came to light that a single trader, Navinder Sarao, operating an HFT algorithm from the bedroom of his parent's house in London, may have contributed significantly to the crash (Reuters 2015). He flooded the market with bogus orders—at one point, his orders represented more than 20 per cent of the US futures market. We wonder what is of greater concern, the fact that a single trader could bring the world's most sophisticated market to its knees or that it took authorities five years to find out and begin taking action?[16]

During the flash crash, some leading US stocks traded as low as one cent and as high as $100,000 per share. This was a frightening level of volatility with no connection with anything happening in the real economy but with potentially significant consequences to individual investors. It was all the *bots*' doing, but no-one knows and no one *can* know what really happened among the *bots*. The unit of time on the stock market has moved well beyond the human ability of observation and record keeping. The *bots* must be making money since the firms that run them are investing millions of dollars in a technological arms race for a microsecond advantage in computer speed. The money skimmed from financial markets goes into the pockets of rather obscure and secretive HFT firms with names you are unlikely to have heard such as Virtu Financial and Tradebot. If we stipulate that the finance industry is parasitic on the 'real economy,' then HFT firms are parasites feeding on the back of larger parasites. Economic rationality is driving HFT, but does it lead to a desirable outcome? In a 2011 speech to the World Economic Association, the Bank of England's Director for Financial Stability, Andrew Haldane (2011) commented on the speed trading arms race: 'there is a risk that the individually optimising actions of participants generate an outcome that benefits no-one.'

The proponents of HFT argue that increased liquidity—the volume of shares traded in the market—is its primary justification. Liquidity enables markets to function smoothly, with plenty of buyers and sellers, and is often considered a virtue beyond dispute because it makes markets more efficient in determining stock prices. However, the claimed benefits of HFT in enhancing this process are not just overstated but often illusory (Lewis 2014). In the end, the *bots* may completely out-calculate humans and be condemned to forever trade among themselves, pointlessly chasing profits in a financial version of anti-utopia.[17]

A company called Spread Networks spent hundreds of millions of dollars tunnelling through the Allegheny Mountains of Pennsylvania to shave three milliseconds off the travel time for a signal (laser light travelling through optic fibre) to go from the Chicago futures exchange to stock markets in New York. In the capitalistic sense, this was a 'good' use of the money since it produced ample returns to investors, but was it a rational use of the Earth's and society's resources?

Sometimes the lightening speed of HFT may have unintended consequences. For example, on 1 August 2012, US firm Knight Capital unleashed a new trading algorithm onto the New York Stock Exchange. Unfortunately for them, it did not function as planned but bought shares at a high price and sold at a low price. The losses on most trades were small, but with thousands of trades per minute, the company was accumulating losses at more than $10 million a minute. At these speeds, it is impossible for human operators to monitor trading in real time. Even so, it was lax of Knight Capital to continue losing money for more than half an hour before noticing the error in the programme. They notched up a loss of $440 million before the morning coffee break, which almost bankrupted the company (Philips 2012). We are pleased to report that the New York Stock Exchange refused to reverse the 'erroneous' trades; if Knight Capital made half a billion 'in error,' they would have been most unlikely to complain.

Booming and Busting in the Twenty-first Century

Trying to get rich, or even just trying to make one's living in a casino can hardly be defended as a rational strategy. The 'rational' approach to the stock market—judiciously buying a diversified collection of quality stocks and keeping them long term—is a minority approach these days. In times of economic prosperity, the 'irrational exuberance' (Schiller 2000) of financial traders regularly leads to smaller or larger speculative bubbles followed by their inevitable collapse. Major bubbles occur about once in a decade, enough time for most people to forget their lessons.

The dotcom bubble of 1999–2000 had the same essential ingredients of the stock market mania that led to the Great Crash in 1929. Companies that only existed in the internet reality, with no profits and sometimes no business model either, were acquiring absurdly high valuations in the world's stock markets. Stock market analysts produced reports claiming this was rational since the internet would revolutionise the world—as indeed in many ways it has. Often, the analysts were no more than shepherds leading a stampeding herd of traders.

In October 1998, American equity analyst Henry Blodget[18] predicted that Amazon's share price would reach $400, though at the time it was only half this and the company was yet to make a cent of profit. Within weeks, the price target was reached, possibly on the back of this report working as a self-fulfilling prophecy. After the bubble burst, Amazon's share price fell to a low of approximately 5 per cent of its inflated value.[19] Amidst the frenzy of speculation, there were some furtive and amusing (to those who did not lose money) elements. Table 5.1 shows the assessment of two internet companies by investment bank Merrill Lynch during the dotcom boom.

According to J. K. Galbraith (1954, 4), 'as time passes, the tendency to look beyond the simple fact of increasing values to the reasons on which it depends greatly diminishes.' Eventually, 'at some point in the growth of a boom all aspects of […] ownership become irrelevant except the prospect of an early rise in price' (p. 18). Income from dotcom stocks which, at this time almost invariably was zero, and even their long-term value were rendered unimportant. The frenzy was supported by much discussion in the financial press of the *potential* value of internet companies, though all of this was constructed like a house of cards, with one com-

Table 5.1 Contrast between public and internal assessments of two internet companies by investment bank Merrill Lynch

Company	Public assessment	Internal assessment
Excite @ Home (ATHM) (6 March 2000)	'We do not see much more downside to the shares.' (Merrill Lynch research report)	'AHTM is such a piece of crap!' (Henry Blodget's email)
Lifeminders (LFMN) (12 April 2000)	'We think LFMN presents an attractive investment.' (Merrill Lynch research report)	'I can't believe what a POS [piece of shit] that thing is.' (Henry Blodget's email)

pany valued in reference to another, which in turn was valued in reference to a third, and so on. Warning cries about over-valuing from more astute market observers were ignored. The boom continued beyond all predictions. Even the experienced financial elder George Soros was caught out. His Quantum investment fund lost billions, first speculating on the premature demise of the dotcom bubble, then switching to buying high-tech stocks just before the crash (Conner and Woo 2004). Soros was hardly alone. It is hard to stand in front of a stampede of elephants even if one knows they are behaving irrationally. The collapse finally came in April 2000. As with all financial bubbles, the exact nature of the trigger is of no particular importance since almost everyone involved had long known that a collapse was inevitable but could not resist riding the wave for as long as possible, until it crashed upon the shore (Fig. 5.4).

The story of the collapse of the US housing bubble and the shockwaves it spread around the world in 2007–2008 has been told many times, but it is worth repeating. The central point here is to show how risk was transferred to those who least understood it. Mortgage lenders created loans that were predicated on rising house prices: they were easy to repay for an initial honeymoon period after which the repayments automatically spiked. Buyers on low incomes and of poor credit worthiness could ill afford to continue the loans without the promise of rising house prices that would enable them to refinance. The peak of the bubble was marked by 'self-amortising loans' on which it was not only unnecessary to pay a deposit but on which no payments of any kind were required over the initial period.[20] But why would a lender create a loan that they knew had a high chance of default in the future?

The solution for that was a clever mechanism (a new 'financial instrument') to transfer the risk associated with the dodgy loans. Groups of mortgages were packaged into 'mortgage backed securities' (MBS) and the debt, along with the income stream coming from the interest on the loans—while there still was any—was sold to investors around the world. Packages of less risky mortgages were easy to sell, but this was not the case with the more precarious 'subprime loans.' Imaginative financiers found a solution to that too: MBSs were sliced up and repackaged in such a way that rating agencies would give them triple-A ratings, meaning the lowest-risk investment. Michael Lewis (2011) described how Goldman Sachs (one of the largest American multinational investment banks which in

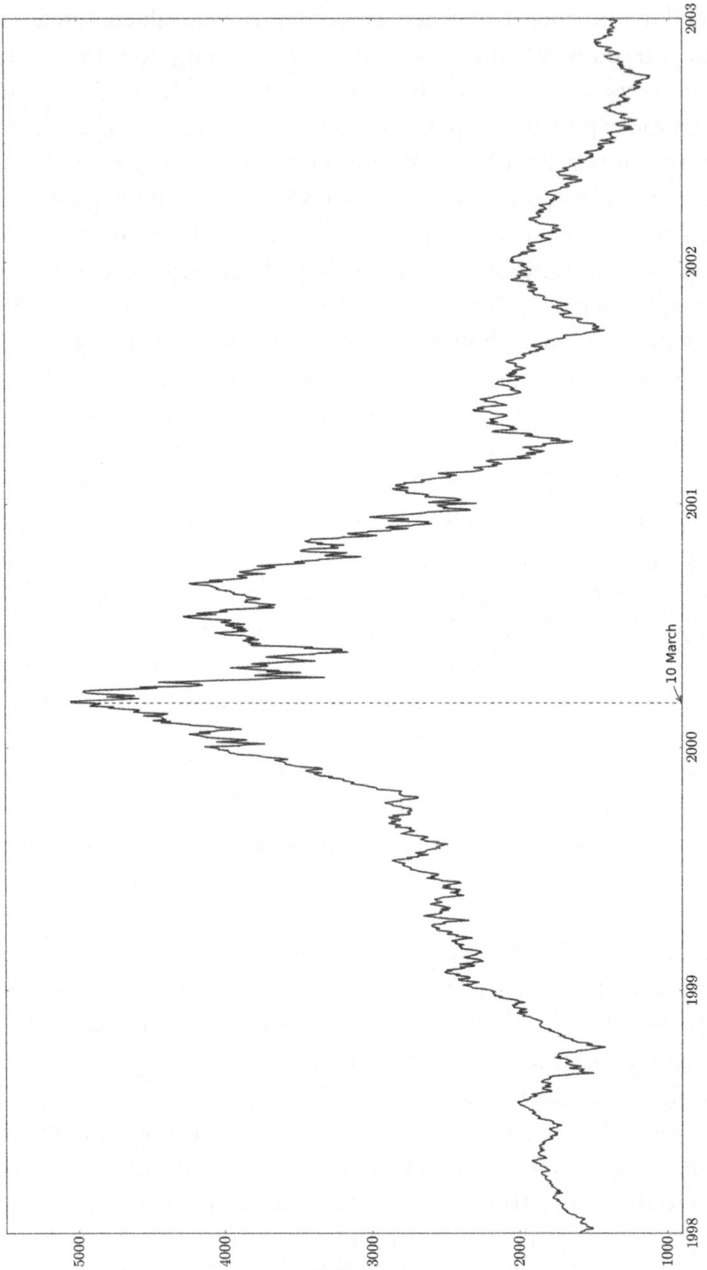

Fig. 5.4 The movement of the NASDAQ index 1998–2003

2013 paid the highest bonuses to their senior staff) created the 'financial philosopher's stone' that 'turned 100 per cent lead into an ore that was now 80 per cent gold and 20 per cent lead [and] would accept the residual lead and turn 80 per cent of that into gold too' (Lewis 2011, 76). In effect, this meant turning high-risk bonds into triple-A-rated bonds. Capital seems to have achieved its dream: creating money with money and therefore perpetuating itself on an ever more fictitious basis.

The investment banks that created the products—now successfully engineered to be triple-A-rated regardless of the fragility of the underlying home loans—then sold them around the world to all sorts of institutions required to invest in 'safe' triple-A products, from German banks, Taiwanese insurance companies, Japanese farmers' unions, European pension funds and Australian local councils. The traders doing the selling pocketed a percentage of the bonds they sold and the CEOs of their companies pocketed large bonuses from the extraordinary profits generated as more and more borrowers, of lower and lower credit worthiness, were fed into the machine. At every stage, the incentive for the lenders, the traders, the Wall Street banks and the ratings agencies was to keep the machine going. The question of default of the underlying mortgages or of the bonds created from them was a matter of indifference since the idea was to hold none of the risk. The more they could create and sell the more profit they could generate for themselves. However, as it happened, the major Wall Street banks were caught holding large numbers of the bonds, or derivatives spawned from them, when the music stopped. According to Lewis (2011, 257), 'the CEOs of every major Wall Street firm were also on the wrong end of the gamble. All of them, without exception, either ran their public corporations into bankruptcy or were saved by the United States government. They all got rich too.'

In the word of finance, it is not rare that failure is amply rewarded: Howie Hubler, the least successful trader in history, who lost $9 billion for Morgan Stanley when the US housing bubble deflated in 2007, was allowed to slip away into retirement keeping the multimillion dollar salary and bonuses he had 'earned' in previous years. Anderson (2008) portrayed a global financial centre, the City of London, as the 'world of pinstripe suits and "sensible" haircuts, soaked in alcohol, heavily sprinkled with cocaine and devoted to debauchery' and admitted that such a place 'successfully cultivated his corrupt side' (pp. 13–14). Anderson went beyond revealing the casino-like properties of the finance industry and exposed appalling levels of irresponsibility and corruption among the cashed-up 'cityboys,' confessing that, in his role of an overpaid financial analyst, he often felt like an 'impostor.' *The Times* newspaper politely described the book as 'an effective indictment of the narcissism and decadence of City life.'

As shown during the GFC, there is a significant moral hazard attached to the financial exuberance of chasing potentially huge profits by 'smart people making complicating bets' (Lewis 2011, 258). As a result of US government intervention, the losses sustained by most of the major Wall Street financial firms in 2007–2008 were covered by taxpayers. This means the rewards of risk-taking go to individuals, but the negative consequences are borne by the public. Global 'banksters' have caused financial trouble so many times they no longer command respect, but the system forces everyone to depend on them. Banks are often accused of being too rich, powerful and exploitative, and most people seem to loath them. However, we all grant them the power by our consuming desires that demand we spend money before we earn it and therefore need to borrow from the banks. They profit from our desire for immediate gratification and the convenience of buying whatever we want, when we want it.

The handsomely remunerated high priests of global finance continue to expound their doctrine that governments should stand aside and allow markets to be the measure of all things. Yet, as discussed above, the markets' task of allocating capital to the most productive enterprises is often more akin to a lottery than to rational decision making and, when things go wrong, governments are 'allowed' to intervene and save financial institutions that are 'too big' and 'too indispensable' to fail. Indeed, the complexity of modern financial markets works to inflate rather than moderate risk, as was amply demonstrated by the GFC. The crisis upset not just the economy but also the Western political order, especially in the Anglosphere. Nearly a decade post-GFC, the global financial system has not become more rational and, according to many commentators, we are now waiting for yet another 'inevitable' financial crisis. The frantic movement of 'unreal' money across global financial markets has expanded exponentially over the past decades. This has more and more to do with traders trying to make a quick buck and less and less about the needs of investors or borrowers whom the markets are meant to serve.

Fig. 5.5 Is there a man more deserving to be immortalised on a banknote than Benjamin Franklin?

Notes

1. If you think the debt of modern-day governments is troublesome, spare a thought for that of the eighteenth-century France. National debt was 3 billion *livres*, more than 20 times the government's annual revenue (Mackay 1995, 5).
2. Also cacao beans from the Americas, the beginning of the modern devotion to chocolate. Pepper was only used by the wealthy, sometimes even as a currency. The expressions *Peperduur* ('pepper-expensive') in Dutch and *papreno* (peppered) meaning 'expensive' in Croatian reflect the bygone era.
3. 'Dutch East India' is now Indonesia.
4. This small street in lower Manhattan became the key metaphor for global finance. In the nineteenth and early twentieth centuries, when paper stock certificates had to be delivered by hand, it was a requirement for stock trading firms, including the major banks, to be physically close to the New York Stock Exchange. Nowadays, the only remaining bank to have its US headquarters in Wall Street is Deutsche Bank.
5. NASDAQ is an acronym for National Association of Securities Dealers Automated Quotations. The Association of Securities Dealers later divested itself of the stock exchange but the name remained.
6. The index is managed by the financial ratings agency Standard & Poor's and replaces the older (but similar) 'All Ordinaries.'
7. The New York Stock Exchange is the world's largest by market capitalisation (the total value of listed companies). The number of listed companies is largely irrelevant; for example, there are more companies listed on the ASX than on the NY Stock Exchange.
8. In 2016–2017, volumes in China eased somewhat, after the bursting of their stock market bubble in mid-2015.
9. Paul Wilmott, author of a number of books on derivatives, puts the figure even higher at $1.2 quadrillion. It is difficult to estimate their values because most derivatives are private contracts between two parties and not listed on public markets.
10. Warren Buffett (b.1930) is the founder, chairman and leading shareholder of the Berkshire Hathaway investment fund, and one of the world's richest people. He made his fortune from scratch by astute investments in the US stock market.
11. Coffs Harbour and Parkes are two councils among a number in New South Wales, Australia, to have lost money in this way (CCA 2012).

12. See https://www.opensocietyfoundations.org/. Soros is a huge fan of Karl Popper and his fund was named after Popper's concept of the 'Open society.'
13. Telstra was the Australian government-owned telecommunications company until 1998 when the privatisation began with one-third of the company being listed on the Australian Stock Exchange.
14. 'Penny dreadful' is a finance slang term for companies whose shares' value has been reduced to a few cents, indicating the firm is struggling financially.
15. The 'E-Mini S&P 500' is based on the prices of the largest 500 US stocks. It is a futures contract: a bet on the future price of these stocks (set at the end of each month) and is a widely followed indicator of market direction.
16. In early 2017, Sarao pleaded guilty to market manipulation and faced a lengthy jail term.
17. There is evidence this is already happening. HFT activity peaked in 2008–2010 and has since declined.
18. Blodget worked for investment bank CBIC Oppenheimer and was later head-hunted by Merrill Lynch for an eight-digit salary. In 2003, he was convicted of civil securities fraud when it was revealed that sentiments in Merrill Lynch's internal emails conflicted greatly with public statements by the company.
19. Over the years since this low in 2001, the share price has fully recovered as Amazon has gone onto become the world's pre-eminent internet retailer.
20. When house prices started to decline, buyers began defaulting en masse. Banks repossessing and selling the houses in order to recoup their money caused house prices to decline further by flooding the market.

Bibliography

Anderson, Geraint. 2008. *Cityboy: Beer and Loathing in the Square Mile*. London: Headline Publishing Group.

Buffett, Warren. 2002. Annual report of Berkshire Hathaway Inc., 2002.

CCA. 2012. GFC Hits Council Investment. *The Coffs Coast Advocate*, 30 July 2012. Accessed 20 June 2017. https://www.coffscoastadvocate.com.au/news/councils-risky-investment-loss/1484544/

CFTC-SEC. 2010. Findings Regarding the Market Events of May 6, 2010. Commodities Futures Trading Commission (CFTC) and Securities and Exchange Commission (SEC) Report, September 2010. Accessed 20 June 2017. https://www.sec.gov/news/studies/2010/marketevents-report.pdf

CME. 2014. Derivatives Market Landscape, Spring 2014. CME Group. Accessed 20 June 2017. http://www.cmegroup.com/trading/otc/files/derivatives-market-landscape.pdf

Conner, George, and Mason Woo. 2004. *An Introduction to Hedge Funds*. Technical Report 002, IAM Hedge Fund Discussion Paper. Accessed 20 June 2017. https://www.iam.uk.com/Portals/0/pdf/lse-publications/An-Introduction-to-Hedge-Funds.pdf

Danckert, Sarah. 2016. Hanlong Exec Gets Largest Insider Trading Sentence in Australian History. *The Sydney Morning Herald*, 11 March 2016. Accessed 19 June 2017. http://www.smh.com.au/business/hanlong-exec-gets-largest-insider-trading-sentence-in-australian-history-20160311-gngjji.html

Das, Satyajit. 2011. *Extreme Money: Masters of the Universe and the Cult of Risk*. New York: Penguin.

Fama, Eugene. 1970. Efficient Capital Markets: A Review of Theory and Empirical Work. *Journal of Finance* 25: 383–417.

Ferguson, Niall. 2008. *The Ascent of Money: A Financial History of the World*. New York: Penguin.

Fisher, Irving. 1929. Speech at the Monthly Dinner of the Purchasing Agents Association. Quoted in *The New York Times*, 16 October 1929, p. 8.

Franklin, Benjamin. 1748. *Advice to a Young Tradesman, Written by an Old One*, cited by Max Weber 1958 [1905]. *The Protestant Ethic and the Spirit of Capitalism*. New York: Scribner, p. 48.

Galbraith, John Kenneth. 1954. *The Great Crash 1929*. New York: Houghton Mifflin.

Haldane, Andrew. 2011. The Race to Zero. Speech to the International Economic Association Sixteenth World Congress in Beijing, 8 July 2011. Accessed 20 June 2017. http://www.bis.org/review/r110720a.pdf

Hildreth, Richard. 1837. *The History of Banks: To Which is Added a Demonstration of the Advantage and Necessity of Free Competition in the Business of Banking*. Hillard, Gray and Co. (digitized by Google).

Joyce, Christopher. 2013. *The Australian Financial Review*, 29 June 2013, p. 18.

Lewis, Michael. 2011. *The Big Short: Inside the Doomsday Machine*. New York: W. W. Norton & Company.

———. 2014. *Flash Boys: A Stock Market Revolt*. New York and London: W. W. Norton & Company.

Litterick, David. 2002. Billionaire Who Broke the Bank of England. *The Telegraph*, 13 September 2002. Accessed 20 June 2017. http://www.telegraph.co.uk/finance/2773265/Billionaire-who-broke-the-Bank-of-England.html

Mackay, Charles. 1995 [1841]. *Extraordinary Popular Delusions and the Madness of Crowds*. Ware, UK: Wordsworth Editions Ltd.

McLeay, Michael, Amar Radia, and Ryland Thomas. 2014. Money in the Modern Economy: An Introduction. *Bank of England*. Quarterly Bulletin 2014 Q1. Accessed 19 June 2017. http://www.bankofengland.co.uk/publications/Documents/quarterlybulletin/2014/qb14q101.pdf

Montgomery, Roger. 2012. Roger Montgomery Re-inventing the Way You Invest. Accessed 19 June 2017. https://rogermontgomery.com/why-the-stock-market-doesnt-work/

Oresme, Nicholas. 1355. *A Tract on the Origin, Nature, Law and Mutations of Money*, cited in B. Carruthers and W. N. Espeland. 1991. Accounting for Rationality: Double-Entry Bookkeeping and the Rhetoric of Economic Rationality. *American Journal of Sociology* 97: 31–69.

Philippon, Thomas. 2012. Finance vs. Wal-Mart: Why are Financial Services So Expensive? In *Rethinking the Financial Crisis*, ed. A. Binder, A. Lo, and R. Solow, 235–246. New York: Russell Sage Foundation.

Philips, Matthew. 2012. Knight Shows How to Lose $440 Million in 30 Minutes. *Bloomberg*, 3 August 2012. Accessed 20 June 2017. https://www.bloomberg.com/news/articles/2012-08-02/knight-shows-how-to-lose-440-million-in-30-minutes

Reuters. 2015. UK Speed Trader Arrested over Role in 2010 'Flash Crash'. *Reuters Business News*, 21 April 2015. Accessed 20 June 2017. http://www.reuters.com/article/us-usa-security-fraud-idUSKBN0NC21220150422

———. 2016. Foreign Exchange, The World's Biggest Market, is Shrinking. *Reuters Business News*, 11 February 2016. Accessed 20 June 2017. http://www.reuters.com/article/us-global-fx-peaktrading-idUSKCN0VK1UD

Russell, Bertrand. 1935. *In the Praise of Idleness and Other Essays*. London: Routledge.

Schiller, Robert. 1984. Stock Prices and Social Dynamics. *Brooking Paper on Economic Activity* 2: 457–498.

———. 2000. *Irrational Exuberance*. Princeton: Princeton University Press.

SCMP. 2015. It's Amateur Hour in China amid Boom in Penny Stocks. *South China Morning Post*, 12 January 2015. Accessed 19 June 2017. http://www.scmp.com/business/china-business/article/1678653/its-amateur-hour-china-amid-boom-penny-stocks

Soros, George. 1998. *The Crisis of Global Capitalism: Open Society Endangered.* New York: Perseus Books Group.

The Economist. 2008. A Nuclear Winter? The Fallout from the Bankruptcy of Lehman Brothers. *The Economist*, 18 September 2008. Accessed 20 June 2017. http://www.economist.com/node/12274112

Yan, Sophia. 2016. It's War! China Blasts Soros over Currency Comments. *CNN Money*, 27 January 2016. Accessed 20 June 2017. http://money.cnn.com/2016/01/27/investing/george-soros-china-attack/index.html

6

Economic Rationality Versus the Earth

In 2009, a British film titled *The Age of Stupid*, set in 2055, depicted the world ravaged by catastrophic climate change.[1] London is flooded, Sydney is burning and Las Vegas is disappearing before the encroaching desert. An unnamed archivist is entrusted with the impossible task of safekeeping human civilisation's vast repository of art and knowledge. He reviews archival footage from the time 'when we could have saved ourselves' (early 2000s) and tries to figure out where it all went wrong. The film, part documentary, part drama set in the not-so-distant future, is an easy-to-digest contribution to the climate change debate and activism. It received excellent reviews from leading global newspapers. However, many people interested in the climate change debate may not have heard of it. There are at least two reasons for this: one, as elaborated in the next chapter, the world's vast repository of knowledge and information at our fingertips is thrilling and exasperating in equal measure, making it impossible to have a reasonable overview even of one's central areas of interest, both profession and personal; two, critical contributions calling for political action tend to be sidelined by mainstream media who prefer to serve 'feel-good' programmes to their audiences lest they defect to another channel.

V. Colic-Peisker, A. Flitney, *The Age of Post-Rationality*,
https://doi.org/10.1007/978-981-10-6259-9_6

Fig. 6.1 The temptations and the detritus of the consumer society in Palermo, Sicily (2009) [Advertising images removed due to copyright restrictions]

The Economy's Chickens Coming Home to Roost

Most public commentators and many ordinary people are concerned about the environmental effects of our economy. The most prominent aspect of the irrationality of the modern Western society is the carelessness with which we treat the earthly resources—from clean water and fresh air to forests and fossil fuels—that sustain our physical survival and our civilisation. An increasing number of economists agree that conventional economics has a major flaw even when judged by its own logic: it is an 'economy of unpaid costs.' These costs, ignored by both individual businesses and national accounts, are primarily environmental, but also social. Since the 1950s, many have argued that capitalism is inherently incapable of regulating its social metabolism with nature in an environmentally sustainable manner. German-born economist Karl William Kapp (1950) pioneered this insight while working in the US during the 1940s and 1950s.

In the pre-industrial past, the productive forces of humanity were modest and the exploitation of natural resources moderate. For many centuries, social change, including population growth, was slow. With the dynamic growth of technology over the past two centuries, the tension between the capitalist economy and the natural environment has become acute. Yet, our leaders refuse to treat the relationship of the economy to the natural environment and society as a political priority. The economic 'bottom line' reigns supreme, and its environmental and social casualties are taken for granted. The most pressing problems are attended to and fixed piecemeal. Profits are private, but the environmental and social costs accrued in economic activity are imposed on everyone. The ramifications of an unbridled economy on nature and society are part of the unaccounted for 'externalities.'[2]

The idea of the social cost of business enterprises dates back to the nineteenth century. In this heyday of European *laissez-faire* capitalism, unfettered by labour laws, the exploitation of workers attracted the attention of critics who advocated 'socialists' reforms. In 1827, while the best known of them, Karl Marx, was still in primary school, Swiss economist and political historian Simonde de Sismondi (1827, 92) wrote:

> The returns of the entrepreneur sometimes represents nothing but the spoliation of the worker; the former makes his money not because his business yields returns far in excess of the cost of production but because he does not pay the total cost of his enterprise; he fails to give an adequate compensation to the worker.

While the most obvious problem of nineteenth-century European capitalism was merciless exploitation of workers, forward-looking thinkers of the time were already warning of the consequences of 'man's conquest of nature.' In the 1850s, Marx (1894) wrote about the 'metabolic rift' between humans and nature created by urbanisation and warned that the exploitation of soils, forests and oceans was unsustainable:

> Even a whole society, a nation, or even all simultaneously existing societies taken together, are not the owners of the globe. They are only its possessors, its usufructuaries, and, like *boni patres familias*, they must hand it down to succeeding generations in an improved condition. (p. 567)

Marx's environmental message has been overshadowed by his more prominent political message and largely lost as part of his intellectual legacy. It is only since the mid-twentieth century that environmental ideas attained wider currency. Kapp (1950, xxvi) argued that capitalism is an 'economy of unpaid costs':

> [S]ocial costs and environmental disruption may be considered the principal contradiction within the system of business enterprise. [...] For the fact that private entrepreneurs are able to shift part of the total costs of production to other persons, or to the community as a whole, points to one of the most important limitations of the present scope of neoclassical value theory, which, [...] has so far been incapable of assimilating to its reasoning and to its conceptual system many of the costs (and returns) which cannot easily be expressed in dollars and cents.

In their 1999 book *Natural Capitalism*, Paul Hawken and Amory and Hunter Lovins argued that the attitude of most corporations has not changed since the start of the Industrial Revolution; even though today's human impact on the Earth's ecosystems is vastly more pernicious, the economic rationality of capitalism has not adjusted to this fact (Hawken et al. 1999). The 1999 *State of the World* report by the Worldwatch Institute introduced the concept of 'the acceleration of history'—the increasingly rapid destruction of ecosystems (WI 1999).

Nowadays seven billion bipedal mammals with oversized brains roam the Earth; we need clean water, lush forests, fresh air and biodiversity in order to survive and prosper. As natural creatures, we critically depend on the survival of ecosystems and our civilisation depends on finite energy and mineral resources. These simple common-sense propositions are ignored: we continue to overexploit natural resources and pollute the environment like there's no tomorrow. Perhaps there isn't?

Trouble in the Anthropocene

Homo sapiens is not only the dominant species on the planet—in advanced capitalism, we have become a geological force. Geologists have proposed naming the current geological epoch accordingly as the

'Anthropocene,' the era of humans, and it seems likely this will be made official (Zalasiewicz et al. 2017). The global mining industry moves four times the amount of earth as the total of all erosion; we have felled or degraded half of the world's forests; since the Industrial Revolution, nearly a third of the carbon dioxide (CO_2) in the atmosphere has been added by human activity. Due to the dominance of humans, animal populations in the wild are increasingly marginal and many species have disappeared or face extinction. The mass of humanity is now ten times that of all wild vertebrates, while the animals we either love or love to eat—pets and farm animals—outweigh mammals in the wild by a factor of 25 (Smil 2011).

Humans began modifying the home planet as soon as they invented agriculture and settled into a sedentary life. Deforestation began in Neolithic times (7000–1700 BC), but the advent of ancient cities caused more extensive problems. Ship building, necessary for trade and for the projection of military power, was a major factor in deforestation in the Mediterranean from the time of the ancient Greeks. The needs of the powerful Roman Empire were greater still. The historian V. G. Simkovitch noted the exploitation of the conquered lands and how 'province after province was turned by Rome into a desert' (Desmond 1973, 52).

Yet, the ancients only had a small fraction of our contemporary power to interfere with nature. Environmental problems were local and remained so until the twentieth century. An industrial town may have had polluted air or a factory may have contaminated the local river. In the nineteenth century, pockets of serious environmental degradation were limited to the highly urbanised and industrialised areas of Europe such as the Ruhr region in Germany and parts of England, including greater London. Anthropogenic pollution became a *global* problem in the late twentieth century.

Margaret Thatcher, the British Prime Minister during 1979–1989, was the first political leader to take the problem of global warming seriously. This is not typical for a conservative politician and a champion of the free market, and it is likely due to her scientific training (a PhD in chemistry) which enabled her to understand the problem in some depth. She recognised that *global* warming meant the problem could no longer be shifted around, usually from developed to developing countries. In her speech to the United Nations on 8 November 1989, she said:

> It is life itself—human life, the innumerable species of our planet—that we wantonly destroy. It is life itself that we must battle to preserve. […] It is no good squabbling over who is responsible or who should pay. Whole areas of our planet could be subject to drought and starvation if the pattern of rains and monsoons were to change as a result of the destruction of forests and the accumulation of greenhouse gases. […] [The] environmental challenge which confronts the whole world demands an equivalent response from the whole world. Every country will be affected and no one can opt out. (Thatcher 1989)

Later in life, Thatcher became truer to her conservative, non-interventionist ideology. In her 2003 memoirs, she stated that 'it [climate change] provides a marvellous excuse for worldwide, supra-national socialism' (Thatcher 2003, 449).

Since Mrs Thatcher's time in politics, the debate over climate change has epitomised the contradiction of capitalist economic rationality and the natural environment. Now well into the debate's third decade, a broad scientific agreement on what is actually happening is muddied by politically motivated renditions. These have confused many ordinary citizens who consequently decided to ignore the issue. Most political leaders are not making it look urgent, and some hold extreme views. The chief business advisor to Australia's 2013–2015 conservative Prime Minister Tony Abbott (2013–2015) contributed to the climate change debate thus: 'This is not about facts or logic. It's about a new world order under the control of the UN […] It is opposed to capitalism and freedom and has made environmental catastrophism a household topic to achieve its objective' (Pearlman 2015).

It is worth noting that the strongest advocate of action on climate change among the current leaders is Angela Merkel, the German conservative *Kanzlerin*, also with a doctorate in (physical) chemistry. Do political leaders need to be female scientists in order to understand the seriousness of our current environmental woes? To be fair, the 2009–2016 American President Barrack Obama was committed to action on climate change but was hamstrung by a Congress dominated by conservatives. A recent Australian survey showed that views on global warming and the necessity of tackling it were determined by political values more than any other variable: only 28 per cent of Australian conservative voters believed that global warming was anthropogenic (Leviston et al. 2015); the figure for US Republican voters was similar at 34 per cent (Leiserowitz et al. 2016).

Political interests have transformed a debate that should be grounded in scientific evidence and rational deductions into an ideological battle between 'believers' and 'sceptics.' Contrary to the examples of Thatcher and Merkel, the 'believers' are typically found on the left side of politics, while 'sceptics' tend to be conservatives investing their faith squarely into the economy (it's the economy stupid!). After Democrat Al Gore lost the 2000 US presidential election to Republican George W. Bush by the smallest of margins and subsequently devoted himself to championing action on climate change, Republicans found it political expedient to take an opposing view, which became entrenched.

Al Gore's 2006 film and book *An Inconvenient Truth* (Gore 2006) and his global lecture tour on climate change brought the subject into mainstream discussion. An increasingly fierce argument ensued via films, books, blogs, public lectures and political speeches and declarations. To take just two examples, in the film *The Great Global Warming Swindle,* Martin Durkin (2009) called the science of climate change 'a multibillion-dollar worldwide industry created by fanatical anti-industrial environmentalists,' while on the other side of the barricade, Craig Rosebraugh's 2012 documentary *Greedy, Lying Bastards* exposed the fossil fuel interests' funding of the climate change 'doubters' in the US.

On top of being obfuscated by political interests, the climate change debate has evolved into a kind of political subterfuge. All the environmental issues discussed for decades—deforestation, air and water pollution, toxic waste, species extinction—have been blended and packaged together into one big issue: anthropogenic climate change. Such packaging allows sceptics to dismiss all environmental issues in one smart blow: if humans are *not* causing climate change, then everything is just fine. We can continue doing what we've been doing: with great enthusiasm, cutting the branch on which we're sitting.

It is not that climate change only recently appeared on the scientific radar and has not had time to sink into the global consciousness and normative vocabulary of public debate. In fact, anthropogenic climate change was 'discovered' as soon as fossil fuels started to be consumed in mass quantities. Early in the nineteenth century, French physicists Joseph Fourier and Claude Pouillet speculated on the role of atmospheric gases in setting the global temperature. In 1859, John Tyndall presented an experiment to the Royal Institution of Great Britain, demonstrating the mechanism of the 'greenhouse effect'—the trapping of heat from solar radiation at the Earth's surface: 'The bearing of this experiment upon the action of planetary atmospheres is obvious [...] the atmosphere admits of the entrance of the solar heat, but checks its exit; and the result is a tendency to accumulate heat at the surface of the planet' (Tyndall 1859; see also Hulme 2009).

In the 1980s, when Author 2 was undertaking his undergraduate course in astronomy, there was a competing theory that anthropogenic air pollution would lead to cooling of the planet by absorbing sunlight before it could reach the ground, possibly precipitating a new ice age. However, evidence accumulated since then established that greenhouse warming dominates the smaller cooling effect of dust and pollution.

A Tale of Two Planets

In the dim past of the last century, when we as children enjoyed a TV science fiction show featuring travel between the planets of the Solar system, Venus was depicted as a hot, steamy world of tropical jungles. At the time, there were no scientific data on Venus, and the sci-fi writers could let their imagination run wild. Reality, though, was far more extreme than anyone could guess.

Venus and Earth are of similar size, mass and composition; they also contain about the same amount of carbon (Miralda-Escudé 2017). However, on Venus all the carbon is in the atmosphere due to extensive volcanism, and there is no mechanism to redeposit the carbon into geological formations. The atmosphere on Venus is 92 times denser than Earth's and consists of 96 per cent CO_2, with the remainder being nitrogen and sulphur dioxide (SO_2; it even rains sulphuric acid). Most of Earth's carbon is locked up in rocks, vegetation and fossil fuels. The average surface temperature of Venus is 462°C. On Earth, it is a somewhat more bearable 14°C (1961–1990 average by World Meteorological Organization).

Geologists may argue that the Earth had much higher levels of atmospheric CO_2 in the past and the climate did not suffer the cataclysmic runaway greenhouse warming that afflicts Venus. Five hundred million years ago, CO_2 levels on Earth were many times today's levels. What is most relevant to the current debate is that during the Pliocene (3–4 million years ago) when atmospheric CO_2 levels were comparable to present-day values (around 400 parts per million), the Earth was 3°C warmer (Robinson et al. 2008) and the sea level was 25 m higher.[3] Is this where we are headed? The amount of CO_2 in the atmosphere is higher now than at any time in which *homo sapiens* has wandered the Earth. Temperatures have risen by an average of 0.8°C since the 1980s (IPCC 2013).

A simple demonstration of the 'greenhouse effect' (the original term used until 'global warming' and 'climate change' took over) can be staged by sitting in a car with the windows closed on a sunny day. Almost all the incoming solar energy is in the form of visible light; it passes through the glass and is absorbed by the car's interior, which re-emits the heat as infra-red radiation. And this is the problem: the longer wave-length infra-red radiation does not pass as easily through the glass and therefore it gets trapped inside the car. As you well know, the temperature of the car rises. Not forever though, due to physical laws we do not wish to bore you with. But you would have surely opened a window before the temperature in the car reaches equilibrium—unless you're sitting in the car on a sunny winter's day and the equilibrium feels just cosy!

Around 30 per cent of the sun's energy is reflected by the Earth from clouds, snow and ice and, to a lesser extent, from land and the ocean surface (NASA 2014). The remainder is absorbed. The average surface temperature of the Earth only needs to be about minus 15°C for the infra-red radiation it emits to balance the solar radiation the planet absorbs. However, certain gases in the atmosphere, notably water vapour, carbon dioxide and methane, act in the same way as the glass in car windows: they are transparent to visible light but absorb much of the infra-red. This results in the Earth warming from the frigid minus 15°C to the above mentioned 14°C, making it a pleasant habitat for the dominant bipedal mammal and most of its four-legged relatives. This is a good greenhouse effect.

Enter civilisation. The question is how much does the extra CO_2 produced by civilisation,[4] as well as anthropogenic releases of methane and other gases, boost the greenhouse effect? To answer this question, scientists have to resort to computer climate models. Computer modelling of the thermal land-sea-atmosphere system is used daily in the weather forecast. Modelling the entire planet for decades into the future is, of course, more difficult, but the science is so advanced that there is every reason to take its predictions seriously.

Dancing Cats and Other Catastrophes

Climate change may be the ultimate, and ultimately global environmental problem, but those that existed before it and independently of it are also serious and need our attention. We would like to remind the reader of a few environmental disasters that acted as catalysts to the development of environmental consciousness and 'green' political movements in the second half of the twentieth century.

The world's first major environmental legislation was precipitated by the 'great London smog' that killed over 4000 people during a 5-day period in December 1952. Another 8000 deaths were attributed to the smog over the subsequent year (Bell and Davis 2001). Bodies did not pile up in plague-like proportions, but within a week, London morgues were full, undertakers ran out of coffins and florists ran out of flowers. At the time, Londoners largely used poor quality coal to heat their homes. This, in combination with the peak of the British post-war manufacturing boom, conspired to produce a highly toxic[5] low visibility environment which not even Jack the Ripper would enjoy. The great London smog was the catalyst for the world's first Clean Air Act (UK) in 1956. Other Western countries followed. Nowadays the smog problem has moved to developing countries. Over the past years, the reports of winter smog in Beijing or New Delhi resemble those of post-war London.

An early story of toxic waste starts in 1908, when the Chisso Corporation opened a fertiliser factory in Minamata, then a small fishing and farming community on the west coast of the Japanese island of Kyushu. Chisso grew into a leading chemical manufacturer by the 1930s. In 1951, a new manufacturing process was initiated that produced methyl-mercury as a waste product. The offending chemical was simply dumped into Minamata Bay.

While the company and its host town enjoyed the post-war boom, the local cats, whose diet was largely fish from Minamata Bay, began to behave bizarrely. They were having convulsions and 'dancing,' some falling into the sea. Before long, similar symptoms started affecting local townsfolk and, in 1956, an epidemic of 'dancing cats disease' was acknowledged. Hundreds of people suffered convulsions, paralysis and many subsequently died. By the end of the year, the cause was traced to mercury poisoning from eating contaminated fish from the bay. Direct evidence linking the mercury to waste from the Chisso plant was only found in 1959, and this evidence was not disclosed to the public for a few more years. Finally, in 1970, Chisso was ordered to pay compensation to its early victims. There have been over 2000 verified victims of what is now called Minamata disease, around half of whom have died (Harada 1995). However, the true numbers are likely to be much higher. In addition, children born to mothers affected by the disease had a much higher rate of birth defects. The factory stopped making the offending chemicals in 1968 but still operates in Minamata. In contrast, the local fishing industry has disappeared due to the permanent mercury contamination of the bay. The story of Minamata Bay briefly achieved worldwide coverage, but then faded from view.

Fig. 6.2 The King River, on the West coast of the Australian state of Tasmania contaminated with heavy metals

The US coming of environmental age was the case of Love Canal in the town of Niagara Falls, New York State, where a school and a residential development were built on a former toxic waste dump. Health effects among the local population began appearing in the 1970s, followed by the discovery of high levels of the known carcinogens benzene and dioxin in the local water. By 1978, Love Canal was a national media event and President Carter announced a federal health emergency—though this was hardly a unique case. The positive spinoff from this episode was the introduction of stricter environmental legislation and an enduring environmental movement.

Skimping on safety is another way in which industry transfers costs to society at large. A gas leak at the Union Carbide plant in Bhopal, central India, in 1984 has been the deadliest industrial accident in history. It resulted from lax safety standards and poor planning. Large tanks of methyl-isocyanate (MIC), a toxic substance used in the production of pesticides, were kept in the centre of the city. At the time of the accident, the plant was run down and scheduled for closure. Minor leaks were frequent, and most experienced workers left for safer workplaces. Late in the evening of 2 December 1984, water began leaking into one of the tanks and reacting vigorously with the MIC, producing large amounts of heat. Over the following few hours, 30 tonnes of vaporised MIC and other toxic products of the chemical process in the tank, including deadly hydrogen cyanide, spread several kilometres down-wind from the site. Initially, Union Carbide officials played down the extent of the accident, but by the morning after the leak, the brutal reality of 2000 dead bodies in nearby streets and houses was obvious. Domestic animals also perished; only birds and rats survived. The official death toll over the first few days was 3787, but this is known to be an under-estimate since many deaths went unregistered. The long-term death toll could have been as high as 20,000 (Varma and Varma 2005). Around half a million people were exposed and over 100,000 suffered long-term health damage including blindness and chronic respiratory problems (ibid.). Even decades later, people still die at the rate of two or three a week from the long-term health effects of the disaster. In their final report on the incident, Union Carbide admitted that safety valves had not been maintained and many safety systems were not operating (Danbury 1985). Although the Indian government initially sought over $3 billion in compensation, in 1989 they agreed to accept a mere $470 million payment from Union Carbide. Twenty-six years after the disaster, the plant was still standing without being cleaned up, continuing to inflict its 'externalities' on the local community. In 2010, the Indian government initiated a clean-up plan, but by 2014, things had barely moved forward (Lakshmi 2010; Elliott 2014).

Over the past decade, the dire environmental consequences of the phenomenal industrial growth and headlong urbanisation of China became plain. Since the late 1970s, when reforms opened the country to private enterprise, 20 per cent of arable land and nearly two-thirds of ground water have been contaminated (Wong 2014, MEP 2014; Reuters 2015). In addition, the growing middle class has replaced environment-friendly bicycles by cars. Air pollution in large cities has prevented people from walking the streets and children from playing outside. In winter, the sun cannot penetrate the heavy layer of smog in Chongqing, Shanghai or Beijing. A landmark 2013 study found that the Chinese living in the highly polluted northern regions had a 5.5 years lower life expectancy than those in the somewhat cleaner South (Chen et al. 2013).

Until recently, the efforts of the Chinese government were focused on keeping the problem under the carpet. After the 'airpocalypse' of February 2013 in Beijing and other major cities, when air pollution rose to 'crazy bad' levels, according to Wong (2013), they were forced to act. New measures were introduced to reduce emissions from heavily polluting industries. In early 2015, a Chinese video titled *Under the Dome*,[6] detailing the extent of air pollution, went viral on the internet with around 300 million views in the first few days—before it disappeared without trace from Chinese websites. Although Chinese authorities have started to address the problem, the urban dwellers still suffer severe air pollution episodes. In one of these, in late December 2016, tens of thousands of 'smog refugees' fled Northern Chinese cities, hampered, ironically, by the closure of many major airports due to the smog (Philips 2016). Despite this, the epicentre of air pollution has moved to India, where New Delhi often exceeds the worst of Chinese cities (Griffith 2016). Worldwide, air pollution leads to an estimated 3.3 million premature deaths each year (Lelieveld et al. 2015).

The Throw-away Society

The economic dynamism of affluent Western capitalism—making lots of things quickly and throwing them away quickly—creates mountains of rubbish and depletes natural resources. Millions of tonnes of wood, metal, plastic, glass and textiles have a short functional life between being made into useful objects and travelling to the tip. If we had to keep a junk mountain in our neighbourhood, we'd take recycling very seriously. However, we know our junk will be taken away, out of sight, out of mind! Vocal middle classes of the Western world have been able to keep rubbish tips and toxic waste at a comfortable distance. While environmental awareness is widespread, research shows that our environmental values do not necessarily translate into 'green' behaviour. We do not even recycle that much; women, young people and left-leaning citizens tend to separate their rubbish more conscientiously. Up to 90 per cent of First World rubbish ends up in landfill (Barr et al. 2001). The world's cities produce around 1.3 billion tonnes of solid waste each year. Per capita waste generation is correlated with wealth: poorer cities in sub-Saharan Africa and Southern Asia produce around half a kilogram per person, while Organisation for Economic Cooperation and Development (OECD) cities average more than four times that amount (Hoornweg and Bhada-Tata 2012, 8–9). Both the rate of urbanisation and per capita waste generation are on the increase everywhere.

As discussed in Chap. 4, preserving our status among our peers is often behind our wasteful behaviour. We waste because we are rich and we can afford to let food rot forgotten in the fridge and never-worn clothes hang neglected in the wardrobe. Importantly, wastefulness, just like greed, is good for the economy. Many common norms of behaviour and some government regulation encourage or even prescribe wasteful behaviour. For example, it is against the law in Australia to feed farm animals with people's scraps, as was done for centuries. As to millions of Western pets, dogs used to get their master's leftovers and cats used to catch mice, but these days pet food is a big industry. To deal with the consequences, and create more 'economic activity,' pet slimming programmes are catching on. Wasting may be irrational individual behaviour, but it is good systemic behaviour.

Built-in Obsolescence

At some stage of their lives, most men decide to buy their first electric shaver. Having used a mediocre hand-me-down from his father for a few years, this moment came for Author 2 around age thirty. After an impressive fifteen years of service the (not so) new shaver began to develop an intermittent electrical fault. He got out the soldering iron and repaired the defective wiring (do not attempt this yourself!). However, after several such repairs he finally decided that, with a degree in physics and a PhD from an electrical engineering department (though completed without ever touching a wire let alone one attached to anything), having 'electrocuted by a faulty shaver' on his tombstone would be just too embarrassing. Given the shaver lasted for nearly twenty years, the rational choice was to buy the same brand again. Yet, the salesperson pointed out that the blades would wear out in a year or two, and they cost more than the shaver. How is this possible? The whole being more than the sum of its parts is understandable, but a part being more than the whole ...? The salesperson wasn't being atypically honest—he simply wanted to sell an additional product, a lubricant that would extend the life of the blades. The logic was compelling, provided it was all true, but the lubricant turned out to have the aroma of a potent, cheap after-shave, and so was hardly ever used. It turned out the salesperson *was* telling the truth about the blades. In less than a year they were pulling hairs out rather than cutting them. Then, in a flash of stingy brilliance Author 2 thought, why not simply transfer the blades from the old shaver into the new one? The blades are now beyond their twentieth year and are still cutting facial hair; they have never been sharpened. Maybe he just got lucky? Whatever the case, twenty plus years ago companies could make blades for an electric shaver that lasted for decades. Now some wear out in a year.

An impressive example of built-in obsolescence comes from the *Phoebus* cartel. Light bulbs manufactured in the early twentieth century typically lasted 1500–2500 hours. But on 23 December 1924, a group of businessmen representing major international lighting manufacturers met in Geneva and had their light-bulb moment: why not boost sales by cooperating to design light bulbs to last no more than 1000 hours? The *Phoebus* cartel was born; it included Germany's *Osram*, France's *Compagnie des Lampes*, the Dutch *Philips* and the US's *General Electric*. Anyone can make a flawed light bulb that will last only a short time, but it took the best engineers considerable time to design a bulb that would reliably fail after 1000 hours. Over a number of years, the average lifetime was 'successfully' brought down from 1800 hours in 1926 to 1200 hours by 1934 (Krajewski 2014), with a commensurate jump in sales.

The job of planned obsolescence was taken very seriously. Every factory in the cartel had to send samples to Switzerland for testing, with fines imposed if the bulbs lasted too long. The rationale presented to the public was that the newer bulbs burnt brighter and more efficiently. In the 1930s, cheaper bulbs from Japan began to undermine the cartel, which was ultimately brought to an end by the Second World War. But the idea of planned obsolescence has not gone away—rather it has gone into overdrive. Fashion plays a leading role in making goods redundant, not just in the most obvious case of clothing but also in our ever-faster updating world of electronic gizmos. How many TVs, laptops and mobile phones clutter your home or have been thrown out, many in good working order? Apple has ensured planned obsolescence by fitting their extraordinarily popular iPhone[7] with special 'pentalobe' screws that cannot be removed by any commercial screw driver, making the phones unrepairable except by Apple's technicians. Recently, there has been some fight-back against this trend with the opening of 'repair cafes,' and organisations such as *iFixit* offering free repair guides for many common items, contributed by volunteers over the internet. However, built-in obsolescence—either by fault or fashion—remains a dominant force, providing extra profit for producers and a shorter path for natural resources heading to the rubbish tip, via short-lived material products.

Our Daily Bread Is Not What It Used to Be

When Author 1 was a pre-schooler, she used to rise at dawn, as young children tend to do, annoying their tired elders. As her grandparents often had her in their care at the time, they found a good use for her early rising. Her grandmother would place a few carefully counted coins in her little hand and send her a few paces down the road to join a 5 am bread queue at the village general store. The dawn bread queue was a summer phenomenon on the island: due to tourist invasion, the supply of bread could not keep up with the demand. At age 5, Author 1 enjoyed being given the responsibility of getting the daily bread for the household and being patted on the head by co-queuing neighbours for being a 'good girl.' Those who arrived after 5 am would often go home empty handed and had to bake their own bread, which was not fun in the Mediterranean summer. But there was no waste! Family fridges were tiny by today's standards, usually level with kitchen benchtops. Most grandmas, including her own, were pleasantly plump and soft, but there was no obesity epidemic.

Nowadays, even if we drop into the supermarket late in the evening, we do not see empty bread shelves. We expect choice, and this is what we get. Any time, day or night, any season, there is an ample selection of everything in our *super*markets. Do we ever wonder what happens to all the unsold bread, thawed fish and sliced ham once the store closes (if indeed it ever does)? It most likely goes into the bin. In the UK, 4.2 million tonnes of edible food and drink is wasted each year (Quested et al. 2013); in the US, a mind-boggling 60 million tonnes is thrown away annually (Buzby et al. 2014), while at the same time nearly 16 million households in the US struggle to put food on the table at some point during the year (Coleman-Jensen et al. 2016). In Australia, an estimated 20–40 per cent of fruit and vegetables are discarded even before they reach the shops because they look less than perfect. Bananas that are a little too small or too large never leave the farm (ABC 2017). The 'ugly food' movement is one answer to this issue, but it is only making a small dent in the problem (Mitchell 2015). Australian food waste could feed their entire 'cousin country' New Zealand (population 4.6 million). According to the UN's Food and Agriculture Organization, around one-third by weight or one quarter by calories of all produced food is wasted (Lipinski et al. 2013).

Supermarkets lock their dumpster bins and often intentionally spoil discarded food to prevent it from being rescued by 'dumpster-divers.' The stated rationale is preventing food poisoning by products past their use-by date. In a capitalist economy, spoiling thrown-away food makes sense: if the poor or homeless require food and cannot buy it, then charities should buy it from supermarkets and feed them. There is no such thing as a free lunch—not even from a bin!

In recent years, there has been some blowback against this practice. In 2009, protests broke out in Belgium after a dumpster-diving eco-activist was arrested for taking food out of a supermarket bin. In May 2015, French MPs, appalled by the growing mountain of food waste, passed a law that requires supermarkets to give excess food to charities or, if unfit for human consumption, to use as animal feed. According to Guillaume Garot, a Socialist MP and a former food minister who proposed the bill, 'it is scandalous to see bleach being poured into supermarket bins' (Chrisafis 2015). Some daring chefs took it upon themselves to prove that supermarket bins can be sourced for a dining experience which can satisfy the most refined palates (Maitland 2009; Ting 2013).

Industrial Food: Quantity over Quality

Waste is only part of the problem that the affluent West has with food. A huge appetite for meat in Western countries, a practice that is being enthusiastically embraced by growing middle classes in developing countries, is itself anti-environmental. However you measure it, water or fossil fuel use, or land area required, the biggest offender is beef. The pleasant image of cows grazing in a meadow we see as we drive to our weekend destinations obscures the reality of grain-fed cattle in giant feedlots, where it takes seven kilograms of grain to produce one kilogram of beef. Per capita meat consumption has doubled since 1950, and livestock now consumes 35 per cent of the world's grain crop (EPI 2011) and use a staggering 30 per cent of the Earth's ice-free land (Herrero et al. 2013). The contribution of farm animals to greenhouse gas emissions is comparable to the transport sector at around 14.5 per cent of the total (FAO 2013)—the main culprit being methane produced by cattle. Increased meat consumption also contributes to expanding waistlines. A thought about the tortured life of industrially farmed caged animals has not yet managed to ruin the appetite of most Westerners (see Lymbery and Oakeshott 2014).

One of the deepest ironies of advanced capitalism, the emphasis on quantity over quality in just about every domain of life, may be most easily illustrated by food, where it affects everyone. Food is industrially produced, abundant, diverse and cheap. We do not have to wait for summer in order to eat tomatoes or strawberries: food travels around the globe, accumulating thousands of 'food miles' on the way to our local supermarket. In addition, industrially produced food has considerably lower nutritional value and is likely to contain any combination of pesticides, herbicides, hormones, antibiotics, preservatives, heavy metals and other toxic chemicals, including those coming from fertilisers. Those who believe that 'an apple a day keeps the doctor away' are definitely behind the times. The apples—along with other fruit and vegetables—Westerners ate in the 1940s and 1950s contained more vitamins and minerals than those grown today (Thomas 2003; Davis et al. 2004). Today, about three apples a day would be needed to keep the doctor away, but unfortunately, in this amount one would also digest many unwanted substances that place apples near the top of the 'dirty dozen' of the fruit and vegie selection—those containing the highest amount of pesticides and other contaminants (EWG 2017).

In response to the industrial food production that leads to mass obesity and contributes to many diseases of civilisation while at the same time being unsustainable and cruel to animals, there is an alternative food movement devoted to 'farmers markets,' advocating locally grown organic food, including meat. But this is still only a marginal middle-class movement: 'alternative' organic local food is considerably more expensive. It is better for our health and the health of the planet, but most of us will still choose more of the cheap stuff over less of the good stuff.

The Hunger for Energy

When then US President Jimmy Carter installed a solar hot water heater on the roof of the White House in 1979, he said,

> [...] a generation from now, this solar heater can either be a curiosity, a museum piece, an example of a road not taken, or it can be a small part of one of the greatest and most exciting adventures ever undertaken by the American people.

The next US President Ronald Reagan decided to contribute to the first scenario. In 1986, he quietly had the solar panels removed while resurfacing the White House roof. Several of the former White House solar panels have ended up in museums: in the Smithsonian's National Museum of American History and in the Solar Science and Technology Museum in Dezhou, China (Biello 2010). However, Carter has had the last laugh. At the age of 92, he has installed a solar energy project on his former peanut farm: 3852 solar voltaic panels capable of supplying much of the electricity for his local town of Plains, Georgia (Blinder 2017).

In Australia, due to widespread rooftop solar energy use, electricity usage from the grid has gone down since 2009—good news from the sparsely populated, sunny continent, where most people live in self-standing family houses and which is therefore an unsurprising global leader in domestic solar energy. However, solar energy accounts for only a tiny proportion of global energy consumption which grows ever upward. By definition, non-renewable energy resources (the main being coal, oil and natural gas) will run out one day—perhaps during our lifetime. Even though Jevons (1866) raised the question of the depletion of coal reserves in the mid-nineteenth century, he could not even start to imagine the levels of coal consumption in the twenty-first century: more than 200 tonnes a second! However, coal is on the decline: China, the world's largest consumer of coal, 'peaked' on coal in 2013. The four US coal companies with the largest market capitalisation in 2011 were all bankrupt by 2016. The fortunes of oil are still strong, but the finiteness of the resource on which our civilisation crucially depends was made clear by the oil shock of 1973, and no amount of new oil discoveries can change this immutable fact.

It is therefore no wonder that one of the key policy concerns is how to meet the West's voracious energy needs. Global energy consumption in 2014 ranged from a low of 690 kWh per year for the average resident of South Sudan to 208,000 kWh per year for the average Icelander: one Icelander uses the same amount of energy as 300 South Sudanese. The figures also vary among developed countries: US energy consumption per capita is more than double that of the UK (World Bank 2014). Overall, OECD countries with 18 per cent of global population consume 42 per cent of global energy. The Chinese use their fair share of energy, proportionate to the population, while the remainder, nearly two-thirds of humanity living in developing countries, uses only 37 per cent of global energy production.[8]

Nuclear energy was once thought of as the power source of the future, having a low carbon footprint and producing a small amount of waste—in volume, at least. Its exploitation started in the 1950s and intensified in the 1980s, currently accounting for 11 per cent of global electricity production. France satisfies around three-quarters of its power needs from nuclear energy, far more than any other country. Although there are over 60 reactors currently under construction in 15 countries, mostly in Asia and Russia, public resistance to the use of nuclear energy is considerable, fed by a fear of the invisible—radiation cannot be seen, smelt or felt but can nonetheless be very damaging to human health.

This resistance became entrenched after the explosion at Chernobyl, Ukraine, in April 1986, and further magnified after the accident at the Fukushima nuclear plant in Japan in March 2011. The technological complexity of nuclear power pushes against the boundary of our ability to manage unforeseen risks, such as the record-sized tsunami that hit the Japanese coast triggering the Fukushima disaster. A smaller part of the public resistance is motivated by rational concerns about the long-term disposal of radioactive waste (some of which remains radioactive for centuries) and the proliferation of nuclear weapons that often accompanies the peaceful use of nuclear energy. In any case, uranium is a finite resource that can only serve as a bridge towards a sustainable energy future based on renewable sources.

However, the resistance to renewable energy sources is considerable too. Australia is one of the worst offenders in terms of per capita greenhouse gas emissions (five times the rate of China) and yet, in 2014, Australia's treasurer described wind farms as a 'blight on the landscape' and 'utterly offensive' (2GB 2014). One can be impressed by a nuclear plant, but hardly anyone would consider it beautiful, not to mention a coal-powered plant billowing suffocating smoke. In Australia, wind turbines are required to be at least two kilometres from people's homes, but a coal-fired power station need only be one kilometre from local residences. A coal mine can be as close as 100 metres.

Fig. 6.3 The nuclear plant Cruas-Meysee (operating since 1983) on the bank of the river Rhône, France

Junk: Space High, Ocean Deep

Our hi-tech civilisation is highly dependent on plastic. Bakelite, the first fully synthetic plastic (you will be thrilled to know its chemical name is polyoxybenzylmethylenglycolanhydride), was developed in the early twentieth century, but mass production of plastics did not begin until the 1950s. Increasing much faster than the world population, annual plastic production reached 50 million tonnes by 1976, doubled by 1989, doubled again by 2002 and currently sits at more than 300 million tonnes (PE 2016). According to chemical manufacturer Bayer, around 5 per cent of extracted oil is used to produce plastic. Much of this plastic—a shopping bag blowing in the wind, a bottle top in the gutter or a soft drink container left on the beach—eventually gets washed into the world's oceans.

The sea has always been the final home for the detritus of civilisation, but unlike most rubbish of times past, plastics do not biodegrade, resisting even the most ravenous bacteria. Instead, floating plastic objects are broken apart into smaller and smaller pieces by the action of waves and the impact of sunlight. In 1989, Robert Day and his team were the first to guess that the North Pacific Gyre—a large region of slowly rotating currents in the subtropical waters north of Hawaii—could be a locus for floating rubbish (Day et al. 1989). The region is rarely visited, being too poor in marine life to attract fisherman and not windy enough to attract sailors. In 2003, Charles Moore, returning from a Los Angles to Hawaii sail race, discovered the 'Pacific trash vortex' (Moore 2003). He was duly impressed:

> I often struggle to find words that will communicate the vastness of the Pacific Ocean to people who have never been to sea. Day after day, *Alguita* was the only vehicle on a highway without landmarks, stretching from horizon to horizon. Yet as I gazed from the deck at the surface of what ought to have been a pristine ocean, I was confronted, as far as the eye could see, with the sight of plastic.

Most plastic that is washed into the ocean ends up as a 'plastic soup' of small particles suspended in the surface layer of water. According to the CSIRO,[9] an estimated 3 per cent of total plastic production (8.4 million tonnes) entered the world's oceans in 2010. Even on remote, uninhabited Henderson Island, thousands of kilometres from the madding crowds, researchers found millions of items of plastic that had been swept there by the currents of the Pacific Ocean (Lavers and Bond 2017). Tonnes of rubbish floating in the vast ocean seem far from everyday concerns, but it seriously affects marine life. For example, in 1960 only 5 per cent of seabirds were found to have ingested plastic; by 2010, the figure had risen to 80 per cent (CSIRO 2015). If the present rate of increase in plastics entering the world's oceans was to continue until 2050, there would be more plastic (by weight) than fish in the sea (EMF 2016)—not something to look forward to!

Rapacious modern humans are capable of polluting not only their home planet and its atmosphere but also Earth's 'inner space.' Space junk is becoming a real problem: in low Earth orbit (less than 2000 km above the Earth), there is an estimated half a million pieces of debris (NASA 2013), from tiny specs a centimetre across to whole defunct satellites.

A derelict Russian military satellite collided with a communications satellite in 2009 and contaminated its orbit with a large quantity of fragments. If an orbit is too polluted with debris, it becomes too dangerous to use. During NASA's space shuttle programme (1981–2011), each mission had an estimated 1/300 chance of a dangerous collision with space junk. Indeed, the International Space Station has been manoeuvred to avoid incoming fragments a number of times and has taken slight damage from minor impacts (Van Zijl 2016). There are documented instances of people being injured by space debris falling from the heavens—though one has to be fairly unlucky to fall a victim of high-tech civilisation this way.

Can Capitalism Clean Its Act?

There are fundamental limits on Earth's capacity to supply our ever-increasing demands for clean air, water, space and natural resources. The only way to solve the problem is reducing the demand. There are three ways to achieve this: stabilisation and even reduction of world population; improvements in technology; and far-reaching socio-economic transformations through implementation of 'green' policies. Most demographers agree that the world population is gradually stabilising and will peak at around 10–11 billion in the second half of this century. This will not in itself solve the problem, if per capita consumption of materials and energy continues to rise, so the search for a solution has to include the other two aspects.

Upon inflicting significant damage on Earth's ecosystem, humans did manage to repair some of it through green policy and technological development. The ozone hole—the damage to the Earth's protective shield against ultra-violet (UV) radiation—was the earliest successfully tackled, global environmental problem. In 1972, James Lovelock[10] was the first to detect significant amounts of atmospheric chlorofluorocarbons, synthetic chemicals used in refrigerators, air-conditioners and as propellants in aerosol cans. Scientists soon learnt that these compounds could cause the breakdown of ozone in the upper atmosphere[11] (Molina and Rowland 1974), though definitive evidence supporting this claim had to wait until measurements made in Antarctica were published in 1985 (Farman et al. 1985).

Unlike the current stalemate with climate change, scientists succeeded to persuade politicians and the response was impressively swift. The 1987 Montreal Protocol, signed by every country in the world including even the Vatican, mandated the phasing out of the dangerous chemicals. Governments had to stare down some industry detractors, but most businesses quickly set about developing alternatives. Some took advantage of profitable opportunities to develop replacement chemicals. A significant contribution to global warming was also averted, since chlorofluorocarbons are potent greenhouse gases. Due to the long lifetime of the offending chemicals, the ozone hole, which expands out from Antarctica each winter, has not yet been eliminated, but its severity has decreased. The successful response to ozone depletion stands as a beacon to how science, governments and industry can work together.

Global warming is a very different kettle of fish, however. Methods to tackle it need to be on a much grander scale. In order to be taken seriously in the world where economic calculations claim a monopoly on rationality, the advocates of action on global warming follow the logic of all public argument—the rationality expressed in dollars and cents—and put forward the 'cost of global warming.' How much would we lose in 'tourist dollars' if global warming bleaches the corals of the Great Barrier Reef, that 'wonderful tourist resource' of tropical Australia (ABC 2012)? How much will it cost Switzerland or New Zealand if their famous glaciers melt? How much damage will extreme weather events inflict on our villages, towns, infrastructure and agriculture? How much will it cost to adapt our cities to the changing climate?

Many people can be persuaded that we should let the magic of market forces engender solutions to environmental problems. An associated convenient solution is what Naomi Klein (2014) calls 'magical thinking': waiting for a technological fix, be it advances in renewable energy generation or geo-engineering to alter the climate—delivered through the 'market.' Waiting for technology-cum-market solutions is a convenient excuse for political inaction. Also, such solutions are almost certain to be a case of 'too little too late.' Economists whispering in politicians' ears can 'put a price on carbon,' but the price is likely to be too low and the unpaid environmental cost will remain mostly unpaid. The logic that led the world into this serious environmental predicament is unlikely to lead us out of it. Market forces will not lead to a major shift in public policy. A switch to renewable energy has to be negotiated through political process and supported by the taxpayer. Political leadership is sorely needed, but conspicuously absent.

Even if framed in the usual economic terms, action on climate change seems warranted. Data from Munich Re, the world's largest re-insurance company, shows the cost of weather-related destruction (by storms, floods, bushfires) is rising much faster than that of geophysical disasters (earthquakes, tsunamis, volcanoes) (Schuster 2013). It is estimated that three-quarters of heat extremes are due to anthropogenic warming (Fischer and Knutti 2015). Though not the first, and certainly not the last, to consider the economic impact of climate change, the 2006 Stern Review has been the most comprehensive. It estimated the cost of reaching a stable level of atmospheric greenhouse gases to be 1 per cent of global GDP per year until stabilisation is achieved, while the cost of not acting would be at least 5 per cent of GDP per year permanently, and possibly much higher (Stern 2006).

In 2011, Michael Raupach, former director of the Australian National University's Climate Change Institute and co-founder of the Global Carbon Project, bluntly expressed the consequence of the lack of action: 'The combination of a 2°C warming target with high probability of success is now unreachable' (Raupach et al. 2011, 2). The best scientific evidence suggests that if we want to achieve an 80 per cent probability of limiting warming to the 2°C target adopted in Paris in 2015 and endorsed by all governments (with the withdrawal of the Trump-led US announced in June 2017), then the world economy would need to become carbon neutral by 2020. Clearly, this is not going to happen. Mixing the uncertainty of long-term climate modelling and the uncertainty of long-range economic forecasting has provided sceptics with plenty of room to raise doubts and slow down reaching a political solution.

To understand climate change scepticism, we need to consider the issue of socially constructed beliefs. People advocate narratives that make sense to them and their peers and that support their interests. As children, we unquestioningly absorb the narratives and 'truths' we are exposed to and few of us review the evidence in adulthood. On specific issues, we often form opinions in a haphazard fashion, led by emotions, prejudices and various unchecked 'facts.' Unsurprisingly, current events impress us the most and long-term thinking does not come naturally. During Australia's millennial drought (1997–2009), there was strong public support for urgent action on climate change, but the arrival of the *La Niña* weather pattern in 2010 bought cooler temperatures and flooding rains to parched eastern Australia, and the urgency was instantly forgotten.

Momentum for action on climate change reached an early consensus in Kyoto in 1997 when developed nations agreed on (somewhat) binding targets to reduce their carbon emissions collectively by a modest 4.2 per cent by 2012. The developing nations, including China, which has in the meantime became the world's leading carbon emitter (in absolute terms), had observer status in Kyoto. Subsequent global action was far from satisfactory. The Republican-dominated US Congress blocked ratification of the treaty; the then conservative government in Australia followed suit, despite having successfully argued in Kyoto to be allowed to *increase* its emissions by 8 per cent. Australia finally ratified the Kyoto Protocol in 2007 after a change of government. At the end of 2011, Canada announced it would withdraw from the treaty when it became clear that the country would fail, by a substantial margin, to reach its target, and thus suffer a serious financial penalty. Europe succeeded in meeting its target, not through any radical action but due to the loss of heavy, polluting industry following the dissolution of the centrally planned economies of Eastern Europe and the former Soviet Union.

The 2009 Copenhagen summit aimed to replace the Kyoto Protocol by an agreement that included a broader range of countries, but it stalled amidst disagreements on burden sharing between the developed and developing nations. In contrast, the 2015 Paris summit was a global love-in with everyone agreeing, but little has been achieved by the time we write these lines (June 2017). Yet, regardless of a global agreement or a lack of it, some countries have acted. The European Union has set an ambitious but non-binding target for a 40 per cent reduction in greenhouse gas emissions by 2030. China and the US surprised many at the end of 2014 by announcing a bilateral agreement on carbon emissions, with China aiming for its emissions to peak by 2030. This will involve the installation of up to 1000 GW of zero-emission power—comparable to the total current US electricity production. China's progress in the area of renewable energy over the past few years gives good grounds for optimism that the country will meet this target, but the US side of the equation is looking increasingly shaky under the Trump presidency. Only four countries have so far committed to reducing their carbon emissions sufficiently to be consistent with the stated goal of limiting warming to 2°C above pre-industrial levels—Bhutan, Costa Rica, Ethiopia and Morocco[12]—and they are hardly the great polluters.

The agreement at the 2015 Paris UN Climate Change Conference, where all participants pledged to reduce emissions and to 'pursue efforts to limit the temperature increase to 1.5°C,' has been greeted with enthusiasm. A rational global debate is in the air, but will the appropriate action follow? Even if Donald Trump, who declared climate change 'a Chinese conspiracy' during his election campaign, never became the US president, chances are high that the economic rationalist dogma would hollow out the 'Paris consensus.' The danger lies in the dogma's rational guise—it's all numbers and (economic) logic, the logic we are culturally conditioned to trust.

Indian author and activist Arundhati Roy (2009) provided a witty summary of the pernicious relationship of advanced capitalism and its economic (ir)rationality with the planet Earth: 'Capitalism is destroying the planet. The two old tricks that dug us out of past crises—War and Shopping—simply will not work.'

Notes

1. *The Age of Stupid* is a 2009 British futurist docu-drama by Franny Armstrong, produced by John Battsek. See http://www.imdb.com/title/tt1300563/. Accessed on 6 June 2017.
2. In economics, an externality is a cost or benefit to a third party not directly involved in the activity that causes the cost or benefit. For example, industries that cause air or water pollution impose health and clean-up costs on the local area or the whole society. See http://www.investopedia.com/terms/e/externality.asp
3. The sea levels were higher due to the lack of ice and the thermal expansion of the oceans. Sea level refers to the mean global sea level ('eustatic' sea level). See the British geological survey at http://www.bgs.ac.uk/discoveringGeology/climateChange/general/coastal.html?src=topNav. Accessed 6 June 2017.

4. Water vapour is the dominant greenhouse gas, but the amount of it in the atmosphere is driven largely by temperature. Under clear skies, CO_2 contributes about 26 per cent of the total greenhouse warming, but it makes a smaller contribution in overcast conditions (Kiehl and Trenberth 1997).
5. The pollution in the atmosphere included 1000 tonnes of smoke particles, 2000 tonnes of carbon dioxide, 140 tonnes of hydrochloric acid and 14 tonnes of fluorine compounds; 370 tonnes of sulphur dioxide gas combined with moisture in the atmosphere became 800 tonnes of sulphuric acid. See the UK Meteorological Office: http://www.metoffice.gov.uk/learning/learn-about-the-weather/weather-phenomena/case-studies/great-smog. Accessed on 7 June 2017.
6. Directed and produced by Chai Jing, released 28 February 2015. If you are not in China, copies of the video with English subtitles can still be found on YouTube. https://www.youtube.com/watch?v=V5bHb3ljjbc. Accessed on 7 June 2017.
7. Electronics manufacturer Foxconn churns out an amazing half a million iPhones *every day* from its factory in Zhengzhou, China, known to the locals as 'iPhone city.'
8. Figures derived from Word Bank data (World Bank 2014).
9. The Commonwealth Scientific Industrial Research Organization (CSIRO) is the leading scientific institution in Australia. Details of CSIRO researcher Chris Wilcox' work on plastic pollution in the ocean can be found at http://people.csiro.au/W/C/Chris-Wilcox.
10. James Lovelock (b. 1919) is a chemist, earth scientist and author, most widely known for his Gaia hypothesis that treats the biosphere and the inorganic surrounds of the Earth as a single complex system.
11. Paul Crutzen, F. Sherwood Rowland and Mario Molina shared the 1995 Nobel Prize in chemistry for their work on damage to the ozone layer.
12. According to climateactiontracker.org

Bibliography

2GB. 2014. Interview with Joe Hockey on Radio 2GB (Sydney), 1 May 2014.

ABC. 2012. Comment by Queensland Premier (2012) Campbell Newman, Australian Broadcasting Commission (ABC) Radio National. *Morning News*, 13 April 2012.

———. 2017. War on Waste. *ABC TV*, 16 May 2017.

Barr, S., A.W. Gilg, and N.J. Ford. 2001. A Conceptual Framework for Understanding and Analysing Attitudes Towards Household Waste Management. *Environment and Planning A* 33: 2015–2048.

Bell, M.L., and D.L. Davis. 2001. Reassessment of the Lethal London Fog of 1952: Novel Indicators of Acute and Chronic Consequences of Acute Exposure to Air Pollution. *Environmental Health Perspectives* 109: 389–394.

Biello, David. 2010. Where Did the Carter White House's Solar Panels Go? *Scientific American*, 6 August 2010. Accessed 24 June 2017. https://www.scientificamerican.com/article/carter-white-house-solar-panel-array/

Blinder, Alan. 2017. Jimmy Carter Makes Stand for Solar, Decades After the Cardigan Sweater. *The New York Times*, 11 February 2017. Accessed 24 June 2017. https://www.nytimes.com/2017/02/11/us/jimmy-carter-solar-energy-plains-ga.html

Buzby, Jean C., Hodan F. Wells, and Jeffrey Hyman. 2014. The Estimated Amount, Value, and Calories of Postharvest Food Losses at the Retail and Consumer Levels in the United States. *Economic Information Bulletin Number 121*. US Department of Agriculture.

Chen, Yuyu, Avraham Ebenstein, Michael Greenstone, and Hongbin Li. 2013. Evidence on the Impact of Sustained Exposure to Air Pollution on Life Expectancy from China's Huai River Policy. *Proceedings of the National Academy of Sciences (USA)* 110: 12936–12941.

Chrisafis, Angelique. 2015. France to Force Big Supermarkets to Give Unsold Food to Charities. *The Guardian*, 23 May 2015. Accessed 21 June 2017. https://www.theguardian.com/world/2015/may/22/france-to-force-big-supermarkets-to-give-away-unsold-food-to-charity

Coleman-Jensen, Alisha, Matthew P. Rabbitt, Christian A. Gregory, and Anita Singh. 2016. Household Food Security in the United States in 2015. *Economic Research Service Report*. US Department of Agriculture, September 2016.

CSIRO. 2015. Almost All Seabirds to Have Plastic in Gut by 2050. *Commonwealth Scientific and Industrial Research Organisation (CSIRO) News*. Accessed 6 June 2017. https://www.csiro.au/en/News/News-releases/2015/Marine-debris

Danbury, C.T. 1985. Bhopal Methyl Isocyanate Incident. *Investigation Team Report*. Union Carbide Corporation.

Davis, Donald, Melvin Epp, and Hugh Riordan. 2004. Changes in USDA Food Composition Data for 43 Garden Crops, 1950 to 1999. *Journal of the American College of Nutrition* 23: 669–682.

Day, R.H., D.G. Shaw, and S.E. Ignell. 1989. The Quantitative Distribution and Characteristics of Neuston Plastic in the North Pacific Ocean 1985–88. In *Proceedings of the 2nd International Conference on Marine Debris*, ed. R.S. Shomura and M.L. Godfrey, Honolulu, Hawaii, April 1989.

Desmond, Annabelle. 1973. The World's Great Cities: Evolution or Devolution? In *Selected Articles in Social Ecology*, ed. James Wittman, digitized by Google.

Durkin, Martin. 2009. *The Great Global Warming Swindle* (A documentary film).

Elliott, John. 2014. India: After 30 Years, Bhopal is Still Simmering'. *Newsweek*, 1 December 2014. Accessed 21 June 2017. http://www.newsweek.com/india-after-30-years-bhopal-still-simmering-288144

EMF. 2016. The New Plastics Economy: Rethinking the Future of Plastics. *Ellen MacArthur Foundation Report 2016*. Accessed 6 June 2017. https://www.ellenmacarthurfoundation.org/assets/downloads/EllenMacArthurFoundation_TheNewPlasticsEconomy_15-3-16.pdf

EPI. 2011. Data Highlights: Rising Meat Consumption Takes Big Bite Out of Grain Harvest. Earth Policy Institute, 22 November 2011. Accessed 8 June 2017. http://www.earth-policy.org/data_highlights/2011/highlights22

EWG. 2017. EWG's 2017 Shopper's Guide to Pesticides in Produce. Environmental Working Group (EWG). Accessed 8 June 2017. https://www.ewg.org/foodnews/summary.php

FAO. 2013. Tackling Climate Change Through Livestock. Report of the Food and Agricultural Organization (FAO) of the United Nations, 2013.

Farman, J.C., B.G. Gardiner, and J.D. Shanklin. 1985. Large Losses of Total Ozone in Antarctica Reveal Seasonal ClO_x/NO_x Interaction. *Nature* 315: 207–210.

Fischer, E.M., and R. Knutti. 2015. Anthropogenic Contribution to Global Occurrence of Heavy-Precipitation and High Temperature Extremes. *Nature Climate Change* 5: 560–564.

Gore, Al. 2006. *An Inconvenient Truth: The Planetary Emergency of Global Warming and What We Can Do about It*. New York: Rodale.

Griffith, James. 2016. New Delhi is the Most Polluted City on Earth Right Now. *CNN*, 8 November 2016. Accessed 21 June 2017. http://edition.cnn.com/2016/11/07/asia/india-new-delhi-smog-pollution/index.html

Harada, M. 1995. Minamata Disease: Methylmercury Poisoning in Japan Caused by Environmental Pollution. *Critical Reviews of Toxicology* 24: 1–24.

Hawken, Paul, Amory Lovins, and Hunter Lovins. 1999. *Natural Capitalism: Creating the Next Industrial Revolution*. New York: Little, Brown and Company.

Herrero, Mario, Petr Havlík, Hugo Valin, An Notenbaert, Mariana C. Rufino, Philip K. Thornton, Michael Blümmel, Franz Weiss, Delia Grace, and Michael Obersteiner. 2013. Biomass Use, Production, Feed Efficiencies, and Greenhouse Gas Emissions from Global Livestock Systems. *Proceedings of the National Academy of Sciences (USA)* 110: 20888–20893.

Hoornweg, Daniel, and Perinaz Bhada-Tata. 2012. What a Waste: A Global Review of Solid Waste Management. *Urban Development Series Knowledge Papers*. World Bank. Accessed 21 June 2017. https://siteresources.worldbank.org/INTURBANDEVELOPMENT/Resources/336387-1334852610766/What_a_Waste2012_Final.pdf

Hulme, Mike. 2009. On the Origin of 'The Greenhouse Effect': John Tyndall's 1859 Interrogation of Nature. *Weather* 64: 121–123.

IPCC. 2013. *Climate Change 2013: The Physical Science Basis, Contributions of Working Group I to the Fifth Assessment Report of the Intergovernmental Panel on Climate Change*. Ed. T.F. Stocker, et al. Cambridge, UK and New York: Cambridge University Press.

Jevons, William Stanley. 1866. *The Coal Question: An Inquiry Concerning the Progress of the Nation, and the Probable Exhaustion of Our Coal Mines*. London: Macmillan.

Kapp, Karl William. 1950. *The Social Cost of Private Enterprise*. Cambridge, MA: Harvard University Press.

Kiehl, J.T., and K.E. Trenberth. 1997. Earth's Annual Global Mean Energy Budget. *Bulletin of the American Meteorological Society* 78: 197–208.

Klein, Naomi. 2014. *This Changes Everything: Capitalism vs. the Climate*. New York: Simon & Schuster.

Krajewski, Markus. 2014. The Great Light Bulb Conspiracy. *IEEE Spectrum*, 24 September 2014.

Lakshmi, Rama. 2010. India Moves to Clean Up Site of Deadly 1984 Union Carbide Gas Leak. *Washington Post*, 9 July 2010. Accessed 21 June 2017. http://www.washingtonpost.com/wp-dyn/content/article/2010/07/09/AR2010070903209.html

Lavers, Jennifer L., and Alexander L. Bond. 2017. Exceptional and Rapid Accumulation of Anthropogenic Debris on One of the World's Most Remote and Pristine Islands. *Proceedings of the National Academy of Sciences (USA)*, 114: 6052–6055.

Leiserowitz, A, et al. 2016. Politics and Global Warming, Spring 2016. Yale University and George Mason University, New Haven, CT: Yale Program on Climate Change Communication. Accessed 6 June 2017. https://www.eenews.net/assets/2016/04/27/document_cw_01.pdf

Lelieveld, J., J.S. Evans, M. Fnais, D. Giannadaki, and A. Pozzer. 2015. The Contribution of Outdoor Air Pollution to Premature Mortality on a Global Scale. *Nature* 525: 367–371.

Leviston, Z., M. Greenhill, and I. Walker. 2015. Australian Attitudes to Climate Change 2010–2014. *CSIRO Technical Report EP158008*, November 2015.

Lipinski, Brian, Craig Hanson, James Lomax, Lisa Kitinoja, Richard Waite, and Tim Searchinger. 2013. Reducing Food Loss and Waste. *United Nations Environment (UNEP) Working Paper*. World Resources Institute, June 2013.

Lymbery, Philip, and Isabel Oakeshott. 2014. *Farmageddon: The True Cost of Cheap Meat*. London: Bloomsbury.

Maitland, Jonathan. 2009. The Bin-Banquet: How to Cook Up a Gourmet Feast for 500—Cooked Entirely from Food Chucked Away by Our Wasteful Supermarkets. *Daily Mail Australia*, 9 September 2009. Accessed 21 June 2017. http://www.dailymail.co.uk/femail/food/article-1211094/The-bin-banquet-How-dish-gourmet-feast-500--cooked-entirely-food-chucked-away-wasteful-supermarkets.html

Marx, Karl. 1894. *Capital*. Vol. III, part VI. New York: International Publishers.

MEP. 2014. The Ministry of Environmental Protection and the Ministry of Land and Resources Issued a National Bulletin Survey on Soil Pollution (China). Accessed 7 June 2017. http://www.mep.gov.cn/gkml/hbb/qt/201404/t20140417_270670.htm

Miralda-Escudé, Jordi. 2017. Lecture 6: Earlier History of Earth's Climate. In *Introduction to the Science of Climate Change (Course)*. Universitat de Barcelona. Accessed 6 June 2017. http://www.am.ub.edu/~jmiralda/fsgw/lect6.html

Mitchell, Dan. 2015. Why People are Falling in Love with 'Ugly Food'. *Time*, 28 March 2015. Accessed 21 June 2017. http://time.com/3761942/why-people-are-falling-in-love-with-ugly-food/

Molina, Mario J., and F. Sherwood Rowland. 1974. Stratospheric Sink for Chlorofluoromethanes: Chlorine Atom-Catalysed Destruction of Ozone. *Nature* 249: 810–812.

Moore, Charles. 2003. Trashed: Across the Pacific Ocean, Plastics, Plastics Everywhere. *Natural History Magazine*, November 2003.

NASA. 2013. Space Debris and Human Spacecraft. National Aeronautics and Space Administration (NASA). Accessed 6 June 2017. https://www.nasa.gov/mission_pages/station/news/orbital_debris.html

———. 2014. Measuring Earth's Albedo. NASA Earth Observatory, 21 October 2014. Accessed 6 June 2017. https://earthobservatory.nasa.gov/IOTD/view.php?id=84499

PE. 2016. Plastics—The Facts 2016: An Analysis of European Plastics Production, Demand and Waste Data. Report by Plastics Europe (The

Association of Plastics Manufacturers in Europe). Accessed 8 June 2017. http://www.plasticseurope.org/documents/document/20161014113313-plastics_the_facts_2016_final_version.pdf

Pearlman, Jonathon. 2015. Australian PM Adviser Says Climate Change is 'UN-led Ruse to Establish New World Order'. *The Telegraph*, 8 May 2015. Accessed 21 June 2017. http://www.telegraph.co.uk/news/worldnews/australiaandthepacific/australia/11591193/Australia-PM-advisor-says-climate-change-a-UN-led-ruse.html

Philips, Tom. 2016. Smog Refugees Flee Chinese Cities as 'Airpocalypse' Blights Half a Billion. *The Guardian*, 21 December 2016. Accessed 21 June 2017. https://www.theguardian.com/world/2016/dec/21/smog-refugees-flee-chinese-cities-as-airpocalypse-blights-half-a-billion

Quested, Tom, Robert Ingle, and Andrew Parry. 2013. Household Food and Drink Waste in the United Kingdom 2012. Report by the Waste and Resource Action Programme (WRAP), UK.

Raupach, Michael Robin, Ian N. Harman, and Josep G. Canadell. 2011. Global Climate Goals for Temperature, Concentrations, Emissions and Cumulative Emissions. *Centre for Australian Weather and Climate Research (CAWCR) Technical Report No. 42*, September 2011.

Reuters. 2015. RPT-More than 60 pct of China's Underground Water Rated Unfit for Human Contact. *Reuters*, 4 June 2015. Accessed 21 June 2017. http://www.reuters.com/article/china-environment-water-idUSL3N0YQ3CV20150604

Robinson, J., H.J. Dowsett, and M.A. Chandler. 2008. Pliocene Role in Assessing Future Climate Impacts. *EOS Transactions American Geophysical Union* 89: 501–502.

Roy, Arundhati. 2009. *Capitalism: A Ghost Story*. London: Verso.

Schuster, S. 2013. Natural Hazards and Insurance. In *Climate Adaptation Futures*, ed. Jean P. Palutikof et al., 133–140. Cambridge, UK: John Wiley & Sons.

Simonde de Sismondi, Jean-Charles-Leonard. 1827. *Nouveaux principes d'economie politique* (Paris, 2nd edition), Vol. I, cited in (and translated by) K. William Kapp (1950, p. 31).

Smil, Vaclav. 2011. Harvesting the Biosphere: The Human Impact. *Population and Development Review* 37: 613–636.

Stern, Nicholas. 2006. *The Stern Review on the Economics of Climate Change*. London: HM Treasury.

Thatcher, Margaret. 1989. Speech to the United Nations General Assembly, 8 November 1989. Accessed 5 June 2017. http://www.margaretthatcher.org/document/107817

———. 2003. *Statecraft: Strategies for a Changing World.* London: Harper Perennial.

Thomas, David. 2003. A Study on the Mineral Depletion of the Foods Available to US as a Nation over the Period 1940 to 1991. *Nutrition and Health* 17: 85.

Ting, Inga. 2013. From the Rubbish Bin to the Restaurant Table. *Goodfood*, 28 May 2013. Accessed 7 June 2017. http://www.goodfood.com.au/eat-out/news/from-the-rubbish-bin-to-the-restaurant-table-20130527-2n73n

Tyndall, John. 1859. On the Transmission of Heat of Different Qualities Through Gases of Different Kinds. *Proceedings of the Royal Institution* 3: 155–158.

Van Zijl, Johannas. 2016. Space Debris Hit the International Space Station Causing Small Crack in Window. *The Science Explorer*, 13 May 2016. Accessed 6 June 2017. http://thescienceexplorer.com/technology/space-debris-hit-international-space-station-causing-small-crack-window

Varma, R., and D.R. Varma. 2005. The Bhopal Disaster of 1984. *Bulletin of Science, Technology and Society* 25: 37–45.

WI (Worldwatch Institute). 1999. *State of the World 1999: A Worldwatch Institute Report on Progress Toward a Sustainable Society.* New York; London: W.W. Norton & Company.

Wong, Edward. 2013. On a Scale of 0 to 500, Beijing's Air Quality Tops 'Crazy Bad' at 755. *The New York Times*, 12 January 2013. Accessed 21 June 2017. http://www.nytimes.com/2013/01/13/science/earth/beijing-air-pollution-off-the-charts.html

———. 2014. One-fifth of China's Farmland Polluted, State Study Finds. *The New York Times*, 17 April 2014. Accessed 21 June 2017. https://www.nytimes.com/2014/04/18/world/asia/one-fifth-of-chinas-farmland-is-polluted-state-report-finds.html

World Bank. 2014. Energy Use (Kg of Oil Equivalent per Capita). *The World Bank*. Accessed 8 June 2017. http://data.worldbank.org/indicator/EG.USE.PCAP.KG.OE?end=2014&start=1960&year_high_desc=false

Zalasiewicz, Jan, et al. 2017. Making the Case for a Formal Anthropocene Epoch: An Analysis of Ongoing Critiques. *Newsletters on Stratigraphy* 50: 205–226.

7

The Promise and Threat of the Internet Age

In 1974, science-fiction author and futurologist Arthur C. Clarke was asked what the world of computers would be like in 2001. Mentioning his young son, he said that '[…] he will have in his own house […] a console through which he can talk to his friendly local computer and get all the information he needs for his everyday life: his bank statements, his theatre reservations, all the information you need over the course of living in a complex modern society […]'[1] How right he was, including the precise timing! By the beginning of this century, the internet became ubiquitous in our daily lives, catering for an increasing number of our needs: communicating, shopping, learning, banking, participating in civic initiatives, socialising, dating, travel, news, maps, music, movies, videos …you name it! It seems that only a few years earlier we could easily live without the internet, but now it was indispensable: a real revolution, with a nearly unlimited promise. We, the twenty-first-century Westerners, became used to a quick succession of techno news, telling us about new things that are now at our fingertips. The whole world was in our computers, accessible at any time.

Only few years later, our hyper-connected computers appeared in a pocket size, so that we never need to be separated from them. It has now

V. Colic-Peisker, A. Flitney, *The Age of Post-Rationality*,
https://doi.org/10.1007/978-981-10-6259-9_7

been a decade since people, at least the younger half of Western populations, have walked the streets immersed into their little smartphone screens, not noticing other people, oblivious to what's going on around them or what they are walking into—unless they downloaded an app showing them what's in front of them! By now we have gotten used to people who walk the streets talking loudly, seemingly to themselves, but in fact using their hands-free smartphone kit to have a phone conversation. Do not try to ask anyone for directions these days! First of all, why don't you ask Google maps instead of bothering other people? Secondly, most people will have wires dripping out of their ears and they won't hear you if you try.

Starting from the 1950s, sociologists have been lamenting both consumer conformism and individualist fragmentation of Western (primarily English-speaking) societies as well as a decline of community connectedness (Riesman et al. 1950; Putnam 2000). Individualism and consumerism seem to have merged in a new phenomenon of 'smartphone isolationism.' It may be a paradox of super-connectedness that we, isolated from reality and people that surround us, share our private emotions and occasions with hundreds and sometimes thousands of online 'friends,' 'connections' and 'followers.'

Governments were compelled to pass legislation outlawing the use of hand-held mobile phones while driving; in Japan, only the silent use of mobile devices is allowed on public transport. In the West, unfortunately, such regulation would probably be considered an attack on personal liberties, even though people who disturb others with their loud talking most certainly impinge on others' rights. In the decade since the smartphone appeared, the vast majority of Westerners, and many in the developing world, not only own one, but are psychologically dependent on it (ABC 2013). For under-30s, what their smartphones have to offer is almost invariably more interesting than the physically present family or friends (ibid.). If you do a quick survey of tables around you when you're next in a café, you'll find that even in this most sociable of situations, at least half of patrons stare at their little screens, ignoring the person(s) with whom they are 'having a coffee,' although it is just as probable that their companions are doing likewise. While the disapproval of the smartphone trance and attempts to enforce smartphone etiquette is no doubt age-related, there are serious questions about phone addiction, traffic safety and other hazards.

Unless you are under 25 (in 2017), and therefore a 'digital native' who takes the hyper-connected computers, big and small, for granted, you have to admire where we've got to with the internet revolution. You may also be able to remember the more innocent, slower, less connected times. If you are a middle-aged citizen, you may well have some concerns about the galloping technological change, the use and misuse of new technologies and perhaps you worry about your privacy while big brother Google is watching you. You may also be aware that only a small majority of humans live in a comfortable high-tech, digital world; the rest of humanity that Greenfield (2015) calls 'The Vast Majority' live outside it. You may share a sense that scientific and technological advancements, a collective product of the accumulated knowledge of humanity, should serve the common good, not only within our Western societies, but also globally.

Yet, in the 'more = better' paradigm of economic rationality, new technologies are adopted when and because someone can profit from them. The market decides and the potential usefulness of the innovation, or harm from it, is a secondary consideration. However, should we accept that all the amazing new devices and updates are a general improvement of our individual lives and the society we live in?

Recent research on education has shown that the increased use of computers in the classroom is not necessarily a good idea. An Organisation for Economic Cooperation and Development report (OECD 2015) on the use of computers in schools showed 'no appreciable improvements in student achievement in reading, mathematics or science in the countries that had invested heavily in ICT [information and computer technology] for education.' Furthermore, those students who are heavily computer reliant at school have much poorer education outcomes than those who use them moderately. It is worth noting that many of the leading Silicon Valley digital entrepreneurs choose to send their children to the Waldorf School of the Peninsula where there is not a computer or smartphone to be seen. Beverly Amico, Executive Director Advancement at the Association of Waldorf Schools of North America, claims that, ironically, students learning in a low technology environment are more likely to acquire the innovative skills that employers in high-tech industries desire (Jenkin 2015). Will this educational research's unequivocal finding of the impact of computer dependence make schools reconsider their enthusiastic embrace of technology in the classroom? Not likely! Guided by the imperatives of economic rationality, our schools are more likely to produce good digital consumers and obsessive updaters than creative, critical and well-balanced adults.

Technology and Economic Rationality Versus Society

On a recent interstate flight, Author 1 was amused by a depiction of a brave new world of 2055 (the First World, presumably) published in an in-flight magazine (Farrelly 2015). In this feel-good story, people (our children and grandchildren) realised the error of their ways and abandoned their thoughtless and wasteful practices. They now lived in a smart, high-tech, recycling, caring and sharing world. An esteemed British neuroscientist and a member of the House of Lords Susan Greenfield (2004) offers a scientifically informed and imaginative vision of a future high-tech world—a dark and a light version. She asks not just how people can harness new technologies but also how to reconcile new technologies with the care for the natural environment and us as a species. She proposes that 'wallowing in techno-luxury' poses considerable challenges: collectively, to work towards a more equitable and harmonious world and also to preserve what she calls our 'private egos'—our individuality and rationality threatened by unwise uses of technologies (Greenfield 2004, 270–271). As is often the case, the wisdom is hidden somewhere halfway between technophilia and technophobia.

Advanced technology is a central marker of Western civilisation. The mechanisation of the Industrial Revolution and automation over the last half-century has freed people from many physically taxing, unpleasant and repetitive tasks. We should be able to enjoy our lives more as a result, particularly in the affluent West. Due to technology, many occupations have died out—remember chimney sweepers, phone operators, typists?—while many new ones have been created, especially in the information technology (IT) sector. We can conclude that technology has benefited everyone in a general sense; for example, our household chores are not day-long physical drudgeries (hand-washing clothes!), and travel and communications are much faster and cheaper. There are public spaces where the benefits of technology are shared such as roads and public libraries, and some use of technology is 'free,' for example, free-to-air television. At the same time, there is a distinct feeling that technology, when employed by economic rationality, threatens many people's jobs and livelihoods—the virtual disappearance of manufacturing (except food production) from Western countries is a much-debated case in point. Technology is also accused of isolating people and diminishing community connectedness in spite of enabling hyper-communication. Technology may also threaten our common sense, sanity and privacy—think internet gaming and gambling addictions, internet relationship and financial scams, online bullying, identity thefts, revenge porn, and much more.

Many problems are created by the fact that technologies are used in an economically rational sense, rather than rationally in a broader sense, to the benefit of most, if not all. As it is, new technologies, in their capitalist form as patents, are sold and bought, ensuring someone has an 'innovative edge,' which means competitive advantage in achieving record profits. Economic considerations trump all others. New digital technologies have created a class of super-rich youngsters (with Mark Zuckerberg, the creator and major owner of Facebook on top of the pyramid) and made other youngsters hopeful to become rich before they finish high school by inventing yet another 'app' which the whole super-connected world would want to use, at least for a little while. In the virtual world of the twenty-first century, where news spreads like wildfire on social media, it is in fact possible to become rich and famous overnight. Many people are drawn to this possibility.

The problem of the unequal use and the inequitable distribution of benefits of modern technology is as old as technology itself, and a direct result of the rule of economic rationality. The issue did not escape the apostle of nineteenth-century liberalism, J. S. Mill (1970, 116):

> Hitherto it is questionable if all the mechanical inventions yet made have lightened the day's toil of any human being. They have enabled a greater population to live the same life of drudgery and imprisonment, and an increased number of manufacturers and others to make fortunes. They

> have increased the comforts of the middle classes. But they have not yet begun to effect those great changes in human destiny, which it is in their nature and in their futurity to accomplish.

A similar point came from the pen of Oscar Wilde (1912, 40–41), a Victorian England celebrity playwright and novelist:

> Up to the present, man has been, to a certain extent, the slave of machinery, and there is something tragic in the fact that as soon as man had invented a machine to do his work for him he began to starve [...] One man owns a machine which does the work of five hundred men. 500 men are, in consequence, thrown out of employment, and having no work to do, become hungry and take to thieving. The one man secures the produce of the machine and keeps it, and has 500 times as much as he should have [...] At present machinery competes against man. Under proper conditions machinery will serve man [...].

Yet, over a century later, these 'proper conditions' did not materialise: machinery 'serves man' only secondarily, if this happens to align with the interest of profit-seeking capital. Cutting labour costs, which means firing working people when technology can replace them, is considered a legitimate profit-maximisation strategy. The resulting unemployment is considered an unfortunate but unavoidable side effect. During the Industrial Revolution, English textile workers known as Luddites were rebelling and destroying machines, fearful of losing their jobs due to technological progress; the movement spread to other industries. In advanced capitalism, technology has made a significant section of the workforce, both blue and white collar, superfluous, while making richer those whose need to hire labour is reduced. Until recently, there was a general understanding that human services cannot be replaced by machines. Yet, the development of artificial intelligence (AI) has led to the latest example of machines replacing people: algorithms are advising judges on sentencing and employers on hiring, and are also replacing share traders and financial advisers; robots can check guests into their hotel rooms and serve food to hospital patients.

Fig. 7.1 The state of the art in mobile electronics circa 1982: Hewlett-Packard 41CV calculator with a 12 character display and memory of a few kilobytes

In spite of various victims of capitalist progress (the natural environment, many animal species and many categories of people), it is obvious that since the time of Mill and Wilde, technology-based mass production has dramatically improved the material comforts of life of even the poorest Westerners and many people in less developed countries. Yet, the central complaint remains: technology has not liberated us. In spite of the enormous increase of labour productivity and the huge output of goods and services churned out by modern economies, we have not cut our working day to four hours, as Bertrand Russell (1935) suggested was possible back in the 1930s. He argued that so much 'stuff' had already been produced—and our great-grandparents at the time he wrote this did not even have fridges, let alone smartphones!

About the same time as Russell, Keynes (1931, 326) predicted that the three-hour working day would prevail in his grandchildren's generation—that is, us. Instead, many have been made redundant from their jobs, while official statistics show that those employed often work long hours, beyond the statutory eight-hour working day won by the labour movement more than a century ago. Thus far there is no sign that the computerisation of the world over the past 30 years has liberated humanity from work either, though the nature of work has changed.

The Internet Revolution and the Digital Economy

Given our ageing population, most Westerners (half of us are over 40) can recall the days before smartphones and laptops, before the World Wide Web (WWW), before email, even before computers entered people's homes. In the mid-1970s, computers were as big as a room and only existed in far-off scientific and military institutes. At the time, Author 2 was thrilled to be able to use a terminal in his local (Australian/Tasmanian) high school, linked to a computer 250 km away that was able to process a few kilobytes of information. Yes, kilobytes! It took a decade or so of the relatively widespread use of computers before the internet revolution took hold—the time when they became connected to everything, everywhere. How did it all start?

The Advanced Research Project Agency Net (ARPANET), which went live on 29 October 1969, linking the University of California, Los Angeles with the Stanford Research Institute, is considered to be the precursor of the internet as we know it. The first communication exchange was less than auspicious: after transmitting 'L' and 'O,' the effort of transmitting 'G' proved too much and the system crashed (Gromov 1995). However, with the benefit of hindsight, we can see that history was made. The term 'internet' was first used in a 1974 *Request for Comments* document (Cerf et al. 1974) about the emerging computer networks. The now ubiquitous email emerged in the early 1980s. In the late 1980s, the Centre for European Nuclear Research (CERN) in Geneva, Switzerland, was looking for ways to connect large numbers of scientists in separate geographical locations, so they could collaborate on a single experiment. Physicist Tim Berners-Lee (1989) proposed an 'information management system,' and the WWW was born. For several years, the WWW was managed from the CERN computers in Geneva. The system went public in 1993 when the world's first web browser, called Mosaic, was created.

From then on, the internet grew at an amazing pace. Towards the end of the millennium, the present giants of the internet world emerged. Amazon started its life in 1994 as an online bookstore. Investors were rewarded for holding faith through years of losses, and the business kept expanding. Amazon moved beyond books into all sorts of consumer goods and has gone on to become the world's largest online store, eclipsing most bricks-and-mortar retailers and driving some of them to liquidation. In early June 2017, its share price reached over $1000 from a mere $72 10 years earlier, a 13-fold increase over the period. In 1996, Google came from the minds of Larry Page and Sergey Brin, then PhD students at California's Stanford University. Google was not the first search engine created for the rapidly expanding WWW, but judging by its current ubiquity and usage, it has developed to become the best. Social media arrived a little later. Myspace—you may be able to vaguely remember it—was started in 2003 and, for a few years, it was the world's pre-eminent social media platform. It even briefly outshone Google as the most visited website in the US. However, it did not last. A combination of economic rationality and ever-advancing technology made the internet a world of fast-changing fortunes. In 2004, Mark Zuckerberg created Facebook to link a group of friends at Harvard University. The social media platform reached 100 million users by 2008, obliterating Myspace. Facebook now has close to two billion active users and is not just a social media site and advertiser *par excellence*, but a major political tool. In an interview on the American CBS TV's *60 Minutes*, Donald Trump declared: 'The fact that I have such numbers on Facebook, Twitter, Instagram, etc., I think it helped me win all these races where they're spending more money than I spent' (CBS 2016).

Much of the WWW is controlled by Google (under the parent company Alphabet), Facebook, Amazon and a few other online behemoths. They are now among the most valuable publicly listed companies in the world and are approaching monopoly status in their respective domains. It is somewhat counterintuitive that the internet, praised for enabling universal, democratic access to just about everything, from information, banking, education and business ventures, actually produced huge near-monopolies. According to advertising research company eMarketer, spending on digital advertising in 2017 will account for 38 per cent of total advertising spending worldwide, overtaking TV, with Google and Facebook combined attracting the majority of the online advertising revenue (eMarketer 2016). The digital economy is how we do capitalism in the twenty-first century!

The Future of Work: From the 'Gig Economy' to Wikipedia

The internet-mediated economy is rapidly expanding. Many businesses, from retail to news media, are now online, with a general effect of job loss and casualisation of work. Apart from traditional businesses transitioning online, a new form of economy, variously known as the sharing, gig, platform or on-demand economy, has spread to many industries. Most impressively perhaps, at least for social scientists, is the fact that the internet is also home to entirely new kinds of collaborative effort that completely escapes the economic rationality of capitalism. As elaborated below, Wikipedia is the best-known example of 'internet socialism' where people contribute according to their abilities and use the collaborative product according to their needs—no questions or money asked!

The best-known example of the 'sharing economy' is the taxi substitute Uber, along with rivals Lyft, Didi and a host of smaller ventures, which allow people to earn money by using their own cars for providing a paid transport service previously limited to registered and publicly recognisable taxi cabs. The appearance, establishment and, finally, legal recognition of Uber have not happened without controversy. Unsurprisingly, taxi drivers protested against the less regulated and generally cheaper competitor, and the battle is ongoing.[2] The second best-known sharing economy venture is Airbnb, which enables people to hire out anything from a spare room to an entire house to tourists and visitors. While Airbnb is internally well regulated, its relationship to the broader world is still in flux. In most popular tourist destinations, Airbnb is squeezing out regular long-term renters because owners can earn more from offering their rental properties (or even rooms in their homes) to tourists (Samaan 2015). The lack of regulation and the unbearable lightness of becoming an Uber driver or an Airbnb host irritate many people and especially the conventional, regulated service providers. There is also a risk that both sides of the transaction may slip into a grey area with poor consumer protection. Yet, none of these fears have had an impact on the growth of the sharing economy platforms.

More recently, the idea of a shared internet economy has evolved to include any number of handypersons or specialists who perform necessary tasks in the requester's home, mediated through online platforms such as Airtasker, Freelancer, TaskRabbit, Geeks2U and many more. Prospective workers compete for tasks, and there are almost always multiple bidders for any project. Want an apartment cleaned or someone to help with a large lunch gathering? Post the task on your local online platform with an indicative price and soon there will be a number of offers of assistance from which to pick the most affordable or best qualified candidate. The task can also be of an intellectual nature and performed at a distance, for example, updating a website or editing a piece of writing.

Is this a further example of hyper-competition infecting our lives? For some people, getting odd jobs online may be a means to make a living while looking for more traditional employment or to make extra money on the side. The supporters of 'gigging' claim that it gives people freedom and independence to work as much or as little as they want, at a time and place that suits them. Those requiring a service have the luxury of multiple offers in an almost instantaneous competitive tender process that keeps prices down, while quality is maintained without any overbearing regulation through the posting of online reviews. It is not just large corporations that can outsource their call centres, IT and other productive services to India or elsewhere where labour, both low- and high skilled is cheaper—now anyone can do it! Undergraduates can order their written assignments to land in their smartphone!

Yet, for an increasing number of people, this kind of gig-economy work may not be a welcome flexibility and choice, but the only option they have in mobilising their skills and earning an income, or at least eking out an existence for some time. Is this the future of work in the brave new fast and flexible world? If yes, what may it mean for all of us: on-demand work, no job security, no career path and none of the perks and benefits of traditional employment, either financial or social? In terms of financial benefits and income security, internet gigging provides no retirement savings, no medical insurance, no sick leave or paid holidays. In terms of social benefits, isolated workers behind their computer, or darting from place to place, have no chance to bond with work colleagues, establish 'real' social networks or gain any social status from their work. Yet, these internet platforms seem to be an innovative, economically rational idea and are therefore likely to keep their momentum and grow further. There are platform companies that try to provide greater benefits to their workers but, due to the higher cost of running these businesses, they face difficulty raising finance and struggle to compete with the more 'efficient' firms. Peter Cappeli, a professor of management at the University of Pennsylvania, notes how 'vociferously the investment community seems to object to being nice to employees' (Kolhatkar 2017).

If we look at this kind of internet entrepreneurship from a social angle and what it means for the individual, isolated workers, this 'future of work' starts to look rather like the work of old, before workers' rights were codified in regulation. Adam Smith would have been proud that the 'invisible hand' has been allowed so much freedom to act in the digital economy of the twenty-first century. Working conditions in the nineteenth-century were often inhumane; the mid-twentieth-century corporate workplace with its unionised workforce, government regulation and triplicate forms had its own share of problems, but it brought stability and protection to many working people. The twenty-first-century workplace replaces these with the ultimate flexibility. The term 'sharing economy' sounds inviting, yet it may turn out to be the final exclamation mark to neo-liberalism whose unforgiving economic rationality has trickled down to the individual micro scale.

Therefore, the sharing economy, alongside its participatory, liberating and environmental potential, also has a potential for fragmentation of the workforce, leading to unregulated and precarious employment, underpayment and exploitation by internet entrepreneurs, the owners of the digital 'sharing economy' platforms. The unfettered competition of the internet-mediated economy amounts to the radical cutting of the proverbial 'red tape'. Without the visible hand of organisation, unionisation and government regulations, the internet economy may become a tool for an extreme casualisation of work. However, it is hardly surprising that the ruling economic rationality also asserts itself on the internet. How can governments even start to regulate this global economy *par excellence*, which so easily crosses national borders?

Trebor Scholz (2017), associate professor of culture and media at The New School, New York, advocates 'platform cooperativism': worker-owned cooperatives running platforms in competition to the dominant players such as Uber. This is the sort of utopian vision made possible by the internet, but it is not clear how well it would work in practice since the globalised world of the digital economy has become very much a winner-takes-all domain.

However, there are some niches of the economically rational WWW that seem to live up to the ideal of a cooperative and sharing world. Wikipedia is the best-known example: founded in 2001, this online encyclopaedia is written and maintained entirely by a cooperative effort of many volunteers. The funding necessary to maintain its physical presence on internet servers is gathered solely through donations, making it free from advertising and therefore closed to interference by corporate interests. Wikipedia boasts an accuracy level as good as any traditional commercial rival, including the most famous one, the Encyclopaedia Britannica (Giles 2005). Within a span of a few years, Wikipedia has become the most comprehensive and the most used encyclopaedia in existence. As of May 2017, there were articles in 296 languages; the English edition alone contains over 5 million entries.

By now taken for granted by most of us, Wikipedia is nonetheless an extremely important phenomenon that defies the competitive commercial logic of the capitalist economic rationality; it is a social collaborative effort which has managed to survive 'outside of markets and without state support' (Wright 2012, 18). Wikipedia is not perfect, of course; it has been shown that the demographic most likely to contribute to it, younger generations of educated white males, brings with them their biases. Yet, the utopian significance of Wikipedia is beyond doubt. It testifies to the emancipatory potential of internet-based ventures and media. The willingness of those who volunteer their time to contribute to a freely shared resource, even without being acknowledged for it, shows that there is life outside planet capitalism. Will there be more such ventures? What else, apart from knowledge, are we able and willing to freely share?

Other cooperative online efforts include numerous forums where useful information is shared and discussed, largely free of commercial bias. Almost anything, from a DIY problem around the house such as how to change an oven light bulb, to a technical aspect of a programming language and a recipe for an old-fashioned pasta dish, will have an instructional YouTube video, obtainable by a minute's search. Generally, the individuals providing the information do so without any reward apart from the nice feeling of being helpful, or perhaps showing off a little (if they features in the video). The Linux operating system, habitat of many computer geeks and one of the big three computer operating systems after Windows and Apple's Mac OS X, is a free and open resource (anyone can look at and modify the code), in sharp contrast to the commercial products of Microsoft and Apple. Linux is constantly being refined by its many aficionados who receive no remuneration. Could such a truly sharing economy transcend the realm of nerds and intrude into the world of ordinary people and into a wider, and not just virtual, 'real economy'?

The Internet (and) Democracy

Even before it became the focal point of the twenty-first-century capitalist economy, the internet was touted as a tool of democracy. In the twenty years of intense global interconnectedness, many things have happened and some patterns have emerged. Are we on the way to a global democracy and global civil society, as many had hoped? Apart from being instrumental in instances of quick, massive mobilisation—which can be a democratic mobilisation against tyranny but also mob recruitment for destruction or persecution—the internet is the birthplace of fake news and 'post-truth society'.

Fake News and Post-truth Society

'Fake news' is a recent addition to our vocabulary—it only took off in earnest during the 2016 US presidential campaign. Some well-known instances of fake news were the stories titled 'Pope Francis shocks world, endorses Donald Trump for president' and 'Clinton runs child sex ring from Pizzeria.' The 'Pope for Trump' story first appeared on a site called WTOE 5 News which had a disclaimer on its home page: 'Most articles on wtoe5news.com.au are satire or pure fantasy.' This did not stop the story being taken up by other sites and gathering nearly a million Facebook engagements, according to Buzzfeed. The bizarre conspiracy theory about Hillary Clinton originated in some highly imaginative misinterpretations of emails from the Clinton campaign chairman John Podestra that appeared on Wikileaks. Even such improbable 'news' may be able to convince and influence some people; they may represent a distraction from more important issues for others.

It should not be forgotten that the phenomenon of fake news—though not necessarily under this name—has been around as long as the mass media. However, the internet has supercharged its spread. At the dawn of the internet era, in June 1996, an article headlined 'Cleaner polishes off patient' appeared in the *Cape Times* of South Africa, reporting a series of deaths of patients in the same hospital bed over a period of several weeks. According to the *Cape Times*, hospital authorities investigated and discovered that a cleaner came in every Friday morning and unplugged the life-support system to plug in her floor polisher. Upon completing her task, she would reconnect the life-support. With the help of the internet, the story was rapidly republished in leading newspapers around the globe. However, the story was an urban myth created after a single death of a patient was queried by the family (Goldstuck 2007).

In the same way that it makes real news and information widely available, the internet is also the world of unreality, in which people did not land on the moon, the US government arranged the 9/11 attacks in order to justify invading Iraq, childhood vaccines cause autism and wind turbines cause cancer. As the then US President Obama put it in a 2016 post-election interview with the *New Yorker*, it (internet) is a media ecosystem where 'everything is true and nothing is true' (Remnick 2016).

'And the capacity to disseminate misinformation, wild conspiracy theories, to paint the opposition in wildly negative light without any rebuttal—that has accelerated in ways that much more sharply polarise the electorate and make it very difficult to have a common conversation,' he said. Not a great tool of democracy, if we are to agree with Obama.

The tense finale of the 2016 US elections brought another new concept—'post-truth'—into the mainstream (cf. Kucharski 2016). The online Oxford Dictionary (2017) defines 'post-truth' as

> Adjective: Relating to or denoting circumstances in which objective facts are less influential in shaping public opinion than appeals to emotion and personal belief: '*in this era of post-truth politics, it's easy to cherry-pick data and come to whatever conclusion you desire*'; '*some commentators have observed that we are living in a post-truth age.*'

'Post-truth' society is not just about fake news items that do not correspond to reality, usually aiming to achieve a certain effect on public opinion. It is also about the consumers of news being prepared to believe whatever suits their world view, and 'make up their mind' on the basis of emotions and beliefs rather than using verified facts and reasoning to reach a decision on a matter of consequence, including for whom to vote. The problem is not just in the fact that politicians and other public figures lie or at least (mis)interpret issues to suit their interests—this is now confounded by the post-truth society where their lies, even when easy to expose as such, no longer matter. In addition, the situation of constant information overload is similar in its effects on rational decision making and rational choice to the situation where we have no information at all—we follow our hunches and the opinions of our significant others.

Over recent years, it has become unremarkable for public figures to disseminate their messages through social media and for their supporters to spread it to the wider audiences of their 'friends, 'contacts' and 'followers.' The US President Trump has used Twitter to announce his political wisdom to his followers from his very first day in office. However, many messages posted on social media, rather than informing, are aimed at achieving a certain effect. They may be deliberately manipulative or outright fake. In a rather creative twist, the label 'fake news' has been often used by President Trump to dismiss stories that are actually true, but not aligned with his interests. His ongoing war with the established media has focused on this particular pursuit: deciding what is fake news and what is true without presenting any evidence, befitting the post-truth society. Trump sets an example and spreads the message: trust your mates on Facebook and those you chose to follow on Twitter, not the New York Times!

With the loss of advertising revenue as well as the disinclination of many people, the young in particular, to pay for online news and other media content, the business model of traditional media—print, radio and television—is under increasing pressure. This is having a debilitating effect on independent journalism, with almost all traditional media companies reducing staff substantially in the last few years (Battersby 2017; Slattery 2017). We may be heading to a state where everyone armed with a smartphone is an amateur journalist who can post photos and videos on social media in a matter of minutes, following an event they find worth publicising. Perhaps this is good and democratic, making conventional, independent media superfluous?

Yet, without independent media with its professional standards and ethical guidelines, the situation where everyone can be a journalist and a publisher is likely to degenerate into a cacophony of voices, many peddling false or misleading stories. How are we to tell the wheat from the chaff? If we are inevitably heading into a post-truth era, how can we make informed choices, as consumers and as citizens? The blurring of the line been reality and fiction has to erode democracy. Professional journalists are expected to be able to summarise complex events and situations in a comprehensible fashion and to keep us reliably informed. Independent, professional journalism has been crucial to the functioning of the mass nation-state-based democracy from its outset; it is hard to see representative democracy surviving its destruction. As early as 2013, the World Economic Forum listed the spread of 'massive digital misinformation' as a major source of risk to global society (WEF 2013). This applies even more to the national realm, where people's votes actually count.

Social Media as 'Echo Chambers'

Alongside their democratic potential, social media have populist potential to spread demagoguery and outright lies and to create ideological 'echo chambers'—another new concept for the internet age. In the changing internet mediascape, social media may erode democracy: through Facebook, Twitter and other social media with their customised news feeds, people are even more exposed to like-minded views and isolated from alternative views than they were in the era of conventional media (Kucharski 2016). Two-thirds of US adults have Facebook accounts and two-thirds of those get some or all of their news stories from it. YouTube and Twitter are also significant sources of news for around 10 per cent of US adults (Gottfried and Shearer 2016). For many people, particularly the young who are likely to keep their habits into their later life, daily news are mediated by their 'friends' and groups of their choosing, and from Facebook 'trending' which tells them continuously what are the hottest daily topics. Facebook knows its users' political leanings and on the basis of this information selects news stories that it expects will grab its users' attention. These personalised news feeds lead to an 'echo chamber' effect where our own ideas are reflected back to us, reinforcing our existing (mis)conceptions and biases. Are we heading into a populist anti-utopia, where social media and internet mobs gradually erode the democratic debate, representing a symptom of the perversion and decay of Western democracy?

According to psychologists (e.g. see Nickerson 1998), we all suffer from 'confirmation bias': we tend to believe stories that confirm our pre-existing beliefs and doubt those that contradict them. Repeated exposure to selective news can lead to 'cognitive inoculation' against alternative viewpoints. Conspiracy theories are shown to spread rapidly online (Del Vicario et al. 2015). Once formed, false beliefs are highly resistant to correction, particularly when they reinforce a pre-existing world view. However, we cannot just blame the 'big bad Facebook': in the conditions of full literacy and freedom to choose, the consumers of news are not passive victims devoid of agency. We choose our social media friends, and the choice has a greater influence on the news stories to which we are exposed than do Facebook's algorithms (Hosanagar 2016).

In the lead-up to the 2016 US presidential election, *The Guardian* ran an experiment to test the effect of political polarisation on social media. Five 'conservatives' were asked to log-in to a 'left-wing' news feed, while five 'liberals' switched to a conservative news source. Reactions varied. Todd Macfarlane, a conservative, decided to abstain from voting after being convinced that Trump might be bad for America; liberal Nikki Mougno said going to the other side was 'like being locked into a room full of those suffering from paranoid delusions.' For comedian, Nato Green, however, the lessons of the 2016 US election were starker: 'Maybe we should stop having social media [...] maybe the ability with social media for people to construct their own reality to create a mob is not worth it' (Wong et al. 2016). Of course, no Western government will ban or abolish social media. The only way for them to disappear is to die a 'natural,' economic death. The current serious, if not terminal, economic illness of the traditional media provides an inkling that this is possible.

Another important issue is that the content of Facebook posts is not entirely 'free'. There is filtering by Facebook staff who can take down posts that peddle fake news or violate the so-called 'community standards'. Attempts to produce tools to verify online information have had limited success. Once a false story takes hold, it is difficult to refute and its content can have a major impact (Graham 2017). Three months before the 2016 US presidential election, the top five fake news stories received more Facebook engagement than the top five real news stories (Silverman 2016). Almost all the fake news stories were pro-Trump or anti-Clinton. The Pope endorsing Trump and Wikileaks confirming that Clinton sold weapons to ISIS led the pack. Yet, attempting to monitor and censor—we can also call it publishing ethics or editorial policy—is extremely difficult, given there are two billion Facebook users. In addition, it may not have the desired effect. Real-time correction of misinformation can sometimes have the result of provoking users into defending misconceptions consistent with their prevailing outlook and confirmation bias (Garret and Weeks 2013, 1047–1058). In addition, monitoring users' posts gives remarkable power to a single for-profit online business. No other single media company has ever had such power to shape the opinions and lives more generally, of so many people globally.

The amazing power of Facebook has been shown on many occasions. For example, it is now widely accepted that Obama skilfully used Facebook in mobilising young voters in the 2008 elections (Carr 2008). Facebook has also been credited—or blamed—for starting the 2011 'Arab Spring' (Vargas 2012), a significant political upheaval with ongoing wide-ranging consequences for a number of Arabic countries and the broader world. The Tahrir Square revolt in Egypt has been called the 'Facebook revolution.' The security forces beating, and subsequent death, of young Egyptian Khaled Mohamed Said was publicised through the Facebook page *Kullena Khaled Said* ('We are all Khaled Said') produced by a Google marketing executive Wael Ghonim on 8 June 2010 (Ghonim 2012). It quickly gained a large Facebook following and helped fuel growing discontent in Egypt in the lead-up to the Tahrir Square protests in 2011. It took less than 3 weeks of demonstrations to overthrow a dictatorship of 30 years. Do these examples provide evidence that social media have democratic potential or are these simply instances of an artful use of their wide reach for specific political purposes? Potentially it is both, and the power of Facebook is growing at a remarkable rate. Everyone seems to be on Facebook; not just individuals but also common interest groups, sports clubs, businesses, universities and political parties. To not be on Facebook is to barely exist!

It is hard to say whether the communication revolution mediated through the internet and social media is bringing us any closer to a truly inclusive participatory democracy. It has been argued that internet-based social media represent an unprecedented opportunity for grassroots democracy. In *The Assault on Reason*, Al Gore (2007) bemoans the influence of the 30-second television sound-bite, with its emphasis on personalities and the superficial. Perhaps Gore envisaged something like Zuckerberg's idea of a Facebook utopia where everyone is engaged, socially connected and has a public voice, when he said that 'the Internet is perhaps the greatest source of hope for re-establishing an open communication environment in which the conversation of democracy can flourish' (Gore 2007, 260). However, it is unclear whether the new information technologies and social media spell a new equality of public voice. As social media become mainstream, the leader-followers and author-consumer formations are likely to be perpetuated. The large-scale use and abuse of social media is likely to reflect the distribution of power in society rather than heralding a profound social change (Curran et al. 2012). Those who possess political power directly through political office, or indirectly through wealth or celebrity, are likely to dominate social media.

The Death of Expertise?

In his younger years, when Author 2 studied computer programming on a clunky school computer circa 1980, there was a joke circulated about an amazing 'new' information storage device that required no electricity, was easy to use, was robust and portable, and which could be 'opened' at any position. It was called Built-in Orderly Organized Knowledge, or BOOK for short. Much rubbish has been printed over the years since the first book rolled off the Gutenberg press. To take just one example, an incredible 5000 books have been written about the doubts over the authorship of Shakespeare's plays, all based on scant evidence, since no one questioned the authorship of his plays (at least in print) until more than 200 years after his death (Bryson 2007). The filter of time and the common sense and professionalism of librarians means that hardly any of these books are to be found in your local library. Generally, books that have stood the test of time can be trusted but can we say the same for digital information? In the post-print, digital age, we are swimming in an ocean of information—factual or otherwise—all available in an instant, anytime or place, with a swipe of a finger. It is hard to stay focused. The attention span of even the 'official learners' such as university students is becoming shorter. And why bother to learn when Google knows everything and is always with us, sharing its endless online repository of sources in a split second? In a recent book dramatically titled *The Death of Expertise*, Tom Nichols (2017, 2), a professor of national security affairs at the US Naval War College, argues that 'never have so many people had so much access to so much knowledge and yet have been so resistant to learning anything.' We do hope he is wrong on the last count.

In a highly individualistic country such as the United States, the lack of trust in experts is hardly new. In the early part of the nineteenth century, French sociologist Alexis de Tocqueville (2014, Chap. 1) noted that 'The practise of Americans leads their minds to other habits, to fixing the standard of their judgement in themselves alone' and that '[...] they are constantly brought back to their own reason as the most obvious and proximate source of truth.' In a democracy where 'all men are created equal,' people may feel that all opinions are created equal as well and deserving of equal respect regardless of their information and knowledge base. Physicist and science broadcaster Brian Cox[3] (2011) puts the issue thus:

> The problem with today's world is that everyone believes they have a right to express their opinion and have others listen to it. The correct statement of individual rights is that everyone has the right to an opinion, but crucially, that opinion can be roundly ignored and even made fun of, particularly if it is demonstrably nonsense.

The Trump era, starting with the election of a poorly informed science denier, and continuing through his evidence-ignoring and experts-shunning policymaking, may be a harbinger of the veritable age of post-rationality. The WWW has supercharged the demise of expertise; people can now scan the internet to find the information they desire, discover others who share and reinforce their view, and anoint themselves 'experts.' In other words, the internet simultaneously provides these people with a mouth-piece as well a platform where their opinion can be legitimised. As much as it is great to have access to plentiful sources of information, it is also a serious problem if we cannot evaluate the accuracy of what we find or appraise the credentials of the source. Anonymous posts and blogs mean that anyone can argue anything under a semblance, or pretence, of legitimate expertise and yet the true experts are not merely doubted, but there seems to be positive hostility towards them. According to Nichols (2014), we are entering 'a Google-fuelled, Wikipedia-based, blog-sodden collapse of any division between professionals and laymen, students and teachers.' He lamented a 'rejection of science and rationality, which are the foundations of Western civilization itself.' Our civilisation and its technological primacy are based on science and reasoned argument—to discard them is to dismantle the civilisation itself.

The internet has also democratised review and assessment. Why trust the opinion of a single person, however well qualified, when we can weigh up the thoughts of a hundred? A British wine critic and journalist, recently complained that she had 'gone from being a unique provider of information to having to fight for attention' (Fischer 2015). Peer review of everything—cars, films, restaurants, hotels, wine, books, you name it—has replaced the considered opinion of professionals. Sometimes this can be helpful but the sheer volume of 'noise' may make it impossible to come to any reliable conclusion. This may be yet another example where quantity trumps quality.

Traditional media are often compliant in the rise of misinformation and poorly informed opinions. In the interest of balance, a TV show, especially on public television, may be compelled to present both (political) sides of an argument. While this may sound fair, reasonable and egalitarian, often it gives voice to those who ignore the available evidence and choose to align with the 'alternative facts.' The climate change debate is a case in point: over 97 per cent of published, peer-reviewed science papers support the view that humans are causing global warming (Cook et al. 2013), yet climate change sceptics get considerable media space.

Two US psychologists, Kruger and Dunning (1999), have given their name to an effect known since antiquity: fools are too foolish to know they are fools, and are therefore more confident in their opinions. The Dunning-Kruger effect means that those most strident in their views are often the least well informed on the issue, while the well informed are likely to be hesitant since they are aware of what they don't know. William Shakespeare expressed the idea in *As You Like It*: 'The fool doth think he is wise, but the wise man knows himself to be a fool.' In a recent interview, renowned American astrophysicist and science populariser Neil deGrasse Tyson expressed his concern over politicians who make momentous policy decisions while ignoring crucial scientific evidence (ABC 2017).

Our complex modern society needs experts. Even though they often disagree with each other, experts are the right people to inform democratic discussion. Debate used to be primarily between experts who followed well-known rules about what constitutes legitimate evidence. Frequently, these debates resembled a jousting match in jargon that excluded the lay person. However, this is changing. Academics and experts are no longer in the ivory towers of their abstractions and concepts but having to argue their case among non-elites. But if we disregard them completely, we descend into a free-for-all wrestling match with no rules, and that sort of slugfest will have no conclusion and no positive real-life outcome.

* * *

Many people may feel that in the high-tech world of the twenty-first century, the conditions are ripe for both global democracy and Orwellian surveillance-based tyranny. The amazing technologies at our disposal can be used and abused in many different ways. We need to think about it and discuss it through established democratic channels, rather than leaving the market to determine our future. In our super-connected world, democratic deliberation is more possible than ever—but is that what we're actually doing with the omnipresent social media and other communication platforms?

The pace of technological and in its wake, inevitably, social change is faster than ever, making the job of crystal-ball gazers all the more difficult. Rather than asking what we want the future to be—because we may not be able to even imagine its possibilities in decades, let alone centuries to come—perhaps we should focus on what we do not want our societies to become. For example, are we concerned about surveillance by governments and creepy individualised marketing? Do we want a world where our every move is monitored and where our lives are increasingly de-naturalised as we learn, communicate, work, love and seek entertainment in virtual reality, in front of ever smaller screens, rather than in interaction and collaboration with flesh-and-blood people? Neurologists are already discussing the effect new technology is having on the way our brains are wired (Carr 2010; Greenfield 2015). Dazzled by new technologies and overloaded by information, our critical faculties may be dulled, rather than enhanced.

In a recent interview for Australian public television (ABC 2017), Neil deGrasse Tyson summarised the main problem we have discussed in this chapter thus:

> [...] I think the internet landed in our lap and we all celebrated the access to information, but I don't think we foresaw what are the consequences of

it, which is, with brilliant search engines, you can have whatever idea, however fringy it is, type it into the search engine and you will find every other person in the world who has exactly that same idea, giving you false affirmation of it being true. And now you say, 'We are true and everyone else is not,' and what it has done is, it has fractured the world. I don't know that we all saw that coming. So what we need is a tandem way in the educational system to inoculate us against being distracted by false information that's out there. This should be a fundamental part of what it is to be educated, being able to judge what is true and what is not.

Notes

1. Originally broadcast on ABC TV in 1974, quoted by Robinson (2017). A. C. Clarke (1917–2008) was a pre-eminent British science-fiction and non-fiction author who envisaged many future technologies, including communication satellites and the internet.
2. Uber and its kin are still banned in a number of European countries, parts of the US and India, and are heavily restricted in Japan and Taiwan.
3. Brain Cox was once a band member of Dare and D:Ream, and is now a professor of particle physics at the University of Manchester and presenter of popular science programmes for BBC TV and radio.

Bibliography

ABC. 2013. Australia Becoming Smartphone Addicted: Report, Peter Ryan, *The World Today*, 13 February 2013, Australian Broadcasting Corporation (ABC) Radio National. Available at http://www.abc.net.au/news/2013-02-13/australia-becoming-smartphone-addicted-report/4516938

ABC. 2017. Interview with Neil deGrasse Tyson, Astrophysicist. *Lateline*, ABC TV, 6 June 2017.

Battersby, Lucy. 2017. News Corp Guts Photography Departments Amid Job Cuts at City Tabloids. *The Sydney Morning Herald*, 11 April 2017. Accessed 22 June 2017. http://www.smh.com.au/business/media-and-marketing/news-corp-guts-photography-departments-amid-jobs-cuts-at-city-tabloids-20170406-gvfdu9.html

Berners-Lee, Tim. 1989. Information Management: A Proposal. Accessed on 29 May 2017. https://www.w3.org/History/1989/proposal.html

Bryson, Bill. 2007. *Shakespeare: The World as Stage*. New York: Harper Collins.

Carr, David. 2008. How Obama Tapped Into Social Networks' Power. *The New York Times*, 9 November 2008.

Carr, Nicholas. 2010. *The Shallows: What the Internet is Doing to Our Brains*. New York: W. W. Norton & Company.

CBS. 2016. President-elect Speaks to a Divided Country. *60 Minutes*, CBS TV, 13 November 2016. Script. Accessed 22 June 2017. http://www.cbsnews.com/news/60-minutes-donald-trump-family-melania-ivanka-lesley-stahl/

Cerf, Vinton, Yogen Dalal, and Carl Sunshine. 1974. Specification of Internet Transmission Control Program (Request for Comment 675). Accessed 29 May 2017. https://tools.ietf.org/pdf/rfc675.pdf

Cook, John, et al. 2013. Quantifying the Consensus on Anthropogenic Global Warming in the Scientific Literature. *Environmental Research Letters* 8: 024024.

Cox, Brain. 2011. Interview—Prof Brain Cox and Robin Ince. *The List*, 24 March 2011. Accessed 22 June 2017. https://www.list.co.uk/article/33462-interview-prof-brian-cox-and-robin-ince/

Curran, James, Natalie Fenton, and Des Freedman. 2012. *Misunderstanding the Internet*. Abingdon, UK: Routledge.

Del Vicario, Michela, Alessandro Bessi, Fabiana Zollo, Fabio Petroni, Antonio Scala, Guido Caldarelli, H. Eugene Stanley, and Walter Quattrociocchi. 2015. The Spreading of Misinformation Online. *Proceedings of the National Academy of Sciences of the USA* 113: 554–559.

eMarketer. 2016. Digital Ad Spending to Surpass TV Next Year. *eMarketer.com*, 8 March 2016. Accessed 22 June 2017. https://www.emarketer.com/Article/Digital-Ad-Spending-Surpass-TV-Next-Year/1013671?ecid=NL1001

Farrelly, Elizabeth. 2015. What Life Will Be Like in the Year 2055. *Virgin Inflight Magazine*, November 2015.

Fischer, Bill. 2015. The End of Expertise. *Harvard Business Review*, 19 October 2015. Accessed 25 June 2017. https://hbr.org/2015/10/the-end-of-expertise

Garret, R.K., and B.E. Weeks. 2013. The Promise and Peril of Real-time Corrections to Political Misconception. *Proceedings of the 2013 Conference on Computer Supported Cooperative Work*, ACM, New York.

Ghonim, Wael. 2012. *Revolution 2.0—The Power of the People is Greater than the People in Power: A Memoir*. New York: Houghton Mifflin.

Giles, Jim. 2005. Internet Encyclopaedias Go Head to Head. *Nature* 438: 900–901.

Goldstuck, Arthur. 2007. Legends from a Small Country. Accessed 30 May 2017. http://thoselegends.blogspot.com.au/2007/09/cleaner-polishes-off-patient.html

Gore, Al. 2007. *The Assault on Reason*. London, New York and Berlin: Bloomsbury.

Gottfried, Jeffrey, and Elisa Shearer. 2016. News Use Across Social Media Platforms. Pew Research Center. Accessed 1 June 2017. http://www.journalism.org/2016/05/26/news-use-across-social-media-platforms-2016/

Graham, Jefferson. 2017. Hillary Clinton—Tech has to Fix Fake News. *USA Today*, 31 May 2017. Accessed 22 June 2017. https://www.usatoday.com/story/tech/talkingtech/2017/05/31/hrc-tech-has-fix-fake-news/102357904/

Greenfield, Susan. 2004. *Tomorrow's People: How 21st Century Technology is Changing the Way We Think and Feel*. London: Penguin.

———. 2015. *Mind Change: How Digital Technologies are Leaving Their Mark on Our Brains*. New York: Random House.

Gromov, Gregory. 1995. Roads and Crossroads of the Internet History. Accessed on 29 May 2017. http://history-of-internet.com/history_of_internet.pdf

Hosanagar, Kartik. 2016. Blame the Echo Chamber on Facebook. But Blame Yourself, Too. *Wired Opinion*. Accessed 30 May 2017. https://www.wired.com/2016/11/facebook-echo-chamber/

Jenkin, Matthew. 2015. Tablets Out, Imagination In: The Schools That Shun Technology. *The Guardian*, 2 December 2015. Accessed 22 June 2017. https://www.theguardian.com/teacher-network/2015/dec/02/schools-that-ban-tablets-traditional-education-silicon-valley-london

Keynes, John Maynard. 1931. Economic Possibilities for Our Grandchildren. In *Essays in Persuasion*. London: Macmillan.

Kolhatkar, Sheelah. 2017. Is Socially Responsible Capitalism Losing? *The New Yorker*, 5 June 2017. Accessed 22 June 2017. http://www.newyorker.com/magazine/2017/06/05/is-socially-responsible-capitalism-losing

Kruger, Justin, and David Dunning. 1999. Unskilled and Unaware of It: How Difficulties in Recognizing One's Own Incompetence Lead to Inflated Self-assessments. *Journal of Personality and Social Psychology* 77: 1121–1134.

Kucharski, A. 2016. Post-truth: Study Epidemiology of Fake News. *Nature* 540: 525.

Mill, John Stuart. 1970 [1848]. *Principles of Political Economy with Some of Their Applications to Social Philosophy*, Books IV and V, ed. and with an introduction by D. Winch. Harmondsworth: Penguin Classics.

Nichols, Tom. 2014. The Death of Expertise. *The Federalist*, 17 January 2014. Accessed 4 June 2017. http://thefederalist.com/2014/01/17/the-death-of-expertise/

———. 2017. *The Death of Expertise*. New York: Oxford University Press.

Nickerson, Raymond S. 1998. Confirmation Bias: A Ubiquitous Phenomenon in Many Guises. *Review of General Psychology* 2: 175–220.

OECD. 2015. Students, Computers and Learning: Making the Connection. *Organization for Economic Cooperation and Development Report*, 15 September 2015. Accessed 4 June 2017. http://www.oecd.org/education/students-computers-and-learning-9789264239555-en.htm

Oxford Dictionary. 2017. *Oxforddictionary.com*. Accessed 22 June 2017. https://en.oxforddictionaries.com/definition/post-truth

Putnam, Robert. 2000. *Bowling Alone: The Collapse and Revival of American Community*. New York: Simon and Schuster.

Remnick, David. 2016. Obama Reckons with Trump Presidency. *The New Yorker*, 28 November 2016. Accessed 22 June 2017. http://www.newyorker.com/magazine/2016/11/28/obama-reckons-with-a-trump-presidency

Riesman, David, Nathan Glazer, and Reuel Denney. 1950. *The Lonely Crowd: A Study of the Changing American Character*. New Haven and London: Yale University Press.

Robinson, Andrew. 2017. Technology: He Wrote the Future. *Nature* 541: 286–288. Accessed 22 June 2017. http://www.nature.com/nature/journal/v541/n7637/full/541286a.html

Russell, Bertrand. 1935. *In Praise of Idleness and Other Essays*. London: Allen & Unwin Ltd.

Samaan, Roy. 2015. Airbnb, Rising Rent, and the Housing Crisis in Los Angeles. *Los Angeles Alliance for the New Economy (LAANE) Report*, March 2015. Accessed 30 May 2017. http://www.laane.org/wp-content/uploads/2015/03/AirBnB-Final.pdf

Scholtz, Trebor. 2017. *Uberworked and Underpaid: How Workers are Disrupting the Digital Economy*. Cambridge, UK: Polity Press.

Silverman, Craig. 2016. This Analysis Shows How Viral Fake Election News Stories Outperformed Real News on Facebook. *BuzzFeed News*, 17 November 2016. Accessed 1 June 2017. https://www.buzzfeed.com/craigsilverman/viral-fake-election-news-outperformed-real-news-on-facebook?utm_term=.jfqkAbmmr#.gblb7ryyR

Slattery, Claire. 2017. Fairfax Media Announces Further Job Losses, Slashes $30 million from Editorial Budget. *ABC News*. Accessed 22 June 2017. http://

www.abc.net.au/news/2017-04-05/fairfax-media-announces-further-job-losses-amid-$30m-budget-cut/8419584

Tocqueville, Alexis de 2014 [1840]. *Democracy in America*, Vol. II. Translated by Henry Reeve, 1899. ebooks@Adelaide, University of Adelaide Library. Accessed 19 June 2017. https://ebooks.adelaide.edu.au/t/tocqueville/alexis/democracy/complete.html

Vargas, Jose Antonio. 2012. Spring Awakening: How an Egyptian Revolution Began on Facebook. *The New York Times*, Sunday Book Review, 17 February 2012. Accessed 30 May 2017. http://www.nytimes.com/2012/02/19/books/review/how-an-egyptian-revolution-began-on-facebook.html?_r=0

WEF. 2013. Digital Wildfires in a Hyperconnected World. *World Economic Forum (WEF) Report on Global Risks*. Accessed 30 May 2017. http://reports.weforum.org/global-risks-2013/risk-case-1/digital-wildfires-in-a-hyperconnected-world/

Wilde, Oscar. 1912 [1899]. *The Soul of Man under Socialism*. London: Arthur L. Humphreys.

Wong, Julia Carrie, Sam Levin, and Olivia Solon. 2016. Bursting the Facebook Bubble: We Asked Voters on the Left and Right to Swap Feeds. *The Guardian*, 16 November 2016. Accessed 22 June 2017. https://www.theguardian.com/us-news/2016/nov/16/facebook-bias-bubble-us-election-conservative-liberal-news-feed

Wright, Erik Olin. 2012. Transforming Capitalism Through Real Utopias (American Sociological Association 2011 Presidential Address). *American Sociological Review* 78: 1–25.

8

Into a Bright (Post-capitalist) Future?

[…] The mind is not satisfied with merely tracing the laws of the movement; it cannot but ask the further question, to what goal? Towards what ultimate point is society tending by its industrial progress?

J. S. Mill (1970/1848, 111)

A map of the world that does not include Utopia is not worth even glancing at, for it leaves out the one country at which Humanity is always landing. […]

O. Wilde (1912, 43)

Since the collapse of communism in the late twentieth century, capitalism, and in particular its unfettered neo-liberal variant, has reigned supreme. Economic rationality, the dollars-and-cents argument, became the final word in public and political discourse. The social dislocation and increasing inequality wrought by neo-liberalism have created an undercurrent of discontent that has had major political consequences, particularly in the Anglosphere, but also globally. Communism has been called 'the God that failed' (Koestler et al. 1949), but twenty-first-century capitalism has left many feeling similarly disappointed and cynical (Ferguson and Johnson 2010).

V. Colic-Peisker, A. Flitney, *The Age of Post-Rationality*,
https://doi.org/10.1007/978-981-10-6259-9_8

In this book, we have proposed that the Western rulebook has become heavily skewed towards wealth accumulation, on a social and individual level, and that this can bear a heavy cost (pun not intended) on our society and the natural environment, threatening our very survival as a species. Given that the Western world and the Anglosphere as its global avant-garde has seen itself, for several centuries, as an eminently rational civilisation based on free thinking, science and democratic dialogue, we articulate the current crisis as 'the age of post-rationality.' We argue the West is in need of a new enlightenment through a gradual change of the public discourse and a broadly conceived, consensus-based policy reform. In the preceding chapters, we analysed specific aspects of Western culture, economy and technology that have reached their hyper-mode and slipped into a terrain of irrationality.

The West has tended to depict its modern (post-Renaissance) history as a near linear progression—though with some significant hiccups along the way such as the slave trade, inquisitions, Nazism and extreme varieties of communism. More recently, there has been a loss of self-confidence that the future will bring better times. Technological and economic progress is beyond doubt, but its social and environmental consequences have been largely neglected, denied or misrepresented. We could also ask about moral progress: is society getting 'better' —and what should 'better' actually mean? The ruling dogma has been: all is good while we can quantify our progress, usually as GDP per capita. We propose this is a root cause of the current Western woes.

As we argued in the previous chapters, the relationship of the West with the Rest has been a several centuries long history of ruthless domination, but this seems to be changing as we move into the 'Asian century.' This shift in global power will no doubt require a significant change in our thinking and perspective. The 'last wave' of globalisation has been largely based on the penetration of Western capital and with it the culture of capitalism into the rest of the world, including its most remote corners, by means other than military conquest and colonialism. This successful expansion of Western capitalism and the creation of global capitalism had many unintended consequences.

A decrease in global inequality between the West and the Rest[1] (Roser 2017) has been complemented by rising inequality within Western countries (Piketty 2014). Part of the problem in the West is the disappearance of the decently paid working-class jobs which have been 'outsourced' to countries where labour is much cheaper. Not only are most consumer goods produced in China, but the West is also transporting some of its rubbish to China to be recycled there (ABC 2017)! Western workers have often protested against the loss of their jobs to foreign countries and governments have cried crocodile tears about it, but employers have never hesitated to follow economic rationality at the expense of society. The most pressing concern for any business is to keep the shareholders happy. Donald Trump's 2016 presidential campaign exploited the concerns of the (entitled, native, white) American working class, but it is unclear how can a president, or even the whole of the government, give them back their jobs, unless they are ready to seriously shake up the basic ethos of capitalism: capital must seek to maximise profit, unconcerned about social or ethical issues.

At the same time, immigrants from developing countries fill the low-skilled service jobs in Western cities and low-skilled agriculture and other food industry jobs outside cities. For more than half a century, foreign workers, both legal and illegal, work in jobs the natives of the Western countries shun (Colic-Peisker and Tilbury 2006). This is connected with another unintended consequence of capitalist globalisation: the unprecedented global mobility of people, including the virtually unstoppable 'irregular migration' (Donato and Massey 2016). This mobility has been enabled by the synergy of the internet communication revolution, the increased ease and affordability of transportation, and deep inequalities in levels of security and opportunity between the West and the Rest.

These two developments—the rise in inequality in the developed countries and the rise in global mobility, especially post-GFC—are at the core of the current wave of popular dissatisfaction in the West that engendered Brexit, Donald Trump as the US President, and the growing power of right-wing parties in Western countries whose ideological platform is anti-globalisation, anti-immigration and 'economic nationalism.' This, paradoxically, leaves the proponents of capitalist—and according to many, neo-colonial—globalisation to be seen as advocating a left or centre-left position. In other words, in order to oppose the populist anti-globalisation and isolationism, left-leaning parties find themselves arguing pro-globalisation. In any case, the genie of globalisation cannot be put back into the bottle. Cutting global communication and physical mobility pathways is not an option. It would require draconian authoritarian measures which we hope, in spite of some recent surprises,[2] will not get electoral support in the West.[3]

The dogmatic rule of economic rationality, bolstered by globalisation, has to be moderated by serious considerations of the social and environmental cost of the neo-liberal capitalist version of progress. Whatever the method of reforming neo-liberal globalisation, it can only be done on a global scale, through politically re-imagining of globalisation as responsible cosmopolitanism. This is as utopian as it is necessary, given that we are on an unsustainable course. The West should lead this process and indeed be compelled to globally redistribute some of its power. Such rational-utopian loss of power leading to a more equitable world is vastly preferable to a dystopian and ultimately irrational struggle for technological, economic and geo-political dominance while the planet, our common home, sinks into irreversible environmental destruction based in adversarial *Realpolitik*. If survival of the human species and its sophisticated civilisation is a rational goal, then this would be a rational course of action. Yet, it is unlikely. Our governments follow the old script of economic rationality, but in a larger scheme of things they do not act rationally.

The main problem with neo-liberal globalisation seems to be that we have become its hostages entangled in a 'prisoner's dilemma' (see below): the (neo-liberal) imperative of globalisation is the central argument for the status quo. In other words, nothing can change because everyone needs to change at once: we cannot unilaterally increase taxes, because capital will escape elsewhere; we cannot tackle climate change because it will 'damage our economy but not help the earth' unless other countries do the same; being less than ruthless in cutting costs (e.g., reducing staff or shifting work to cheaper countries) will make a business 'globally uncompetitive.' Therefore, it is wholesale global change, or nothing. Political realists say that under the current rules of engagement, this almost inevitably means 'nothing.'

The December 2015, Paris summit on climate change offered some lofty promises about global action, but in May 2017, the US President Trump dismissed it and promised to pull out of the accord and re-invigorate the US coal industry. The miners of West Virginia are currently optimistic about their future. However, is there a long-term future in such a reckless dismissal of science and the reviving of a dying industry for short-term political gain? Examples of short-termism abound in Western politics. Are Western constituencies able to see and vote beyond such a close horizon in spite of the political rhetoric scaring them into it by alarmist economic argument: jobs will be lost, economic growth will stall, and so on?

The Prisoners' Dilemma: All That We Could Do If Others Did Too

John Forbes Nash[4] believed that beings from other planets spoke to him and gave him insights into complex mathematical problems. At one point he thought he was the emperor of Antarctica. But Nash was indeed a mathematical genius whose 1950 PhD thesis, a mere 28 pages in the nascent field of 'game theory,' contained profound insights for which he was later awarded the Nobel Prize in Economics. One archetypical 'game' in the theory is known as the 'prisoners' dilemma.' The two protagonists in the game—let's call them Angela and Donald—must decide on a strategy without knowing what the other player is going to do. Their choice is to be nice ('cooperate') or to stab the other person in the back ('defect'). Angela reasons thus: if Donald cooperates I gain quite a bit if I also cooperate, but I get even more if I defect; if Donald defects, then I better not be a patsy and cooperate—I am better off if I defect as well. Therefore Angela, being a self-interested specimen of *homo economicus*, decides that defection is the best strategy regardless of what Donald does. Donald is in the same position and reasons the same way. The result, the *Nash equilibrium*, is that both defect, which is a pity since they *both* would have been better off if they both cooperated. The result is a dilemma, some form of which, usually in its many player version, is responsible for much of the misery in the world.[5]

Real-life approximations to the prisoners' dilemma abound: in tackling global climate change, we would all benefit from cooperating, but unilateral action has a cost and little benefit. Therefore, it seems more advantageous to be selfish and do nothing. In elite sporting competition, all athletes would be better off if no one took performance-enhancing substances, but individuals are worse off if they abstain while others use drugs.

Is the *homo economicus* behaviour, starting from the competitive assumption that life is a zero-sum game (if you gain, I lose), our destiny? There are other imperatives of human behaviour. In an experiment now famous among game theorists, Robert Axelrod, a professor of political science at the University of Michigan, ran a tournament between different computer algorithms for playing prisoners' dilemma. The winning programme was called 'tit-for-tat': it started out being cooperative towards all opponents and would only retaliate if an opponent defected. It never beat any individual opponent but did best overall by being better at eliciting cooperation (Axelrod and Hamilton 1981; Axelrod 1984). Axelrod's conclusion was: don't be envious of others' success and try to undermine them, but simply try to do well enough for yourself. While there are wise people who follow this principle, most of us suffer from competitive status anxiety and the feeling of relative deprivation.

Can We Design the Future?

Trying to plan and control the future is part of being human, but especially so for modern 'Western' humanity. We erased God and fate from the equation and took destiny into our own hands, considering our social future the collective product of human endeavour. Given the extent of global economic and political entanglement, nation-states cannot plan their own futures in isolation—they are caught in a planetary scale prisoners' dilemma. The global future is our shared global responsibility, though the dominant West bears the largest portion of the responsibility.

Throughout the ages, astrologers, seers, palmists and witch-doctors have claimed the ability to peer into the inky blackness of the future. With ever-faster technological and social change, we remain eager to gaze into the 'crystal ball.' Governments regularly engage experts to model future policies. Principally, the task of anticipating the path of unborn time falls upon economists. The specialisation of 'futurists' emerged in the second half of the twentieth century, trying to model future scenarios beyond economic number-crunching. Utopian and dystopian visions abound: euphoric expectations of a soon-to-be super-convenient high-tech heaven compete with dark warnings about environmental cataclysm, the third world war and the end of the human species (e.g., see Greenfield 2004; Farrelly 2015; Hamilton 2010; Lovelock 2009). Streeck et al. (2016, 170), for example, see a future anomic society with decaying institutions and successive, deepening crises and conflicts.

In presenting our case studies in post-rationality, we do not seek to join the 'decline and downfall of the West' camp. We call it 'crisis' only reluctantly; as discussed in the introduction, it is possible to argue some sort of crisis at any time. However, we do see the current global developments—technological, economic, social, political—as a challenging time of transition. A rational debate about this transition is predicated upon upholding the best Western traditions of democracy, dialogue and tolerance, against the clearly existing Western legacy of power politics, violence and intolerance (Russell 1935).

Even though some models and future projections claim scientific backing, strictly speaking the future is not a province of science. Prognoses, even short-term ones, are usually wide of the mark. Crises always surprise us, perhaps due to humans' undying optimism? Through a 20-year study, political scientist Philip Tetlock (2005) showed that political analysts, even those—in fact particularly those—who were prominent in the public sphere, have little more predictive ability than a dart throwing monkey. In spite of the deep crisis of European communism during the 1980s, as late as 1988 no political scientist saw it falling into a heap only a year later. Quantification and high-powered mathematics lends economics an aura of scientific legitimacy and their predictions are taken seriously by governments. Yet, in practise, economic predictions have been hilariously poor. International Monetary Fund economist Prakash Loungani (2001, 430) concluded that 'the record of failure to predict recessions is virtually unblemished.' Just prior to the collapse of Lehman Brothers in September 2008, consensus forecasts were that not a single major economy would fall into recession the following year (Ahir and Loungani 2014).[6] Modern society is an extremely complex system; there are many variables we cannot control and causal connections we cannot clearly see.

An important question is: what are the ideological and moral underpinnings of future scenarios that current policies reflect and support? What are the often-unspoken values they project? We are used to thinking about ideologies and values as 'conservative' or 'progressive.' Equality and freedom have been the most sought-after goals of social development, but many argue they are hard to reconcile and nurture side by side. In modern society, equality has become the key battle cry of the political left, and freedom the most prized conservative value. According to many public commentators, these two positions are drifting further and further apart, fortified in their ideological trenches, which weakens democratic dialogue (e.g., Haidt 2017). The recent US presidential election is a prime example of a deeply divided electorate.

A major issue to be reckoned with when considering crisis and social change is a huge social-systemic as well as individual inertia. Even though technology changes faster than ever, the complex and interdependent systems and mechanisms that hold modern society together change only gradually. At a personal level, inertia is embedded in old habits and expectations, and a fear of change. Take travelling to work in a large city. You drive out in the morning somehow hoping, against all available evidence, that the traffic will be better today. A discouraging morning traffic report will not make you consider leaving your car at home and walking to the railway station. So yet again, you end up crawling at below-bicycle speed. If it is a bad day, you are barely faster than a pedestrian. You are frustrated and resent other drivers clogging the roads. You know this is 100 per cent irrational, but you are still annoyed. The satirical publication *The Onion* (Nov 2000) summed it up thus: 'Report: 98 per cent of U.S. commuters favor public transportation for others.'

Sociologists call this effect 'cultural lag': technological, economic and social conditions change faster than the deep 'culture' containing our perceptions, values, customs and habits. A rational, adaptive response to endless traffic jams would be to consider alternatives: walking, cycling or public transport. Rare individualists adopt new practices against the trend, but the majority is stuck in the cultural lag of habitual inertia. Once a critical mass of our significant others change their ways, we will happily jump on the bandwagon. Most of us are followers rather than trend-setters. However, once an issue becomes a crisis, people do take notice and modify their behaviour. There is hope, at least for our car clogged-cities: Melbourne and Sydney passed 'peak car' in the early 2000s, measured by the number of cars per capita. Most European cities are well into declining car usage.

Can We Agree About the 'Good Society'?

Ethical postulates about the 'good life' and 'good society' vary from culture to culture and from individual to individual, but all cultures and religions contain certain universal basics that are there to secure survival. These include respecting human life and cooperating, especially helping the weak. What distinguishes Western ethics is that, over a couple of centuries, we came to value individual autonomy and 'reason' over faith and unquestioned submission to authority.

In the preceding chapters, we proposed that public language in the Anglosphere and to a lesser degree in other affluent Western countries (i.e., continental Europe) is in the straightjacket of economics. There is no consensus about what social changes are desirable and what actually constitutes genuine progress; the closely related but more specific question about where to channel public money is a matter of ongoing, often heated, debate. In this situation, decision makers fall back on evaluating the results of any programme or project by measuring whether they are 'good business.' If it is good for the economy, expressed in dollars and cents, who can argue with it? Our public language reflects the dominant public rationality, which is that of economics.

In his book *Critique of Economic Reason*, French philosopher Andre Gorz (1989) discussed the limits of economic rationality and the possibility of creating a society which rejects the competitive work ethic in favour of an emancipatory ethic of free time. He argued that the economic conception of 'value' is reductive and impoverished. He pleaded for the transformation of work and working time, where productivity gains made possible by technological developments could be used to enhance individual and social life, rather than intensify ruthless economic competition and social division. Nearly 30 years later, the problem remains the same and we can ask where is the increased leisure and social time that improvements in technology and productivity promised long ago?

The 'good for the economy' imperative primarily benefits business interests, but in public policy language, it is usually presented as a 'more jobs' imperative, which is a 'common good.' This justification is usually spurious. In the twenty-first-century West, reducing the number of (decently paid) jobs is actually good for the economy; jobs have migrated to low labour cost countries on a massive scale. At times, the outsourcing of production and services abroad has reached absurd, though still economically rational, levels. For example, salmon caught off the coast of Alaska are frozen, shipped to China, thawed, filleted and sliced up, refrozen and shipped back to the US (NPR 2014). This hollowing out of the workforce is a major reason the disenchanted American working class chose to vote for the 'economic nationalist' Donald Trump.

A unique view on a good society comes from German philosopher G.W. Leibniz[7] (1951) who, in his 1710 *Essays on the Goodness of God, the Freedom of Man and the Origin of Evil*, proposed that we inhabit the 'best of all possible worlds.' If anything better could have been possible, the omnipotent and omnibenevolent God would have created it. The idea was ridiculed by Voltaire, an atheist and *enfant terrible* of the French

Enlightenment. Dr Pangloss, a character in Voltaire's 1759 novel *Candide*, advocated Leibniz's idea, which gave the name to such a world view: 'Panglossian.' Even if you find Leibniz's idea soothing, its fatalism contradicts the dynamic spirit of the modern West, which has been in constant search for improvement, innovation and update.

To make the topic of improving society—beyond the economic imperative and more = better logic—more complicated, influential thinkers have not been able to agree whether it is even possible to improve society by design. Philosopher-economist F. Hayek was adamantly against government intervention in economic and social affairs in an attempt to engineer a better society. He opposed the idea that society is a product of people's intelligent design as the 'fallacy of constructivism' (Hayek 2005) and dismissed visions of a better society as the 'fatal conceit' of intellectuals (Hayek 1988, 27). Instead, he argued that society develops as a 'spontaneous order' or 'catallaxy' through the market mechanism. This earned him a reputation of an apostle of the free market and the admiration of Margaret Thatcher, and many others.

Another esteemed twentieth-century thinker and a colleague of Hayek at the London School of Economics, the philosopher of science Karl Popper, argued against any form of 'historical prophecy' which would try to define a final goal of social development. He based his argument on the premises that the course of history is influenced by the expansion of human knowledge and that this (the expansion of knowledge) is impossible to predict by rational or scientific methods (Popper 1974). Instead, we need to uphold free inquiry and democratic debate, which, according to Popper, is at the heart of rationality (as discussed in Chap. 1).

Popper was opposed to the 'prophet' Karl Marx, whose critique of capitalism adopted an eschatological view of history as a movement towards a final utopian goal. Marx argued that society inevitably changes following the development of the productive forces of society—technology, as we tend to say these days. While it is clear that technology indeed changes society (as discussed in Chap. 7), Marx has been maligned as a simplistic 'technological determinist.' Yet, his 'technologically determined' historical blueprint deserves a second look. According to Marx, and others inspired by him, people can intervene in the process of social change once the technological and economic conditions are ripe. A certain social class, the carrier of progress in a particular historic period (e.g., bourgeoisie in early capitalism), can be the 'midwife of history' but not its parent, its creator. The opposite Hayekian view, however—that social development should be left to the spontaneous forces of the market—can also be seen as deterministic.

In any case, the 'free market' is a concept, an idea and not something that has ever existed in reality; governments have always intervened. A 'dialogical' intervention, in a Popperian sense, through the existing and (hopefully) further improving democratic mechanisms, needs to continue, because it is the only rational response to social challenges. This does not mean that people will agree about what constitutes a good society any day soon; we cannot even agree on whether advertising junk food in children's TV programmes should be banned. We may agree that the 'greatest happiness of the greatest number' is a fine principle, but we also have to agree that it is a purely formal and abstract one; in an extremely diverse society, 'happiness' remains a matter of unending contention. Therefore, the only way forward is to continue the debate and ground it as much as possible in solid evidence and accumulated knowledge. The 'death of expertise' (discussed in Chap. 7) would therefore mean the end of rational public debate.

When discussing social improvement and what it should prioritise, different social positions represent different vantage points. Individual people may live in the same city, or even neighbourhood, but inhabit parallel social universes. Individuals in different social positions have different interests. Those in privileged positions tend to be conservative: social change shaking the social pyramid may cause those on top to fall off or at least to slide downwards. Homeowners cheer when housing prices rise and consider it an improvement, while those who seek to get a foothold in the housing market consider it bad news. The diverging interest and different social vistas are further separated by the effect of internet 'echo chambers' (Chap. 7). Our peculiar social bubbles reinforce our perceptions and views, as well as misconceptions spread through traditional and even more through social media. Such social segmentation and polarisation may be seen as paradoxical at a time when technology allows us to access many varied sources of information and communicate with a multitude of people. However, most people avoid exposing their views to the scrutiny of established facts and the challenge of other people's alternative realities. Arguing about policies as well as the big picture therefore remains a province of politicians and a small caste of public commentators, while ordinary people, although 'super-connected,' are remarkably disengaged from society's big questions.

How (Not) to Change the World

Acting primarily on ideals and values rarely happens in the pragmatic world of daily *Realpolitik*. With the benefit of hindsight, we know that 'value-driven' politics is risky and can bear a high cost for society: Robespierre, Lenin, Hitler, Mao and Pol Pot were all 'idealists' who acted upon a vision of a perfect society. Their shortcuts to paradise, supported (at least initially) by popular acclaim but unchecked and unhindered by effective democratic institutions, ended in rivers of blood.

Twentieth-century communism was the only large-scale and longer-term attempt to build a perfect society from an ideological blueprint. The process was led by a 'political avant-garde,' which climbed on a high moral horse but in reality brutally crushed all political opposition and soon transformed into a corrupt and usually also incompetent oligarchy. For a time, the project of building a communist utopia was supported by the popular majority and considered legitimate: after all, it was about a noble goal of creating a happy state where 'everyone works according to their ability and is rewarded according to their needs.' Virtually, all real-existing communist countries were backward and rural, and starting from a low economic base, they initially succeeded to modernise society. Yet, a century of real-existing socialism reminds us that every 'enlightened' dictatorship soon darkens.

Amidst stiff competition, one of the most power-drunk communist dictators was Romanian Nicolae Ceausescu. In the 1980s, he announced that the final state of communism would be reached by the year 2000. The extraordinary array of repressive policies meant to achieve this goal ranged from a decree limiting the maximum allowed strength of a light bulb in private homes to the banning of contraception and emigration in order to create a large, powerful nation. However, it was obvious that the nation was neither empowered nor enlarged by his rule. Ceausescu's execution, alongside his wife Elena (who was allegedly the brain behind many of his ideas) against a wall in Bucharest on Christmas Day 1989, after a one-hour trial, was one of the most dramatic moments in the disintegration of Eastern European communism.[8] A pre-eminent scholar of global communism commented that 'ghoulish though the event was, for many Romanians it seemed like a Christmas present' (Brown 2009, 544).

Yet, many Chinese revere Mao to this day as a leader who brought stability to China and enabled the waking of the Chinese giant, even though tens of millions perished during his regime, especially during the period of the Cultural Revolution 1966–1976. This brutal attempt to transform the country was replaced by economic liberalisation, resulting in the Chinese economic miracle. The latter, in itself another revolution, was based on a ruthless version of the free market economy that created colossal inequality, while the country still calls itself communist and prisons continue to be crammed with political dissenters. An extreme level of environmental pollution was another sacrifice inflicted on the nation by its visionary leaders (e.g., see The Economist 2017 or Chap. 6). The simultaneous 'one child policy' created a serious gender imbalance. Contemporary China breaks all the political moulds and postulates of political theory. It is an example of an experimental, top-down designed social change based on extreme ideas and policies. Even though some of the Chinese social engineering was successful according to economic criteria—both the country's GDP per capita and global power increased exponentially since the 1980s—there has been an enormous price to pay.

The Democratic Potential for Change

In spite of the dominance of economic criteria in public policy making of Western countries, and especially the Anglosphere, the debate about the values and ideals that should underpin the 'good society' and the way forward is ongoing. The problem is how to achieve a relative consensus and translate the ideals into political action, without every new government undoing progressive policies of the previous one—the US under Trump is the most prominent recent example, but there are many others.

Democracy, however imperfect and slow, has to be the framework of social change, but within this framework, we also need leaders who have courage to uphold values and a vision of social progress—the qualities largely absent among current Western leaders.

In spite of being a declared Marxist, the distinguished twentieth-century historian Eric Hobsbawm (2007, 11) argued that there are few shortcuts in history. In spite of dramatic images of the August 2011 British riots and violent demonstrations in several European countries confronted with 'austerity measures' in the intervening years, revolution is not likely in the affluent West. The Anglolands are even less known for radical, violent revolutions, and this is, fortunately, unlikely to change. Movements such as *Occupy Wall Street* have been fringe affairs that had little effect on the global financial system or global capitalism, more generally. People are attracted to a revolution if they are desperate and feel they have little to lose. A majority of Westerners have much to lose. However, significant minorities have been left behind by neo-liberal globalisation, and popular discontent of various political colours has reached significant proportions over the past years.

Democratic reform remains the only rational-dialogical and non-violent way to change society. Just like gender equality, a vibrant deliberative and participatory democracy is an ideal to strive towards, not something we already have. Yet, piecemeal reform by democratic means is a slow and frustrating process. In our complex and information-overloaded world, we are not confident that politicians represent our interests and equally importantly, that we are represented by the best and most competent people, let alone those most 'principled.' Most of our leaders are concerned primarily with managing their image in the media and keeping their powerful jobs by winning the next elections.

Apart from self-interested politicians, there are various experts with their impenetrable language and vested interests. Back in 1935, Bertrand Russell wrote: 'it is increasingly difficult for ordinary men and women to form an intelligent opinion on political questions, or even to decide whose expert judgment deserves the most respect' (1935, 80–81). Then there are also big corporations ruthlessly seeking profit and manipulative media (most of them also big corporations) peddling inflammatory stories in search of sales. Rising popular discontent is driven by the perception that these 'elites' amassed too much power and that vibrant democracy is not their most important concern. While the elites may be steering society into an uncertain future as they see fit, following their own interests, the 'ordinary people' are kept happy shopping and scrolling through the tiny screens of their smartphones.

As always, it is 'bread and circuses,' only much more of both. In the society ruled by economic rationality, the consumer is more important that the citizen. If the shopping and spending person is 'confident,' both businesses and politicians are happy. 'Consumer confidence' oils the cogs of capitalism. In contrast, a confident citizen is a dust-stirring person who tends to complain, criticise, sign petitions, march in rallies and direct unpleasant questions to those who make decision in her/his name. The hyperactive competitor and consumer pursuing individual goals has little time or energy to be an active citizen who chooses to deliberate and cooperate with others in achieving a common good. Ginsborg (2008) and others suggested that for the participatory democracy to deliver the 'common good' through a rational debate, the citizen must be strengthened at the expense of the consumer, but also at the expense of lobbyists representing powerful private interests.

In spite of the usual reference to 'market democracy,' consumer capitalism and democracy may not be natural companions, let alone allies. In fact, they are becoming increasingly uncomfortable bedfellows. The US, often claiming to be the 'leader of the free world,' has been a concerning precedent of (un)democratic development, even before President Trump took the stage. To plutocracy and popular apathy, deep ideological divisions among those who are not happy have been added. Hobsbawm (2007, 5) expressed doubt in the substance of twenty-first-century representative democracy. He argued that this 'sacred cow of vulgar Western political discourse' is in crisis. He was especially scathing about America: 'In recent US rhetoric the word [democracy] had lost all contact with reality.'

Yet, however imperfect, a 'mature' democracy is vastly preferable to a massacre in the central square. At this point in the neo-liberal, post-GFC era, it may not be unwarranted to propose that a majority of Western citizens want a rational, democratic debate about social goals that transcend a sheer battle for economic profits and more money in their pockets. A democratic discussion could intensify, as the grassroots input is further enabled by the internet and social media—provided we find efficient ways to deal with the perils associated with the virtual internet jungle, as discussed in Chap. 7. Even though some authors see the 1960–1970s as the golden era of democracy (Reich 2008; Ginsborg 2008), today's full literacy, higher than ever levels of formal education, free media and nearly universal access to the internet in the Western world constitute best-ever conditions for democracy. The sheer mass of (mis)information on the internet may muddy the waters and the future may be full of surprises, but we should act to shape it rather than accepting to be passive victims of the Hayek's 'spontaneous order'—or someone else's will.

Fig. 8.1 Pont du Gard, a Roman aqueduct in the south of France built in 50 AD

Who Wants to Change the World?

What social forces are likely to drive the reforms we seem to need—for example, in achieving environmental sustainability and healthy levels of equality? In his 1969 book *Marshall, Marx and Modern Times*,C. Kerr argued that there are two groups that tend to challenge the [Western developed] society: the 'underclass,' those impoverished and underprivileged who are 'an inevitable but not fatal minority'; and the 'outer-class,' a more formidable, but still not a fatal force, consisting of critical intellectuals. All other social groups, according to Kerr, such as workers, managers, leaders, white-collar employees and self-employed, are the 'inner-class' who compete for social rewards within the framework of the existing social order which they, unlike the underclass and outer-class, accept as fully legitimate. Kerr argued that the underclass and outer-class did not have the combined strength to challenge existing society, except with the support of some dominant groups within the inner-class—which was, in his view, a fairly hopeless prospect. This may be seen as an early version of the end of history thesis: simply, there was no social force that would be interested in bringing down capitalism.

Joseph Schumpeter (2009), one of the most prominent economists of the twentieth century, had a different idea about what the future of capitalism may hold. Like Kerr, he also believed that most intellectuals are critical and even antagonistic towards capitalism and the idea of unfettered entrepreneurship. They are the class that can stand up for the interest of other groups and the class that is likely to lead social discontent and protest. Writing in the 1950s, Schumpeter believed that capitalism would naturally evolve towards industrial democracy and a version of socialism opposed to thriving entrepreneurship. Yet, his predictions did not materialise; if anything, the opposite happened with the advent of neo-liberalism.

In his book *The Culture of Contentment*, J. K. Galbraith (1993) reaffirmed Kerr's thesis with an unhidden regret. He argued that American society was underpinned by a contented majority (what Kerr called the 'inner-class') which supported the status quo. According to Galbraith, since the Second World War, the self-congratulatory ruling classes (big business and politicians) had been joined by the comfortable middle class who are not going to vote for reform if it is likely to disturb their comfort, even if it is just a small tax reform that would take few dollars out of their pockets. In Australia, no recent government dares to tackle the issue of middle-class welfare in various forms, the most debated among which are the preferential tax treatment of investment properties ('negative gearing'), capital gains, the tax-free status of the primary residence regardless of its market value and tax-free retirement savings. However, the debate about these reforms is recurring more and more often, and the voices of dissatisfaction seem louder than before.

A couple of years before his death in 2002, French sociologist Pierre Bourdieu[9] got out of his academic ivory tower, started writing prose for non-academic audiences and gave a number of lectures around the world, urging his outer-class colleagues to 'intervene in the world of politics' through an 'intellectual engagement' (Bourdieu 2003, 13). He thought that intellectuals needed to 'help to create the social conditions for the collective production of realistic utopias' (Bourdieu 2003, 21). Many other public intellectuals and activists have worked tirelessly and passionately for various worthy causes: saving old-growth forests, banning whaling, fighting cruelty to animals, stopping corruption, restoring the dignity of the homeless or occupying Wall Street. Yet, as Kerr (1969) suggested, a real change in society can only take place if a critical mass of citizens, the 'inner-class,' are mobilised. Is something like that likely to happen any time soon?

In recent years, Western sociologists started talking about a new class, the 'precariat' (Standing 2011). The old blue-collar 'proletariat,' the fully employed, respectable working class earning a living wage is gone as a political force to be reckoned with, as globalisation and economic restructuring destroyed their jobs. Left in the wake of economic restructuring, there are now millions of casual workers without secure employment, homeownership or career prospects. Starting from the 1980s, the old proletariat has been replaced by a massive precariat, a class-in-the-making, created by neo-liberal reforms such as deregulation of labour markets, privatisation of public assets and functions—from the postal service to prisons—and weakening of the welfare state's mechanisms of social solidarity. The precariat is a somewhat unpredictable political force, which may reject neo-liberalism and globalisation but also a welfare-state-based social democracy. The precariat may be insecure and demoralised, but it is not ostracised and disrespected in the way the (usually racialised) underclass is. It is therefore not likely to violently rebel, burning cars and smashing shops, but it may become a force of new populism. The disappearance of the reasonably well-off working class and the shrinkage of the well-off middle class have created an 'hourglass labour market' (Allen 2014), with well-paid professionals on the one end and the precariat on the other. Such an imbalance is not likely to last. By definition, the content 'inner-class' must constitute a majority in order for the status quo to be preserved.

Cultural observers and sociologists diagnosed that many people felt they had had enough of the rat race by the time they reach their middle age. 'Sea-changers' and 'tree-changers' are now well-established phenomena. Often, this is an early (semi)retirement, but sometimes young people opt out. Such non-systemic behaviour attracts pity or disapproval but also envy. Is there a new trend, a bandwagon more people may wish to jump on? Whose mandate is it to change the world and perhaps 'save' the (Western) world?

If forces of social change lie dormant, democratically elected governments do not seem eager to awaken them. Western governments, and in the Anglosphere the increasingly similar major parties, operate on the basis of economic rationality and from the premise that people are primarily economically motivated. Government's central mandate is to maintain economic growth and secure an endless rise in 'living standards'. Western governments have short mandates (3–5 years), and if they want to be re-elected, they have to focus on short-term goals and indicators, just like a publicly listed corporation primarily devoted to keeping its shareholders happy year by year or even quarter by quarter. In consequence, governments are not able to provide leadership for long-term reform. According to Australian economist Frank Stilwell (2010), after the GFC:

> [...] there was an expectation that alternative political economic ideas [would get] more traction, both in the academy and in the realm of public policy. It is by now clear that this has not happened: after a shake-up, economic policy has fallen back onto the neo-classical orthodoxy [...] to shore up the existing economic system, rather than transform it.

Given the status quo and inertia cultivated by the major parties, the unsatisfied constituencies are turning to smaller and usually more ideologically extreme parties, or the unforeseen ideological extremes of the major parties epitomised in the ascendency of Donald Trump. If we are to learn from history, we can be sure that the right-wing, nationalist populism tends to be immediately attractive and therefore more successful than the left-wing, green, cosmopolitan alternative. While the capitalist economy operates on a global scale, nationalism is anything but a spent force.

Economy Versus Morality

For many centuries, religion was the moral glue of society. The moral order was written down in a holy book and interpreted with a wide margin of freedom by an accredited caste of clerics. The rules were enforced in an authoritarian fashion, either through the internalised fear of God and eternal punishment or by this-worldly fear of powers-that-be, ecclesiastical or secular. The fear was well founded; excommunication from the church was a considerable calamity, even without becoming a person of interest to the Spanish Inquisition. While most people believed in God, the religious moral order was legitimate—it was reflecting 'God's will' and who can argue with that? Life was unfolding according to strict rules, at least for the powerless majority—and the world was changing very slowly.

The secular state and the modern Western judicial system are still partly based on Christian tenets, the most important of which is the equal moral worth of each individual. This means that the individuals have equal human rights and obligations before the law. Bertrand Russell, an avowed atheist, saw the value of religion as a moral force in society. According to Russell (1935), modern democracy had derived strength from the moral ideals of Christianity, which had done much to divert governments from exclusive preoccupations with the interests of the rich and powerful (p. 115).

However, over the centuries, not only religion's own heretics and dissidents, but also the members of other religions—pagans, infidels, antichrists—were excluded from any rights and ruthlessly persecuted.

Religious wars between Catholics and Protestants were raging in Europe in the seventeenth century. In a strange parallel, similar wars are raging today in the Middle East between those claiming to represent Sunni and Shia branches of Islam. Over time, the moral authority of religion has been eroded, not just by corrupt practices of God's representatives on Earth, but also by a wider process of enlightenment and secularisation.

In his book *Religion for Atheists*, Alain de Botton (2012) suggested that secular societies may have thrown out the ethical baby with the religious bathwater. Modern education teaches us 'how to make a living but not how to live.' Those elements of culture concerned with the latter, such as humanities and literature, religion and philosophy, are considered old fashioned and largely a useless luxury in a pragmatic society that values gain that can be expressed quantitatively and translated to dollars and cents. *Apranihita* ('aimlessness' in Sanskrit) is 'a state as much prized by Buddhism as it is reviled by capitalism' (de Botton, 2012, 156).

Once 'God is dead,' where are we to ground values and ethics? French Enlightenment and German classical philosophy of the eighteenth and nineteenth centuries proposed rational consideration of ethical postulates. People should make rules themselves. One of the best-known rational imperatives is Immanuel Kant's (1967) 'categorical imperative,' an unconditional obligation derived from the concept of duty: 'I ought never to act except in such a way that I can also will the maxim of my action to be a universal law.' Or more simply, we should ask ourselves: 'What would the world be like if everyone behaved like me?'

The economic rationality of capitalism clashes with the central postulates of classical ethics. The rational agents (human persons) have an absolute value and are therefore 'ends in themselves,' who have a 'perfect duty' *not* to use themselves and others 'merely as a means to the satisfaction of their inclination,' and an 'imperfect duty' to further the 'ends of nature in ourselves,' that is, to seek their own perfection. In more contemporary language, after their more basic needs are satisfied, it is people's moral duty to seek the realisation of their potential or 'actualisation,' and facilitate the same process for other people (Maslow 1970). In other words, a person should never be treated (just) instrumentally, as a means for some external purpose.

Contrary to this postulate, the commodification of people is a stark reality of capitalism. Marx, who was an economist and an ethical philosopher in equal measure, called it 'alienation.' Economic rationality dictates the instrumental treatment of people in achieving the ultimate goal: wealth accumulation. In capitalism, people's relationships are mediated through the market. We are therefore reduced to our roles as producers on the one hand and consumers on the other. Systemically, we are a means to someone else's end. We only resist and draw a line when such instrumentalisation is beyond acceptable parameters or too close to home. We may tolerate self-interested and even exploitative employers, but friends, siblings or spouses who unashamedly 'use' us or betray us for money trigger our moral censure.

Confronted by many examples of global misery and violence, and an increasing number of domestic instances of corruption and injustice, many people seem to yearn for an 'ethical position,' which is articulated by left-wing critical intellectuals. In his 2011 presidential address to the American Sociological Association, Eric Olin Wright discussed 'real utopias' as 'emancipatory alternatives to capitalism' as part of his project of developing 'normatively grounded sociology of the possible, not just the actual' (Wright 2012, 1). He proposed three moral principles for judging social institutions and developing viable alternatives: equality ('equal access' rather than just 'equal opportunity'—mitigation of capitalism-generated inequality), democracy (the participation in collective decision making and therefore in political power) and sustainability (an 'intertemporal' justice—a justice principle for people in the future).

Articulating ethical principles and living by them seem an important element of what Wright (2012) calls 'human flourishing.' People are inherently reflective moral beings who espouse non-quantifiable values and have a need to conceptualise quality (the 'good' versus the 'bad'), to judge and not just calculate. The discussion about values and goals can never be fully replaced by financial accounting. Even in the highly utilitarian American context, only a minority conceives 'improvement' purely through economic gain—even though they are constantly urged in this direction (Wilkinson and Pickett 2009). Aside from, and sometimes in contravention to economic gain, people seek love, autonomy, community, justice, truth, beauty, salvation, meaning, communion with nature, wisdom and kindness. These higher goals are often associated with religion, spirituality, art and other pursuits in which it is impossible to reliably calculate cost and benefit.

However, the onslaught of quantification is relentless: aesthetic enjoyment has become a quaint side-benefit of art investment, while communion with nature has to be paid for because the 'tourism industry' treats 'nature' as an economic resource. Hiking trails were once constructed and marked by volunteers for the free enjoyment of all. Now they are often a business like any other.[10] Moral questions remain a side show of capitalism; we are a society with a short attention span. There are too many distractions from pondering justice. Capitalism induces people with laid-back temperaments to be comfortable and 'have fun,' and those more ambitious to accumulate wealth and strive to be famous and powerful. For all, the prevailing wisdom offers a ready-made one-size-fits-all purpose of life: wealth accumulation. Morality fits uncomfortably with this goal, and often mitigates against it: a single-minded pursuit of pecuniary success, social status and power is likely to make one an absent parent, a negligent spouse, an inattentive friend, an exploitative boss, an unpopular colleague, a poor citizen and a neglectful tenant of the planet Earth.

Is a Green Enlightenment Possible?

As discussed in Chap. 6, the 'more=better' paradigm is consuming the planet. Humanity's impact on the Earth is now so great it can no longer be called a 'footprint'—it is rather a boot-print of a giant. We have entered the age of Anthropocene, where humanity itself is a geological force. We are dominating the biosphere, we have modified much of the Earth's surface and we are conducting a risky experiment on the planet's atmosphere. It is clear that humanity, and primarily the profligate West, is on an unsustainable path, endangering the flourishing, and perhaps even survival, of future generations.

If we take as granted that survival—of the human species and advanced human civilisation—is a rational goal, then we have to consider the insistence on limitless economic growth colliding with the environment as irrational. The justification for the irrational behaviour comes from two sources: first, our impact on the environmental is downplayed; and second, given the span of an individual human life, putting short-term goals before long-term ones can be defended as rational—but only if we are ready to say *après moi le déluge* and ignore future generations.

Environmental thinking first penetrated society's mainstream in the 1970s. The world's first 'green' party, the United Tasmania Group, was formed in 1972 in the relatively unspoilt Australian state of Tasmania as a result of a controversial hydroelectric development in the wilderness of its south-west corner.[11] Green parties in Europe arose at the end of the 1970s and have been influential in much of Western Europe, especially in Germany, where the Greens are part of ruling coalitions in 11 of the 16 federal states (mid-2017).

The key reason why international summits on the environment come and go, but we keep polluting, is the preservation of the political status quo. Reducing our environmental footprint requires reconsidering our relationship to other societies (i.e., diminishing the power of the West vis-à-vis the Rest) and reconsidering the power structure within advanced capitalist societies (i.e., diminishing the power of big business vis-à-vis the rest of society). This is a process that the powers that be, national as well as global, are simply not willing to initiate. A call for collective downsizing, a more frugal lifestyle and some redistribution of wealth as an alternative to indefinite growth would not travel well as an election promise within the currently dominant political discourse. 'Political realists,' even those without vested interests, consider a political solution that would include controlled but significant reforms highly unlikely. With the Trump's administration rejection of the 'Paris consensus' on climate change action, its chances of being translated into meaningful policies are diminished, but there is significant opposition to Trump's position, within the US as well as globally.

In spite of some encouraging examples, the chances of a comprehensive 'green enlightenment,' which would lead to a post-capitalist transformation of the economy, seem limited. A review of evidence that we attempted in Chap. 6 suggests that no significant alteration to the current dominant discourse or policy is likely before the West experiences a dramatic environmental degradation. However, the affluent countries will be the last to experience it, having been able, so far, to pass much of the environmental degradation onto the developing world. Transcending the public-discursive dominance of the growth paradigm and thinking outside the economic-rational square are epochal challenges comparable with few in recent history.

Notes

1. Although the average gap between rich and poor countries has decreased, this is not the whole story. At the extremes, the gap between the richest and poorest countries has in fact increased (Hickel 2016).
2. In the first week of his presidency, Donald Trump attempted to ban immigration to the US from seven Muslim-majority countries but ran up against objections from the judiciary that this represented a 'ban on Muslim immigration' (that Trump had promised during the election campaign) and thus violated the constitutional right of freedom of religion.
3. John Keane (2017) has argued that even despotic regimes, where authoritarian governments are based on plutocracy and rule without civil society monitoring (e.g., Russia and other post-Soviet states and a one-party system such as. China), manage to be perceived by their constituencies as democratic.
4. John Forbes Nash (1928–2015) made fundamental contributions to several fields of mathematics including game theory, a branch of mathematics dealing with strategic decision making in conflict situations and widely used in economics and social science. For much of his life, Nash suffered from paranoid schizophrenia but his condition improved with age. He was awarded the Nobel Prize in Economics in 1994.
5. There is an abundance of literature on game theory. For a good non-technical introduction, see Poundstone (1992).
6. By September 2009, to make up for lost time, the consensus predicted 54 of the 49 recessions that occurred in that year (Ahir and Loungani 2014)!
7. Gottfried Wilhelm Leibniz (1646–1716) was a German polymath who contributed to the fields of philosophy, politics, physics and philology (and that is just the 'p-s'). He developed the mathematical technique of calculus at the same time as, but independently of, Isaac Newton.
8. A video is available on YouTube.

9. Pierre Bourdieu (1930–2002) was a French sociologist, anthropologist and philosopher. He became a leading public intellectual in France in the 1990s, fiercely critical of neo-liberalism.
10. To take one example, the Three Capes Track on the south coast of Tasmania, completed in late 2015, cost $25 million and took 17,000 helicopter flights to construct. The privilege of enjoying its delights will set walkers back $500 (ABC 2015). Ironically, *Wild Magazine,* while being critical of the commercialisation of the track, also features advertisements for the walk (Wild 2015).
11. The world's first national level party to campaign predominately on environmental issues was the Values Party in New Zealand, also formed in 1972. The Finnish Green party was the first to become part of a national cabinet in 1995.

Bibliography

ABC. 2015. Bushwalkers to Pay $500 to Explore Three Capes Track on Tasman Peninsula. *Australian Broadcasting Commission (ABC) News*, 17 September 2015. Accessed 23 June 2017. http://www.abc.net.au/news/2015-09-17/bushwalkers-to-be-charged-500-to-explore-three-capes-track/6784448

———. 2017. War on Waste. *ABC TV*, 23 May 2017.

Ahir, H., and P. Loungani. 2014. 'There Will Be Growth in the Spring': How Well Do Economists Predict Turning Points? *Vox*, 14 April 2014. Accessed 23 June 2017. http://voxeu.org/article/predicting-economic-turning-points

Allen, Katie. 2014. Sands are Running Out for Britain's Hourglass Labour Force. *The Guardian*, 7 December 2014. Accessed 23 June 2017. https://www.theguardian.com/society/2014/dec/07/labour-market-britain-hourglass-sands-running-out

Axelrod, Robert. 1984. *The Evolution of Cooperation*. New York: Basic Books.

Axelrod, Robert, and William D. Hamilton. 1981. The Evolution of Cooperation. *Science* 211: 1390–1396.

de Botton, Alain. 2012. *Religion for Atheists*. New York: Random House.

Bourdieu, Pierre. 2003. *Firing Back: Against the Tyranny of the Market 2*. London: Verso.

Brown, Archie. 2009. *The Rise and Fall of Communism*. London: The Bodley Head.

Colic-Peisker, Val, and Farida Tilbury. 2006. Employment Niches for Recent Refugees: Segmented Labour Market of the 21st Century Australia. *Journal of Refugee Studies* 19: 203–229.

Donato, K.M., and D.S. Massey. 2016. 21st Century Globalisation and Illegal Migration. *Annals APPSS* 666: 7–26.

Farrelly, Elizabeth. 2015. What Life Will Be Like in the Year 2055. *Virgin Inflight Magazine*, November 2015.

Ferguson, T., and R. Johnson. 2010. The God That Failed: Free Market Fundamentalism and the Lehman Brothers Bankruptcy. *The Economist Voice* 7: 1–1.

Galbraith, John Kenneth. 1993. *The Culture of Contentment*. London: Houghton Mifflin.

Ginsborg, Paul. 2008. *Democracy: Crisis and Renewal*. London: Profile Books.

Gorz, Andre. 1989. *Critique of Economic Reason*. Translated by Gilliam Handyside and Chris Turner. London: Verso. First published in 1988 as *Metamorphoses du Travail*. Paris: Editions Galilee.

Greenfield, Susan. 2004. *Tomorrow's People: How 21st Century Technology is Changing the Way We Think and Feel*. London: Penguin.

Haidt, Jonathan. 2017. When and Why Nationalism Beat Globalism. *Saturday Extra*, 29 April 2017. ABC Radio National.

Hamilton, Clive. 2010. *Requiem for a Species: Why We Resist the Truth about Climate Change*. Abingdon, UK: Earthscan.

Hayek, Frederick von. 1988. *The Fatal Conceit: The Errors of Socialism*. Chicago: University of Chicago Press.

Hayek, Fredrick von. 2005 [1944]. *The Road to Serfdom*. London: Routledge.

Hickel, Jason. 2016. Global Inequality May Be Much Worse than We Think. *The Guardian*, 8 April 2016. Accessed 22 June 2017. https://www.theguardian.com/global-development-professionals-network/2016/apr/08/global-inequality-may-be-much-worse-than-we-think

Hobsbawm, Eric. 2007. *Globalisation, Democracy and Terrorism*. London: Little Brown Book Group.

Kant, Immanuel. 1967 [1785]. *Groundwork of the Metaphysics of Morals*. New York: Barnes & Noble.

Keane, John. 2017. The New Global Order and the Rise of Despotism. Public Lecture, University of Melbourne, 17 July 2017.

Kerr, Clark. 1969. *Marshall, Marx and Modern Times: The Multidimensional Society*. London: Cambridge University Press.

Koestler, Arthur, Ignazio Silone, Richard Wright, André Gide, Louis Fischer, and Stephen Spender. 1949. *The God that Failed*. New York: Bantam Books.

Leibniz, Gottfried Wilhelm. 1951 [1710]. *Theodicy: Essays on the Goodness of God, the Freedom of Man and the Origin of Evil*. London: Routledge and Kegan Paul Ltd.

Loungani, Prakash. 2001. How Accurate are Private Sector Forecasts? Cross-country Evidence from Consensus Forecasts of Output Growth. *International Journal of Forecasting* 17: 419–432.

Lovelock, James. 2009. *The Vanishing Face of Gaia: A Final Warning*. New York: Basic Books.

Maslow, Abraham. 1970. *Motivation and Personality*. New York: Harper.

Mill, John Stuart. 1970 [1848]. *Principles of Political Economy with Some of Their Applications to Social Philosophy*, Books IV and V. Harmondsworth, UK and Baltimore, MA: Penguin Classics.

NPR. 2014. National Public Radio (NPR), "Fresh Air", Interview with Paul Greenberg, 1 July 2014. Transcript. Accessed 22 June 2017. http://www.npr.org/sections/thesalt/2014/07/01/327248504/the-great-fish-swap-how-america-is-downgrading-its-seafood-supply

Piketty, Thomas. 2014. *Capital in the Twenty-first Century*. Cambridge, MA: Harvard University Press. First published as *Le capital au XXI siècle*, 2013 by Éditions du Seuil.

Popper, Karl. 1974 [1945]. *The Open Society and its Enemies, vol. 2: The High Tide of Prophecy: Hegel, Marx and the Aftermath*. London: Routledge and Kegan Paul.

Poundstone, William. 1992. *Prisoner's Dilemma*. New York: Doubleday.

Reich, Robert. 2008. *Supercapitalism: The Transformation of Business, Democracy and Everyday Life*. Melbourne: Scribe.

Roser, Max. 2017. Global Economic Inequality. Published online at *OurWorldInData.org*. Accessed 23 June 2017. https://ourworldindata.org/global-economic-inequality

Russell, Bertrand. 1935. *In Praise of Idleness and Other Essays*. London: Routledge.

Schumpeter, Joseph. 2009. *Can Capitalism Survive? Creative Destruction and the Global Economy*. New York: Harper Perennial Modern Classics.

Standing, Guy. 2011. *The Precariat: The New Dangerous Class*. London: Bloomsbury Academic.

Stilwell, Frank. 2010. The Political Economy: Challenge to Orthodoxy. *Labour and Industry* 20: 331–343.

Streeck, Wolfgang, Craig Coulhoun, Polly Toynbee, and Amitai Etzioni. 2016. Does Capitalism have a Future? *Socio-Economic Review* 14: 163–183.

Tetlock, Philip. 2005. *Expert Political Judgement: How Good Is It? How Can We Know?* Princeton: Princeton University Press.

The Economist. 2017. The Most Neglected Threat to Public Health in China is Toxic Soil. *The Economist*, 8 June 2017, pp. 18–20.

The Onion. 2000. Report: 98 percent of U.S. Commuters Favour Public Transport for Others. *The Onion*, 29 November 2000. Accessed 22 June 2017. http://www.theonion.com/article/report-98-percent-of-us-commuters-favor-public-tra-1434

Wild. 2015. The Three Capes Track: Tourist Boon or White-elephant. *Wild Magazine*, May 2015. Accessed 23 June 2017. https://wild.com.au/news/three-capes-track-white-elephant/

Wilde, Oscar. 1912 [1891]. *The Soul of Man under Socialism*. London: A.L. Humphreys.

Wilkinson, Richard, and Kate Pickett. 2009. *The Spirit Level: Why More Equal Societies Almost Always Do Better*. London: Allen Lane.

Wright, Erik Olin. 2012. Transforming Capitalism Through Real Utopias (American Sociological Association 2011 Presidential Address). *American Sociological Review* 78: 1–25.

Index[1]

[1] Note: Page numbers followed by "n" refers to notes.

V. Colic-Peisker, A. Flitney, *The Age of Post-Rationality*,
https://doi.org/10.1007/978-981-10-6259-9

The manufacturer's authorised representative in the EU is Springer Nature Customer Service Centre GmbH, Europaplatz 3, 69115 Heidelberg, Germany. If you have any concerns regarding our products, please contact ProductSafety@springernature.com

Printed and bound by CPI Group (UK) Ltd, Croydon, CR0 4YY
30/09/2026
02225451-0007